# The Business of Sustainability in Fashion

## Following the Threads

Iva Jestratijevic, PhD

University of North Texas Press
Denton, Texas

The Printed in the United States of America.

10  9  8  7  6  5  4  3  2  1

Permissions:
University of North Texas Press
1155 Union Circle #311336
Denton, TX 76203-5017

The paper used in this book meets the minimum requirements of the
American National Standard for Permanence of Paper for Printed Library
Materials, z39.48.1984. Binding materials have been chosen for durability.

Library of Congress Cataloging-in-Publication Data

Names: Jestratijević, Iva, author.
Title: The business of sustainability in fashion : following the threads /
    Iva Jestratijevic.
Description: Denton : University of North Texas Press, [2024] | Includes
    index.
Identifiers: LCCN 2024000455 | ISBN 9781574419092 (paperback)
Subjects: LCSH: Fashion merchandising--Environmental aspects. | Clothing
    trade--Environmental aspects. | Clothing trade--Sustainable methods. |
    Textile industry--Environmental aspects. | Sustainable design. |
    Sustainable development. | BISAC: BUSINESS & ECONOMICS / Industries /
    Fashion & Textile Industry | BUSINESS & ECONOMICS / Development /
    Sustainable Development
Classification: LCC HD9940.A2 J478 2024 | DDC
    746.9/20684--dc23/eng/20240131
LC record available at https://lccn.loc.gov/2024000455

The electronic edition of this book was made possible by the support of
the Vick Family Foundation. Typeset by vPrompt eServices.

*To my family,*
*Nikola, Roman, Fedor, Nika, and Nestor Jestratijevic,*
*and to all my students that will play effective roles*
*in the fashion transformation process.*

# Contents

# List of Tables

# List of Case Studies

# Preface

S ustainability presents the most significant issue currently confronted by fashion businesses. However, the selection of published books focused on sustainability in the fashion business is still very limited. This is particularly true when it comes to the topic of sustainable business practices. The book *The Business of Sustainability in Fashion: Following the Threads* provides a broad overview of the main concepts, theories, and methodologies involved in the description and assessment of sustainable business practices. This book's content is suitable for business studies, retail studies, fashion studies, and environmental studies and is for students at the undergraduate and graduate level. The book content highlights the opportunities, benefits, and challenges associated with sustainable business practices and emphasizes both the necessity and the importance of sustainable development in today's fashion industry.

This book is designed to:

1.  emphasize the importance of sustainability in the fashion business/ industry;
2.  review the key sustainability concepts and theories and showcase their application in fashion sourcing, manufacturing, marketing, and retailing;
3.  consider drivers of and barriers to sustainable corporate and consumer behavior;
4.  "analyze case studies to evaluate the various strategies employed in the development of a sustainable business practice";[1] and
5.  support critical and creative thinking about corporate sustainability, emphasizing industry factor interdependence.

The book is divided into six chapters. All the chapters specify the learning objectives and key terms. A glossary of the terms can be found after chapter 6.

The first chapter, **Sustainability as a Business Imperative**, was written by professor, consultant, and sustainability practitioner Dr. Neal Drobny, who is on the faculty of Western Michigan University, where he leads an innovative program designed to impart sustainability problem-solving skills to a broad section of WMU students. In 2016, at the beginning of my graduate school years at the Ohio State University, Dr. Drobny successfully led the component of the Environment, Economy, Development & Sustainability (EEDS) major that focused on sustainability at the Ohio State University. I still remember how he introduced me to different shades of sustainability in practice at the beginning of my graduate school years. He taught us fresh graduate students to "incorporate a systems mindset when thinking about sustainability, explaining that everything is connected to everything else . . . meaning that every function in the business has to work together to pull off a change in culture and a change in business practices to deliver significant value."[2] Similarly, the intention of the first chapter is to overview the key sustainable business concepts and to establish subtle environmental, social, and economic connections so that readers can better grasp *why the status quo is not an option for any industry and why sustainable change is now an imperative across the industries*!

Next, the purpose of the following five chapters, which I wrote alone, is to position and elaborate on sustainable business concepts in the fashion industry context. More specifically, the second chapter, **Sustainable Development in the Fashion Industry**, explores how the Sustainable Development Goals (SDGs) are linked with environmental, economic, and social performance in the fashion industry. By reading materials in the second chapter, students will gain an understanding of what the SDGs are and how improvement in the fashion business and supply chain operations are intrinsically linked with achieving them. Case studies presented in this chapter are for the purpose of illuminating the multilayered sustainability problems in our industry, showcasing how the clothing we wear every day affects the world around us and why the fashion practices are often interlinked with human rights abuses, worker poverty, inequality, and environmental degradation.

The third chapter, **Sustainability in the Fashion Business: Core Principles and Assessments**, presents the core sustainability principles and assessments used to appraise fashion business. The purpose of this chapter is to clarify why sustainability presents the most significant issue currently confronted by fashion businesses. As sustainability becomes a key component of successful decision-making processes, fashion businesses must respond by making decisions that showcase their dedication to sustainable business activity. Consequently, this chapter frames how sustainability-oriented companies can assess their products and their corporate and supply chain practices according to the industry-relevant sustainability standards. Materials and case studies in this chapter introduce the main sustainability drivers, arguing that sustainability represents a valuable lens for the business practitioner to navigate necessary and needed changes in the fashion industry.

The fourth chapter, **Fashion Circularity and Waste Management Strategies**, discusses textile, apparel, and packaging waste generation in the fashion industry and its impacts on the environment and on human well-being. The intention of the chapter is to provide valuable insights into the applications of the circular economy principles within wasteful and linear fashion industry systems. The focus in this chapter is therefore given to various circular strategies to reduce and reuse fashion industry waste, showcasing why in a circular economy waste must be reconsidered as a valuable resource for the next production cycle. A sustainability expert whose work is presented in this chapter is Dr. Jana Hawley, dean of the College of Merchandising, Hospitality, and Tourism at the University of North Texas, because she is one of the first researchers in the United States to conduct research on textile recycling and apparel sustainability.

The fifth chapter, **Sustainability Communication among Fashion Brands**, elaborates on how fashion businesses can manage economic and reputational risks by communicating their sustainability efforts. Although this chapter demonstrates that sustainability initiatives bolster sustainability credentials, it also shows that communicating sustainability is not an easy task. There are various marketing ploys and greenwashing tactics in use, and thus when analyzing promotional tools used by fashion brands, we need to navigate through a myriad of green, natural, organic, and recycled options that all promise the same "sustainable" value. Thus, this chapter is intended to equip students with the knowledge and expertise in sustainable product and certification areas and to help them to remain vigilant so they do not fall into the fashion greenwashing trap.

The sixth and last chapter, **Sustainability and Engagement**, explains why purposeful engagement of various stakeholder groups in sustainability activities is needed to support sustainable transformation in the fashion industry. The idea is quite simple. The SDGs in the fashion industry can be achieved only if all the parties involved in the fashion production and consumption process work together. This means that all actors, including businesses, governments, nongovernmental organizations (NGOs), and consumers, have a role to play in sustainable development, and as discussed in this chapter, this need for stronger partnerships to reach goals is becoming particularly evident now, after the global COVID crisis. The sustainability expert whose work is presented in this chapter is Dr. Elena Karpova, Putman & Hayes Distinguished Professor at the Bryan School of Business and Economics at the University of North Carolina at Greensboro, because she is researching sustainable apparel consumption and she has created a list of simple practices that readers can implement in their daily lives in order to consume fashion more sustainably.

When they have reached the end of this book, students should be well aware of sustainable solutions in the fashion business that would enable any organization to thrive. Now, when universities, colleges, and schools have started or expanded their sustainability focus within fashion, merchandising, and retail programs, it is my hope that this book focused on sustainable business practices in the fashion industry will serve as a great starting point for educating future sustainability professionals that will play effective roles in the fashion transformation process.

# References

1. I. Jestratijevic, MDSE 4560: Sustainability Strategies, undergraduate course syllabus, University of North Texas.
2. N. Drobny, "Green Is Good - Neal Drobny - Ohio State University," Impact with John Shegerian, YouTube video, Oct. 15, 2014, https://www.youtube.com/watch?v=-Y5Skfwv57U.

# Chapter 1

# Sustainability as a Business Imperative

- Chapter Introduction and Learning Objectives
- Sustainability Expert Profile: Dr. Neil Drobny
- Important Terminology
- The Evolution of Sustainability
- Sustainability as a Business Issue
- Getting Started with Sustainable Business: A Brief Guide
- Chapter Summary
- References

## Chapter Introduction and Learning Objectives

The popular and business media have been rampant as of late with messages pertaining to the need for business to take more authentic and significant action to deal with environmental and social matters locally and globally. Collectively, these actions are called sustainability, a broad and difficult to define term, about which more will be said in the next section of this chapter. The call for greater attention to sustainability in business has many reasons. Significant are the following social and cultural developments:

- Interest in healthy lifestyles and awareness of the many threats to healthy living that stem from practices embedded in our culture and economy, from hazardous and toxic substances in products that we rely upon, and from lifestyle practices that deliver highly desired conveniences of various types.
- Consensus that climate change is an economic and civilization survival threat that must be dealt with aggressively, and soon by everyone, ranging from individuals to the largest institutions of government and business.
- Awareness about the limitations of fossil fuels and their connection with both climate and national security risks.
- Recognition that the world's poor must have better access to natural resources, environmental protection, and health safeguards.

As reflected in this book, the fashion industry and its suppliers and consumers rank near the top of the communities that need to make the urgent changes alluded to above. No industries are immune from such responsibilities. Details regarding needed changes, and the strategic recipes that will yield results, vary from industry to industry and from one company to another in the same industry. Nevertheless, there are some common drivers and solutions that are a starting point for understanding essential ingredients and options for strengthening the environmental and social responsibility of any enterprise. These common drivers and solutions are the focus of this chapter. Subsequent chapters will address details as they pertain to the fashion industry and its stakeholders.

The theme of the chapter is that the **status quo is not an option for any industry and change is now an imperative**! Leaders across many industry sectors whose successes can provide guideposts for those who need guidance in setting and executing their sustainability agenda will be cited.

This chapter has the following learning objectives:

- Define sustainability.
- Recognize the key sustainability drivers and business solutions.

- Understand the main concepts of sustainability.
- Describe why sustainability is a business imperative.

**Key Terms**

| | |
|---|---|
| B Corporation | linear economy |
| biomimicry | materiality |
| blockchain | materiality assessment |
| by-product synergy | people, planet, and profit |
| circular economy | product as a service |
| Cradle to Cradle | triple bottom line |
| ecosystem services | resilience |
| embedded vs. bolted-on sustainability | shared value |
| extended producer responsibility | shareholders vs. stakeholders |
| environmental, social, and governance reporting | sharing economy |
| | sustainable |
| green vs. sustainable | Sustainable Development Goals |
| greenwashing | sustainability credentials |
| handprints vs. footprints | sustainability reporting |
| impact investing | sustainability vs. compliance |
| leadership in energy and environmental design | systems thinking |
| lifestyles of health and sustainability | |

# Sustainability Expert Profile: Dr. Neil Drobny

Dr. Neil Drobny is a semiretired academic leader and consultant and holds degrees in environmental engineering from Dartmouth College and the Ohio State University. Prior to retirement, he was a registered professional engineer in several states and a certified sustainability professional as awarded by the International Society of Sustainability Professionals (ISSP), of which he served a term as a board member. Dr. Drobny has spoken extensively and published frequently on sustainability, including authorship of the introductory chapter of the first book on ISO 14000 (family of international environmental management standards), published by Irwin Professional Publishers.

Dr. Drobny has spent his entire professional life focused on matters of environmental protection and, more recently, sustainability. As of this writing, he is a senior projects mentor at the Haworth College of Business at Western Michigan University, where he guides students working on sustainability projects for sponsoring companies. Prior to his semiretirement, Dr. Drobny was senior lecturer and program director at the Ohio State University, with a dual appointment in the College of Business and the College of Food, Agriculture, and Environmental Science. His teaching load included courses in sustainable business practices at the graduate and undergraduate level, for which he received an Outstanding Service Award. In addition to teaching responsibilities, he led the external relations component of a new campuswide major and minor in sustainability. That responsibility involved developing relationships with companies and other organizations that placed student projects with courses that were part of the sustainability curriculum. In 2013 that curriculum won first prize in a national competition for excellence in undergraduate sustainability education. Prior to the academic phase of his career, Dr. Drobny served in several consulting roles. He was an early member of the management team of what is now the ERM Group, a global sustainability consulting organization. Prior to ERM, he was an early leader in the development of environmental research programs at Battelle, a global contract research organization. At Battelle he was a member of the team that developed the first formal methodology for preparing environmental impact assessments, which received national recognition. Other consulting assignments included executive director roles of two recycling organizations and interim CEO assignments for several startup companies.

## Important Terminology

In order to incorporate sustainability principles into one's personal and/or professional life, it is critical to understand applicable terminology. Here we will cover some of the key terms and their interpretation.

**Systems thinking.** Systems thinking is a mindset that promotes thinking holistically about all the components of a problem or issue versus dealing with the components piecemeal. This is essential when working in sustainability because all the components of sustainability problems and solutions are typically interrelated in complex ways.

A recent editorial made the point as follows: "An unfortunate side effect of enacting bold sustainability strategies can sometimes be not seeing the forest for the trees, as it were for example, creating ripple effects when substituting one problematic commodity crop for another; or charging ahead with circularity commitments without the necessary infrastructure in place. On a brighter note, a pioneering light installation could be a game-changer for keeping COVID and future viruses at bay outdoors."[1]

A concrete example would be the task of designing a building with an efficient energy footprint. One would need to consider, for example, not only fuel source options and choices for building materials but also intended use of the building, natural surroundings, building orientation on the site, local weather patterns, transportation networks, and modes available to people that use the building.

**Shareholders vs. stakeholders.** As commonly understood, shareholders are people (or entities) that own part of a company. Their interest in how a company performs is essentially purely financial. In contrast, a stakeholder is any person, organization, or community that incurs environmental, social, or economic impacts caused by the operations of another party such as a business. Stakeholders include, for example, neighbors, employees, investors, regulators, suppliers, and customers. Stakeholders may be not only local but also regional or global. For example, regional stakeholders would be a community that gets its water supply from a watercourse to which a company discharges wastewater.

A popular view held by many economists and articulated in 1970 by economist Milton Friedman was that leaders of corporations had only one primary duty, and that was to deliver financial gain to shareholders.[2] That view was challenged in 2019 in a statement by the Business Roundtable, signed by 181 CEOs, that in part read, "We believe the free-market system is the best means of generating good jobs, a strong and sustainable economy, innovation, a healthy environment and economic opportunity for all,"[3] thereby embracing a stakeholder model of leadership in contradiction to the stakeholder model espoused by Friedman.

**Materiality.** In the context of sustainability, materiality is used to determine what aspects of sustainability, across the full spectrum of environmental, social, and economic issues, really matter to an organization and its stakeholders. For example, for a company that manufactures paper, water conservation would be material from an environmental point of view, whereas for a company with a large network of retail stores that sell products made in Asia, child labor would be a material issue from a social point of view. Typically, companies will identify ten to twenty issues that are material and manageable across all business operations. As summed up by Joe Makower in *GreenBiz*: "As you well know, the number of topics faced by sustainability professionals inside companies has mushroomed over the past two decades, from simply worrying about waste and pollution to fully embracing all aspects of the health and well-being of humans and other living things, all while tracking progress with financial and nonfinancial metrics."[4]

**Sustainability vs. compliance.** Sustainability-type thinking was an outgrowth of interest in natural resource conservation and concern for public health effects of air and water pollution dating back a hundred years or more in the United States. Subsequent to population growth and expansion of industrial activity, especially after World War II, laws and regulations were enacted to put limits on what and how much waste could be disposed of and where and when. These limits were plant and location specific. Though fines existed for noncompliance, enforcement was weak and inconsistent.

Though laws and regulations have been tightened and financial and criminal penalties for noncompliance have become more stringent over the years, that is not what sustainability is all about. Compliance is typically rooted in following the letter of the law and rarely going beyond established legal limits. Sustainability, on the other hand, guides companies to be more responsible with regard to their environmental and social impact. Additionally, compliance is typically focused on the present or reactive to current events, whereas sustainability is focused on being proactive for the future. Accordingly, compliance is more tactical and sustainability is more strategic, which brings into play options for strengthening financial performance. For example, with regard to waste management, a compliance mindset would primarily assure waste materials are sent to permitted waste disposal facilities. A sustainability mindset would seek ways to recycle or reuse waste materials, or better yet avoid creating them in the first place, both of which have the potential to generate revenue and/or reduce cost. Loyalties of stakeholders such as customers, investors, and employees are often reinforced by a company's sustainability agenda and performance but rarely by actions that target compliance and nothing beyond. Clearly, sustainability and compliance share many common interests, such as operating in accord with regulatory demands, risk management, supply chain resilience, and integrity, transparency, and reputation. However, due to differences in focus as outlined above, they draw upon different skill sets and knowledge bases.

**Green vs. sustainable.** Green and sustainable are often incorrectly interchanged. This is understandable because in the early days of sustainability discussions, after the release of *The Brundtland Report* in 1987 (this report was sponsored by the United Nations and introduced the concept of sustainable development and described how it could be achieved), the focus was on the environmental aspect of sustainability. There was little understanding about what the social component meant and few, if any, metrics or frameworks for framing initiatives and measuring results.

For example, one of today's strongest sustainability nonprofit organizations, founded in 1993, is the US Green Building Council (USGBC). At the time it was founded, the primary sustainability issues related to buildings were environmental impacts related to the use of energy and building materials. The social aspects of buildings, well-known today, just were not on the radar. Because of the strong brand strength of its name, USGBC has not moved away from its use of "green" when they really mean "sustainable," and they pay very strong attention to social issues. Inclusion of social issues in the definition of sustainability brings into play factors that are often included in the domain of corporate social responsibility. Such factors include, for example, supply chain practices that might tap into exploitative labor practices, community impacts that might result from 24/7 manufacturing operations, or heavy freight traffic through neighborhoods, and cover up of product safety issues that can be traced to toxic raw materials. Attention to the needs of economically and socially disadvantaged populations is coming from several directions these days. C. K. Prahalad and Stuart L. Hart's work reported in "The Fortune at the Bottom of the Pyramid" is one example.[5] One more example is the work of 2006 Nobel Peace Prize winner and micro financier Muhammad Yunus, as described in his book *Creating a World without Poverty: Social Business and the Future of Capitalism*.[6] In each case the theme is that businesses can and must work to extend the reach of capitalism to all populations, albeit in some creative ways.

**Embedded vs. bolted-on sustainability.** Embedded sustainability describes an organizational approach in which sustainability principles are part of the culture. Sustainability policy and goals are transparent to all stakeholders. All employees know how their duties contribute to sustainability goals and are encouraged to make suggestions. Executives, managers, and supervisors talk frequently about progress on sustainability goals and new goals as they are established. Bolted-on sustainability occurs when selected products or services are given features that contribute a sense of being sustainable. However, overall enterprise culture and operations do not contain a conscious commitment to sustainability.

**Resilience.** Resilience is another concept pertinent to this discussion about sustainability. Resilience is the capacity for systems to survive, adapt, and grow in the face of turbulent change. When applied to a business or any other type of enterprise, resilience speaks to the ability of the enterprise to recover its ability to perform after some shock (a fire, a market downturn, an extended strike, a weather disaster, etc.). Clearly, in order to be sustainable, a business must be resilient, and vice versa. Research is underway at many locations to understand how to improve the resilience of organizations and communities and the environments in which they operate so they can also be sustainable. The COVID-19 pandemic underscored for all businesses the need to build resilience into their systems and operations. The importance of resilience was driven home during the COVID-19 pandemic when organizations of all types tried to find ways to continue operations and then again as they tried to reopen. Many now have planning for the next pandemic as a key element of their sustainability agenda.

**DfX.** DfX is a design acronym where Df stands for "design for" and X is any attribute important to a product, process, or system. Common examples are design for sustainability and design for environment.

**Greenwashing.** Greenwashing is the dissemination of incorrect or incomplete information to convey an impression that the party providing the information is sustainable or environmentally responsible. The goal is typically to attract customers who have a preference for sustainable or environmentally responsible products without making the effort to build those features into the product. Seven forms of greenwashing have been identified, to which have been assigned the following descriptive labels: hidden trade-off, no proof, vagueness, irrelevance, lesser of two evils, fibbing and worshipping false labels.[7] One example of vagueness is to claim that a product is made with no emissions, without saying what type of emissions are being referenced. The community of responsible companies has made efforts to combat greenwashing. They include, for example, industry-based codes of conduct such as the Responsible Care initiative of the chemical industry and the Code of Conduct for Responsible Fisheries. Another initiative out of the UK led by software company Provenance is an online tool "that enables businesses to make substantiated sustainability claims, and shoppers to fact-check them."[8]

**Ecosystem services.** Ecosystems are the interactive networks of plants, animals, microorganisms, and their physical environment, often referred to as mother nature. They provide the organizing framework and the operating system for the earth. Ecosystem services are the functions performed and benefits provided that make human life possible. These include carbon sequestration, providing "clean water, regulating disease and climate, supporting the pollination of crops and soil formation, and providing recreational, cultural and spiritual benefits."[9]

## The Evolution of Sustainability

The word **sustainable** is defined by Webster as "capable of being maintained at length without interruption, weakening, or losing in power or quality."[10]

In an economic context, being sustainable has been a goal for businesses for some time. However, sustainability as a key to the well-being (some would say the survival) of human civilization, the context for this book, is relatively new. More specifically, in 1987 the United Nations issued a clarion call under the name of sustainability for global actions to simultaneously improve environmental, social, and economic conditions on earth.

In that year the UN published the previously mentioned Brundtland Report, also called *Our Common Future.* The report targets issues and approaches for interdependent nations to deal with environmental and social consequences of materialism. The report was produced in nine hundred days by a UN commission under the leadership of Gro Harlem Brundtland, former prime minister of Norway. Accordingly, the document is often referred to informally as the Brundtland Report. An important lasting impact of that work is the definition of sustainable development as "development that meets the needs of the present without compromising the ability of future generations to meet their own needs."[11] While criticized by many as an unexciting statement, that definition has survived as the only widespread definition of sustainability and has served as an organizing framework for organizations and individuals to think about their sustainability agenda. Sustainability is a multidimensional concept. It suggests that attention to environmental and social issues is intended to coexist with attention to economic matters. In fact, the premise upon which the interest and success of sustainable practices rest is that economic prosperity can be enhanced by attention to environmental and social matters. A popular shorthand that developed to convey the essence of this three-dimensional view of sustainability is people, planet, profit.

In 2015, thirty years after the Brundtland Report, the UN released the **Sustainable Development Goals (SDGs).**[12] The SDGs were to serve as a universal call to action to end poverty, protect the planet, and ensure that by 2030 all people (ideally) enjoy peace and prosperity. There are seventeen SDGs, and the underlying detailed road map for action is integrated in the sense that they recognize that action in one area will affect outcomes in others, and that development must balance social, economic, and environmental sustainability. The SDG road map is very comprehensive and includes, for example, recommended actions to end poverty, hunger, AIDS, and discrimination against women and girls.

*Looking to the sustainability future.* Business Week portrayed sustainability as a sixty-generation descendant of the Industrial Revolution that began in 1785 (table 1). As illustrated through this book, that has certainly proved to be the case. If the graphic were revised today, important new topics in the sixth wave would include climate risk, circular economy, biodiversity, and ecosystems valuation, all of which have environmental as well as social dimensions.

Further, postpandemic competition for sustainability-skilled talent attests further to the accelerating importance of sustainability to employers in general.[13]

**Table 1** Sustainability born of the Industrial Revolution*

| Year | Wave | Innovation |
|------|------|------------|
| 1785 | First | Iron, water power, mechanization textiles, commerce |
| 1845 | Second | Steam power, railroad, steel, cotton |
| 1900 | Third | Chemicals, internal combustion engine |
| 1950 | Fourth | Petrochemicals, electronics, aviation, space |
| 1990 | Fifth | Digital networks, biotechnology, software, information technology |
| 2020 | Sixth | Sustainability, radical resource productivity, whole system design, biomimicry, green chemistry, industry ecology, renewable energy, green nanotechnology |

* Table information derived from *BusinessWeek*, February 4, 2008.

## Sustainability as a Business Issue

As a major user of natural resources, employer of people, and generator of wealth, the business community has a responsibility to be a major player, if not the largest player, in the quest for global sustainability.

**Linear economy.** A **linear economy** is based on the take-make-waste philosophy where raw materials are sourced and transformed into products (consumer goods) that are then briefly used, and quickly thrown away, so that new products can replace them. The model of linear economy has prevailed since the second half of the twentieth century.

More precisely, in the years following World War II, business and government leaders faced the question of how to sustain spending and employment at the levels that drove the economy during the war. An answer was provided by economist Victor Lebow in a 1955 article:

> Our enormously productive economy demands that we make consumption our way of life, that we convert the buying and use of goods into rituals, that we seek our spiritual satisfactions, our ego satisfactions, in consumption. The measure of social status, of social acceptance, of prestige, is now to be found in our consumptive patterns. The very meaning and significance of our lives today are expressed in consumptive terms. The greater the pressures upon the individual to conform to safe and accepted social standards, the more does he tend to express his aspirations and his individuality in terms of what he wears, drives, eats-his home, his car, his pattern of food serving, his hobbies. These commodities and services must be offered to the consumer with a special urgency. We require not only "forced draft" consumption, but "expensive" consumption as well. We need things consumed, burned up, worn out, replaced, and discarded at an ever-increasing pace. We need to have people eat, drink, dress, ride, and live, with ever more complicated and, therefore, constantly more expensive consumption. The home power tools and the whole "do-it-yourself" movement are excellent examples of "expensive" consumption.[14]

Essentially Lebow argued that the way to sustain spending and employment was to promote consumerism at all costs. Consumerism has proved to be the foundation for the take-make-waste economy that business and government leaders are now working to replace with the circular economy.

*Defining global events that led to sustainability development.* In the years that preceded and followed publication of *Our Common Future*, a series of business-associated events aligned global sentiment and set the stage for the report's message and especially the role of business practices in place at the time. As an example, in 1989, about eighteen months after the Brundtland Report was published, the oil tanker Exxon Valdez, owned by the Exxon

Shipping Company, struck a reef in "Prince William Sound, Alaska, spilling more than 11 million gallons of crude oil. The spill was the largest in U.S. history and tested the abilities of local, national, and industrial organizations to prepare for, and respond to, a disaster of such magnitude. The spill posed threats to the delicate food chain that supports Prince William Sound's commercial fishing industry. Also in danger were ten million migratory shore birds and waterfowl, hundreds of sea otters, dozens of other species, such as harbor porpoises and sea lions, and several varieties of whales."[15]

The magnitude of the spill and the widespread publicity about its impacts galvanized the oil industry and others to establish the Valdez Principles, an industry code of conduct to guide into a large-scale damage control. One outcome was the publication of the Valdez Principles "to regulate and monitor the conduct of corporations in matters relating to the environment." Of special note, "The sustainable investment movement was inspired by the Valdez Principles which were instituted by sustainable business nonprofit CERES (Coalition for Environmentally Responsible Economics)."[16] Today Ceres is a loud and influential organization that gives voice to the investment community regarding the risk management imperative of sustainable practices across all industries.

Other similar events are probably familiar to many readers. By geographic reference and associated dates they include Love Canal, Niagara Falls, New York (1976); Chernobyl Nuclear Power Plant, Pripyat, Ukrainian Soviet Socialist Republic (1986); Times Beach, Missouri (1982); Bhopal, India (1984); Garbage Barge, Islip, Long Island, New York (1987); Deepwater Horizon (2010); and Fukushima, Japan (2011). Hundreds, if not thousands, of less dramatic and visible events have occurred as well. All attest to the need for businesses generally to be key players in advancing sustainable practices.

*The business case for sustainability.* The business case for transforming a business in the direction of sustainability touches many issues. While the priorities for different companies will depend on individual circumstances, three factors seem to dominate most lists:

- *Reduction of risk.* Sustainable practices will allow a company to minimize the risk associated with rising prices and availability for energy

and water, unmanageable costs for carbon emissions as a result of cap
and trade regulations or new taxes, and fines and penalties for acciden-
tal releases.

- *Competition for talent.* Companies with proactive sustainable business
  practices are a magnet for talent. Companies find it easier to attract and
  retain top talent if they demonstrate that, while they care about making
  money, they also care about the environment and the people who are
  impacted by their activities.
- *Cost reduction or avoidance.* Sustainable business practices will lead
  to the purging of waste and inefficiencies from the system. Examples
  may include energy efficiency and conservation, closed-loop process
  water systems, scrap recovery and recycling, waste elimination, material substitution, and waste heat recovery.

Other elements of the business case for sustainability may include:

- Improved relationships with regulatory agencies.
- Increased productivity, operational efficiency, and effectiveness.
- Improved relationships with neighbors and other stakeholders.
- Increased reputational capital.
- Strengthened brand loyalty.
- Reduced cost of capital.

**Stakeholder engagement.** All components of the business case for sustainability have an underlying need for robust communication with stakeholders.
There are many approaches for building a stakeholder engagement program,
which can be a powerful differentiator in the competitive marketplace for
customers, employees, investors, and other allies.

**Sustainability reporting.** An early effort to codify the relationship of sustainability to business was the work of John Elkington, a British scholar and
entrepreneur who in 1994 coined the phrase **"triple bottom line" (TBL).**[17]
The concept is that businesses should measure, report, and be held accountable to stakeholders for their performance in regard to their environmental
and social impacts as well as their economic performance. Elkington's TBL
was well received as a framework that businesses could use in framing their

sustainability agenda and reporting results. The work provided a significant boost to what has become an industry within an industry—the preparation of annual sustainability reports. As the content of such reports began to expand, many companies, in the full spirit of sustainability, have moved them to a digital format. "Over the past five years, more companies have begun publishing sustainability reports, with 90 percent of the largest 500 U.S. public companies reporting in 2019—an 11 percent increase since 2015."[18] Investors are a prime audience for the reports of public and private investor-owned companies, as they contain information useful in gaging investment risk. Another prime audience is early-career job seekers, as that cohort of potential employees has high standards for the sustainability performance of employers they will consider. In 2019 Elkington published an article in the *Harvard Business Review* in which he proposed a recall of the triple bottom line idea.[19] He felt that there might be better frameworks to promote the corporate behavior and reporting transformations he had initiated. As of yet, however, there has been no landslide of activity promoting wholesale recall of Elkington's triple bottom line.

A reporting trend that has caught on is to couch the sustainability discussion in terms of **environmental, social, and governance (ESG)** issues. This makes sense because it brings into play board-level decisions that relate closely to the strategic dimensions of a robust sustainability agenda. ESG and sustainability are not yet synonymous, but that day may come. Because the financial and nonfinancial elements of sustainability are inextricably interrelated, there has been some effort by various stakeholder groups to encourage combining sustainability reporting with annual/economic reporting into a single integrated report. This has not caught on to a significant degree. A leader in doing so is investor-owned utility American Electric Power (AEP). AEP's 2020 report is called the *Corporate Accountability Report*.[20] Likewise, Dow titled its 2020 report as *INtersections: 2020 Environmental, Social and Governance Report*.[21]

A final important point regarding sustainability reporting frameworks relates to content and format. In the early years of sustainability reporting (the 1990s), every company that issued a sustainability report used its own format, and often the format changed from year to year. This made it difficult for stakeholders to track progress. The Global Reporting Initiative (GRI) was founded in 1997 to bring more uniformity to sustainability reporting and today provides such services to reporting entities in over one hundred countries.[22] GRI Standards offer two levels of reporting: core and comprehensive. Other reporting frameworks also exist.

**Materiality assessment.** Materiality assessment is the process of mapping the list of material issues selected by an organization onto a $2 \times 2$ grid. This shows how well each issue is aligned with stakeholder priorities for that issue with the organization's priorities. Both the core and comprehensive GRI reporting formats require inclusion of a materiality assessment in the sustainability report.[23]

**Sustainability credentials**. Sustainability credentials are a means to communicate commitment to sustainability and are available for buildings, people, companies, and products.

- *Credentials for buildings*. One of the first sustainability credentials was conceived by the USGBC with its program **Leadership in Energy and Environmental Design (LEED)**.[24] Using a point system, buildings can apply to be designated at one of four levels of LEED certification: certified, silver, gold, or platinum. Buildings are scored on six groups of factors relating to location and transportation, materials and resources, water efficiency, energy and atmosphere, site sustainability, and indoor air quality. Over the years since launch of the program in 1998, LEED buildings have gained a reputation for being less costly over their life cycle and healthier, more comfortable places to work. Accordingly, commercial LEED buildings command higher lease rates. Building-related sustainability credential programs exist in Canada, the UK, and in many other countries.

- *Credentials for People*. Credentials for people are of two types. One type requires passing an exam and the other requires completion of specified course work, in person or online. The strongest, of course, require passing of an exam. Three of the exam-based credentials are:

- ○ The LEED Green Associate and the LEED Accredited Professional, which focus on skills and knowledge needed to design LEED buildings.
- ○ The GRI Sustainability Professional, which focuses on skills and knowledge related to sustainability reporting.
- ○ ISSP Sustainability Excellence Associate and the Sustainability Excellence Professional.

Other opportunities may be found online.

- *Credentials for Companies.* The holy grail for companies seeking to outshine the competition when it comes to sustainability matters is the Dow Jones Sustainability Index (DJSI).[25] The index "ranks the stock performance of the world's leading companies in terms of economic, environmental and social criteria."[26] The index is actually a family of indices segmented by industry and geographic groupings.

  A related credential is the S&P Global Corporate Sustainability Assessment (CSA).[27] Both the DJSI and the CSA are used by investors use to apply a best-in-class process to investment decisions. Annually about ten thousand companies are invited to submit data for inclusion in the DJSI rankings, but only about seven thousand companies actually survive the rigorous screening process. Companies invited to participate in the DJSI may also submit to the CSA free of charge. Other companies may participate in the CSA for a fee. Both the DJSI and the CSA employ sixty-one industry sectors. These sectors include airlines, building products, insurance, steel, and tobacco. Other less recognizable industry groupings include casinos and gambling, energy equipment and services, life sciences tools and services, and oil and gas storage and transportation.

  Criteria are organized by ESG categories and include, for example:
  - ○ Environmental criteria (environmental reporting, climate strategy, packaging)
  - ○ Social criteria (labor practices, human capital development, corporate citizenship & philanthropy)
  - ○ Governance and economic criteria (materiality, risk and crisis management, privacy protection)

The criteria vary slightly from one industry sector to another, as do the weights given to criteria, and they may be adjusted slightly from one year to another. While the DJSI and CSA rankings and assessments appeal to larger companies, certification as a **B Corporation** (or B Corp) appeals primarily to smaller companies for whom sustainability is a primary brand identifier.[28] The *B* stands for *benefit*, and to achieve B-Corp certification, a company must undergo an assessment that attests that their business decisions routinely consider the impact of their decisions on their workers, customers, suppliers, community, and the environment. There are over four thousand B Corporations in the world.[29] They are a community of leaders, driving a global movement of people using business as a force for good. Familiar names of companies that have achieved B-Corp certification are Patagonia, New Belgium Brewing, Danone, Stonyfield Organic, and Ben & Jerry's. Also deserving mention at this point is the International Standards Organization (ISO).[30] ISO is the source of highly respected management or process standards that apply to making a product, managing a process, delivering a service, or supplying materials. ISO does not set performance criteria or standards but rather prescribes the management processes that should apply to an activity. Several ISO standards apply to topics pertaining to sustainability matters such as environmental management, health and safety, food safety, and energy management. Certifications available under ISO standards apply not to companies per se but to individual operating units such as plants.

- *Credentials for products.* When considering the sustainability merits of a product the most important lens is the design of the product. Design governs:
  - What a product will be made of and, hence, from where raw materials be sourced, If raw materials are extracted or harvested, what are the environmental and social impacts, such as the depletion of nonrenewable resources and abusive labor practices?

- ○ Manufacturing processes that will be employed, which will most likely have their own set of impacts, such as carbon emissions from energy used.
- ○ What options exist at end-of-life for repair, reuse/repurposing, and/or recycling.
- ○ Disposal options and associated impacts.

**Biomimicry** is a design approach that guides product designers through the myriad of complex considerations outlined above by relying on processes and principles employed by nature.[31] One example is a paint call Lotusan that leaves coating that mimics the self-cleaning characteristics of the lotus leaf.[32]

**Lifestyles of health and sustainability (LOHAS)** is a large and growing market segment of consumers interested in knowing about the sustainability credentials of products. In 2020 the LOHAS market segment was "a $355 billion market in the USA alone and growing at 10% per year. It [was] a $546 billion market worldwide."[33]

**Green Seal** is an independent, nonprofit organization, over thirty years old, that offers certifications for over 3,300 products with a focus on household products versus industrial products. There is a strong focus on environmental versus social matters, as evidenced by the four main goals upon which its product certifications are based: (1) to preserve climate, (2) to protect human health, (3) to ensure clean water, and (4) to minimize waste.[34]

In the for profit space: there is the **Cradle to Cradle (C2C)** product certification. C2C is based on a belief of its founders, William McDonough and Michael Braungart, that waste should be eliminated as a concept. The name is clearly the signal to a 180-degree departure from the traditional cradle to grave approach to product end-of-life approaches. Products are evaluated across five topical categories of environmental and human health: "material health, material re-utilization, renewable energy and carbon management, water stewardship, and social [fitness]. Product certification is awarded at five levels: basic, bronze, silver gold, and platinum."[35] The C2C certification is very rigorous in that overall product certification is based on the lowest level award across the five topical categories.[36]

Two last points regarding product certifications related to sustainability:

- *Organic*, when applied to food, is a certification granted by the US Department of Agriculture that certifies the product has been grown in accord with specified standards, such as without the use of synthetic fertilizers, pesticides, and herbicides. Labels such as "natural" and other words that might suggest some relationship to sustainability have no agreed-upon or enforced connotation.[37]
- *Energy Star* rates the energy efficiency of household and commercial products and equipment. It is a joint program of the US Department of Energy and the US Environmental Protection Agency (EPA). It is a very popular program and has been copied by many other countries. The program has also been adopted to rate the energy efficiency of buildings.[38]

## Getting Started with Sustainable Business: A Brief Guide

Often one hears corporate leaders and executives state that they understand the business case but don't know how to get started on the path to sustainability. This section of the chapter outlines the essential ingredients of a successful program, which are typically customized to fit each company's situation.

- *Create a written policy.* A written policy on sustainability is the way to draw a line in the sand for everyone to see and to use as a benchmark for their behavior and decision making. Stakeholders, especially employees, should frequently see and hear company leadership making reference to the policy and using it as a decision-making guide.
- *Illuminate top management support.* The next step must be declaration by the CEO or business unit leader that there are business reasons behind initiatives and programs being initiated. Then the CEO or business unit leader must reinforce the message by his or her behavior and frequent remessaging, until the tonsils bleed. Reluctant and skeptical employees must be won over. Clearly, this cannot be assigned to a lower-level manager or staff person. That approach is the single most common cause of failure; following that methodology will guarantee

that sustainability initiatives don't work out or just "die on the vine." An excellent example of CEO leadership on sustainability is the late Ray Anderson, founder of Interface Carpet. He came to a realization that his company was plundering the earth with its carpet manufacturing business. He set the company on a path to climb "Mount Sustainability" and he personally visited company plants to tell employees why that was important.[39]

- *Engage all employees.* Under leadership of the CEO or business unit leader, managers and supervisors must ensure that each employee understands how his or her performance and behavior support the sustainability initiative. Job expectations and sustainability roles must be aligned. Formation of a "green team" is often a useful way to create this engagement.

- *Set goals and targets.* Next, set goals and targets with measurable milestones and assign responsibilities for their achievement. Pay particular attention to the metrics that are chosen so they represent true measures of sustainability progress. Remember that not everything that can be measured is worth measuring, and not everything important can be measured in quantitative terms. In setting goals and targets, don't just look within your plant or place of business for improvement opportunities, but also look deeply into the supply chain and consider broadly how company activities affect all stakeholders.

- *Report on results.* Reporting on results is the way to close the loop with stakeholders and sets the stage for transparency. Reporting programs must be designed for replicability. Results must be reported year after year in the same format and with the same metrics so that trends can be easily seen by stakeholders. Reporting also lays the foundation for setting continuous improvement goals. In the spirit of continuous improvement, update the above process periodically.

*Stages to sustainability transformation.* Companies that embark on a transformation to be green or sustainable typically go through several stages. Authors Dunphy, Griffiths, and Benn studied dozens of companies and found that six stages represent the journey of the typical company.

- *Stage 1: Denial.* The attitude of company leadership at this stage is that "all resources—employees, community infrastructure," mineral deposits, timber stands, "and the ecological environment—are there to be exploited by the firm for immediate economic gain."[40] The company has no concern for the negative impacts of its activities on the environment and on other people and actively opposes efforts by governments or citizens to place constraints on its activities. Fortunately, there are only a handful of such companies still in existence today.
- *Stage 2: Non-responsiveness.* "Non-responsiveness usually results from lack of awareness or ignorance rather than from active opposition to a corporate ethic broader than [immediate] financial gain." Human resource strategies are focused on assuring the availability of a productive and "compliant workforce. Community issues are ignored"[41] and negative environmental impacts are considered to be the normal result of doing business.
- *Stage 3: Compliance.* Companies in this stage focus on reducing the risks of failing to meet minimum standards imposed by law. Company leadership holds itself to the standard of "ensuring a safe, healthy workplace and avoiding environmental abuses that could"[42] expose the company to litigation or damaging PR. There is a willingness to accommodate community expectations for green or sustainable practices, but only in a reactive mode.
- *Stage 4: Efficiency.* Companies in this stage have woken up to the fact that there are bottom-line advantages to be realized from green or sustainable practices. Waste is viewed as a "product" that is manufactured at a cost but that can't be sold, and that therefore needs to be minimized or eliminated. Companies begin to train personnel to recognize such opportunities, as well as other expenses to implement green or sustainable initiatives, as investments rather than costs.
- *Stage 5: Strategic proactivity.* Companies in this stage have moved to the point that sustainability is a key part of business strategy. Company leadership has learned that sustainability can be a key to competitive advantage. Sustainable best practices are implemented to the greatest degree possible and are used proactively to attract and retain top talent.

Sustainability initiatives are used to strengthen stakeholder relationships in all directions. In the final analysis, sustainability is motivated by intelligent and enlightened corporate self-interest. Companies in this space include GE, Toyota, and 3M.

- *Stage 6: The sustaining corporation.* In this final stage, the company leadership has strongly internalized the notion of working for a sustainable world and operating sustainably is embedded in the company's DNA, as is transparency. Sustainable operations are viewed as a key to sustaining profits and a key to promoting environmental integrity, as well as community and social values. These companies believe that markets and institutions must be transformed to work for, and not against, sustainability. Only a few companies inhabit this space. They include Interface, Patagonia, and Unilever, for example.[43]

These stages, presented in linear fashion, are obviously an oversimplification of reality. In practice, companies may have different parts of the business at different points in the continuum at any one time. And it is not uncommon to slip back and forth for short periods of time even as forward progress is made over longer periods of time.

*Emerging ideas in sustainability.* Sustainability is a maturing endeavor. The flood of newsletters on the topic, many of which are daily, is more than anyone can keep up with and still have time left to be productive. Summarized are a few ideas that have gained traction but that still have not yet gained mainstream traction. A primary source of sustainability innovation is Scandinavia, where sustainability thinking has been part of the culture almost since the emergence of modern civilization.

**Sharing economy.** The sharing economy, also called collaborative consumption, epitomized by public libraries, has been with us for centuries and is an example of the conserver economy. Driven in the case of libraries by scarcity and affordability of books, present-day interest in sharing some assets is driven by conservation interests. For example, equipment and tools for home maintenance, which can be expensive and/or inconvenient to store and maintain, are desired not for ownership per se but for the service they provide. Many people view automobiles and bicycles in the same manner.

Accordingly, rental and leasing options for various assets have become very popular in many communities, particularly among millennials.

**Product as a service.** Product as a service also builds on the realization that we acquire many of the products we buy not because we want to own the product but because we want access to the service the product provides. Consider the case of lightbulbs. We buy lightbulbs because we want lighted surfaces and spaces. Purchasing lightbulbs and changing them when they burn out is an inconvenience most of us would gladly avoid. Phillips realized this and offers the opportunity for customers to purchase lighted surfaces and spaces according to contractually specified details, and Phillips takes the responsibility to provide the lightbulbs and change them as necessary. This turns the business model around for Phillips. Under this model the company is incentivized to manufacture lightbulbs that will last as long as possible, versus as short as possible when they made money selling lightbulbs. Amsterdam's international airport was an early adopter of this approach. A similar opportunity is taken by Michelin, who offers to provide tires with a miles of service guarantee versus just selling tires. In both the Phillips and Michelin cases, the manufacturer earns money by making products that last as long as possible versus as short as possible, thereby conserving resources in the long run—to the benefit of all stakeholders including the earth.

**Circular economy.** The classical, linear, take-make-waste economy is giving way to the circular economy, in which products are designed to be disassembled, remanufactured, and recycled or upcycled back into economic use. Circular economy ideas have gained traction due in part to the work of the Macarthur Foundation. Caterpillar puts this thinking to work in its remanufacturing program. Through wise design choices, Caterpillar can rebuild construction equipment and offer it for sale with the same guarantee as for new equipment, but at lower prices than new equipment because of the resources conserved.[44]

Another example of the circular economy is **by-product synergy (BPS)**. This is the simple concept that one company's waste may be the input or raw material for another company's production. The Ohio By-Product Synergy network has been operating successfully for some time now, working with manufacturers in Ohio that meet periodically to discuss what they buy and what they discard as waste.[45] During its first ten years of operation, dozens of such synergies have been identified, which save Ohio companies money and conserve resources, many of which are nonrenewable. BPS was conceived by the US Business Council for Sustainable Development in Austin, Texas, and it has spawned BPS networks in several cities.[46] These networks have in turn spawned online materials marketplaces to enable circular economy practices, such as one in Ohio.[47] The concept of BPS was spawned in Kalundborg, Denmark, in the late 1960s when eight companies agreed to colocate on the same site of several hundred acres because they anticipated the opportunity to share waste streams for multiple uses. The Kalundborg center is still in operation and the resident companies exchange twenty-eight streams of waste material and energy. It operates under the label of industrial symbiosis versus BPS, but the concept is the same.[48] Circular economy principles were also a strong building block of the sustainability agenda for the 2021 Olympic Games in Tokyo.[49]

**Handprints vs. footprints.** We are all familiar with footprints as a metaphor for the damage we do to the environment as we go about our business. But what about handprints? Handprints are a new metaphor for the good we can do. There is a significant difference. The best we can do is to reduce our footprints to zero, which none of us will probably ever achieve. But there is no limit to our handprints, the good we can do. To imbed this into corporate goals, many companies are now talking about being net positive, the net impact of footprints and handprints—a laudable aspirational goal. Examples ae that reducing emission to zero would maximize possible footprint reduction, whereas increasing the efficiency of energy use would be a handprint improvement. One company that has done so is Toledo, Ohio-based Owens Corning, which is ranked number one in their category in the coveted DJSI.[50]

**Quadruple vs. triple bottom line.** A core sustainability concept is the previously discussed triple bottom line, which is the notion that enterprises are accountable for performance in three accounts: social responsibility, environmental performance, and economic measures, often abbreviated

**people, planet, and profit (or the 3 Ps)**. Researchers in Australia and New Zealand have suggested a fourth *P*, purpose, suggesting that a sustainable organization should have an aspirational purpose (beyond its mission) that speaks to why the organization exists and why anyone would want to work there. This line of thinking is reflected in a *Harvard Business Review* article titled, "Creating a Purpose-Driven Organization." The article argues, with numerous examples, that when a sense of purpose is embedded in an organization, employees perform at higher levels and are motivated to embrace aspirational goals.[51]

**Blockchain.** Blockchain is an embryonic set of emerging digital technologies for protecting the privacy and security of transactions. A primary value of blockchain technology is that it increases the integrity of transactions among and between the parties to a business transaction, called the network, by making the records of a transaction (i.e., the ledger) available in real time across the network. With regard to sustainability, blockchain has found application to improve the integrity of supply chain transactions.

The key advantage of blockchain technology is the opportunity to create a secure network available to the parties to a transaction without requiring intermediaries such as bankers and others normally needed to facilitate a business transaction. An example would be a coffee shop owner in any location globally who knows of a special coffee bean grown by a farmer in a remote locations (Brazil, for example) that he wants to feature as the ingredient for his signature coffee without competitors knowing his supplier or any related details. Using blockchain, the coffee shop owner and the farmer can create a two-party network not available to anyone else to ensure that the coffee shop owner gets the coffee beans he orders (without risk of tampering), and the farmer gets paid.

**Shared value.** Shared value is the practice of creating economic value in a way that also creates value for society by addressing its needs and challenges. In the context of sustainable business practices, shared value results from policies and practices that contribute to competitive advantage while strengthening the communities in which a company operates. As an example, in one instance Cummins committed to bringing fresh water to 20 million people who otherwise did not have access. At the same time it and produced net water benefits exceeding Cummins' annual water use in all company regions by 2030 and all Cummins communities by 2050. The commitment will be led through its new $8 million global community program.[52]

**Impact investing.** Impact investing refers to investments made into companies, organizations, and funds with the intention to generate a measurable, beneficial social or environmental impact alongside a financial return.[53] Impact investments provide capital to address social and/or environmental issues. Impact investing is in contrast to socially responsible investing, which screens out investments in companies judged by the investor to have negative social or environmental impact.

**Extended producer responsibility (EPR).** EPR, also known as product stewardship, is a strategy to place a shared responsibility for end-of-life product management on producers and other entities involved in the product chain, instead of on the general public, while encouraging product design changes that minimize negative impacts on human health and the environment at every stage of the product's life cycle. This allows the costs of processing and disposal to be incorporated into the total cost of a product. It places primary responsibility on the producer, or brand owner, who makes design and marketing decisions. It also creates a setting for markets to emerge that truly reflect the environmental impacts of a product and to which producers and consumers respond. As of early 2021, thirty-four states had EPR laws governing one or more products.[54] Additionally, some states have local laws. Examples of products covered by various EPR laws include, for example, paint, carpet, mattresses, pharmaceuticals and sharps, mercury thermostats, and pesticide containers.

*Valuing ecosystem services.* Ecosystem services are so prevalent and commonplace as to be taken for granted and not valued in a formal sense. However, forward-looking companies are working on ways to monetize the value of ecosystem services they use or that represent assets of which they are stewards and to use this information in decision-making.[55] An example would be deciding whether to cut down a grove of trees that protect a building from stormy weather to build a parking lot to improve employee access to work spaces.

*Internal carbon pricing.* Internal carbon pricing is a voluntary action taken by a company to prepare for an anticipated future requirement to pay a tax on carbon emissions. Based on whatever inputs the enterprise considers pertinent, an estimated future carbon tax amount is determined. Estimated tax amounts employed across all industry sectors range widely but are in the range of five to twenty dollars per ton. This is used to estimate the likely future cost of operations as a guide to determine the potential future return on investments in carbon-taxed environment.[56]

*Keeping up with sustainability ideas.* A good way to keep up with the flow of new ideas pertaining to sustainability in business is the annual *State of Green Business* report issued by *GreenBiz*. The previously referenced 2021 report led with the statement, "At last, sustainability has emerged from the shadows to be considered part and parcel of corporate success."[57] Another aspect of keeping up is to embrace, not resist, change. Nadya Zhexembayeva, in her book *How to Thrive in Chaos*, prescribes that organizations and individuals commit to reinventing themselves periodically as one means of strengthening their sustainability and resilience agendas.[58]

## Chapter Summary

The first chapter, written by professor, consultant, and sustainability practitioner Dr. Neal Drobny (Western Michigan University), overviews key sustainable business concepts while positioning our firm belief that there is a realistic need for fashion businesses to take more authentic and significant action to deal with environmental and social matters locally and globally. By focusing on corporate negligence, such as the ExxonMobil Corporation oil spill disaster and many other planetary crises caused by negligent corporations, this chapter attests that it is expected from successful and responsible businesses to act as key players in advancing sustainable practices. The benefits of LEEDs certified buildings, BPS networks (e.g., the Ohio By-Product Synergy network), or B-Corp certified businesses (e.g., Patagonia, New Belgium Brewing, Danone, Stonyfield Organic, and Ben & Jerry's) discussed in this chapter furthermore showcase that the status quo in today's business context is not an option and that sustainable change has become an imperative across the industries!

# References

1. Scarlett Buckley, "The Urban Sun: A Light at the End of the Covid Tunnel?" *Sustainable Brands*, July 12, 2021, https://sustainablebrands.com/read/product-service-design-innovation/the-urban-sun-a-light-at-the-end-of-the-covid-tunnel/?utm_source=newsletter&utm_medium=email&utm_campaign=nl_210712.
2. Eric Posner, "Milton Friedman Was Wrong," *Atlantic*, August 22, 2019, https://www.theatlantic.com/ideas/archive/2019/08/milton-friedman-shareholder-wrong/596545/.
3. N. Pedigo, "180 CEOs Redefine Corporate Purpose to Promote 'An Economy That Serves All,'" *Sustainable Brands*, August 20, 2019, https://sustainablebrands.com/read/leadership/business-roundtable-redefines-purpose-of-a-corporation-to-promote-an-economy-that-serves-all.
4. Joe Makower, "Mapping Sustainability Means Connecting the Dots," *GreenBiz*, July 13, 2021, https://www.greenbiz.com/article/mapping-sustainability-means-connecting-dots.
5. C. Prahalad and Stuart L. Hart, "The Fortune at the Bottom of the Pyramid," *Strategy+business*, January 10, 2002, https://www.strategy-business.com/article/11518.
6. Muhammad Yunus, *Creating a World without Poverty: Social Business and the Future of Capitalism* (New York: PublicAffairs, 2009).
7. Lydia Noyes, "A Guide to Greenwashing and How to Spot It," *EcoWatch*, October 21, 2021, https://www.ecowatch.com/7-sins-of-greenwashing-and-5-ways-to-keep-it-out-of-your-life-1881898598.html.
8. "New Rulebook Helps Companies Validate Their Sustainability Claims," Sustainable Brands, July 22, 2021, https://sustainablebrands.com/read/marketing-and-comms/new-rulebook-helps-companies-validate-their-sustainability-claims/?utm_source=newsletter&utm_medium=email&utm_campaign=nl_210726.
9. "Ecosystem Services & Biodiversity (ESB)," *FAO*, accessed January 10, 2022, https://www.fao.org/ecosystem-services-biodiversity/en/#:~:text=Ecosystem%20services%20make%20human%20life,recreational%2C%20cultural%20and%20spiritual%20benefits.
10. "Sustainable," *Webster's Third International Dictionary of the English Language*, (London, Encyclopedia Britannica, 1986).
11. World Commission on Environment and Development, *Our Common Future*, 1987, accessed January 10, 2022, https://www.are.admin.ch/are/en/home/media/publications/sustainable-development/brundtland-report.html.
12. "The 17 Goals," United Nations, accessed February 7, 2022, https://sdgs.un.org/goals.
13. Joe Makower, "Inside the War for ESG Talent," *GreenBiz*, July 19, 2021, https://www.greenbiz.com/article/inside-war-esg-talent?utm_source=newsletter&utm_medium=email&utm_campaign=greenbuzz&utm_content=2021-07-19&mkt_

tok=MjExLU5KWS0xNjUAAAF-XdTdtq45xId043MDctwSjSPo7HgZZd-baE4H5YfJBCU6Yl-z0nxHapEi-M03shC6qYIHicO5un3iWDkq0wcHs8ZfK.

14. Victor Lebow, "Price Competition in 1955," *Journal of Retailing* 31, no. 1 (1955): 5–10.

15. "Exxon Valdez Spill Profile," *EPA: United States Environmental Protection Agency*, November 29, 2022, https://www.epa.gov/emergency-response/exxon-valdez-spill-profile.

16. Matthews, Richard, "Valdez Principles (Ceres Principles) Ceres Pledge," *Change Oracle*, March 2, 2015, https://changeoracle.com/2015/03/02/valdez-principles-ceres-principles/.

17. John Elkington, "Enter the Triple Bottom Line," chap. 1 in *The Triple Bottom Line, Does It All Add Up? Assessing the Sustainability of Business and CSR*, ed. Adrian Henriques and Julie Richardson (London: Earthscan, 2007), accessed on May 23, 2023, https://www.johnelkington.com/archive/TBL-elkington-chapter.pdf.

18. Joel Makower and the editors at *GreenBiz*, *State of Green Business 2021*, accessed on February 7, 2022, https://www.greenbiz.com/article/state-green-business-2021.

19. John Elkington, "25 Years Ago I Coined the Phrase 'Triple Bottom Line.' Here's Why It's Time to Rethink It," *Harvard Business Review*, June 25, 2018, https://hbr.org/2018/06/25-years-ago-i-coined-the-phrase-triple-bottom-line-heres-why-im-giving-up-on-it.

20. AEP Sustainability, *AEP Corporate Accountability Report 2020*, accessed on May 13, 2023, https://www.aepsustainability.com/performance/report/docs/CAR_MID-YEAR%20UPDATE2020.pdf.

21. Dow Corporate, *INtersections: 2020 Environmental, Social, and Governance Report*, accessed on February 23, 2022, https://corporate.dow.com/documents/about/066-00338-01-2020-esg-report.pdf.

22. "GRI mission history," *Global Reporting Initiative*, accessed on February 22, 2023, https://www.globalreporting.org/about-gri/mission-history/.

23. Mia Overall, "How to Make Your Materiality Assessment Worth the Effort," *GreenBiz*, August 15, 2017, https://www.greenbiz.com/article/how-make-your-materiality-assessment-worth-effort.

24. "LEED Rating System," *USGBC*, accessed on February 22, 2022, https://www.usgbc.org/leed.

25. "Dow Jones Sustainability Indices Methodology," *Dow Jones*, September 2023, https://www.spglobal.com/spdji/en/documents/methodologies/methodology-dj-sustainability-indices.pdf.

26. Cecilia Plottier and Yuri Park, *Korean FDI in Latin America and the Caribbean: A Partner for Sustainable Development*, 2020, https://repositorio.cepal.org/server/api/core/bitstreams/19c66a1b-7ce4-469f-9081-596fec164dc6/content.

27. "Getting an Assessment," *S&P Global*, accessed on February 23, 2022, https://www.spglobal.com/esg/csa/getting-an-assessment.

28. "Make Business a Force for Good," *B Lab*, accessed on February 23, 2022, https://bcorporation.net/.

29. B Lab Global, "B Lab announces the Best For The World 2021 B Corps," *B Corporation*, July 13, 2021, https://www.bcorporation.net/en-us/news/press/b-lab-announces-2021-best-world-b-corps-performance-excellence-beyond-just-profit/#:~:text=Today%20there%20are%20more%20than,%2C%20communities%2C%20and%20the%20planet.

30. "ISO Standards," *ISO*, accessed on February 23, 2022, https://www.iso.org/standards.html.

31. "Humanity's Biggest Challenges 2020," *Biomimicry Institute*, accessed on February 23, 2022, http://www.biomimicry.org.

32. "Architectural Coatings," *STO Corp*, accessed on February 23, 2022, https://www.stocorp.com/coatings-us/.

33. "The Lohas Consumer 2019," *Spa Wellness*, accessed on May 1, 2022, https://www.spawellness.com/blog/https/wwwspawellnesscom/blog-page-url/2019/3/15/new-post-title-1.

34. "Green Seal a Universal Symbol of Health and Environmental Leadership," *Green Seal Home*, accessed on February 22, 2022, http://www.greenseal.org.

35. Susan Heinking and Candace Small, "TOXIC! Our 7 Most Useful Materials Certification, Disclosure Systems," *Builtworlds*, January 14, 2015, https://builtworlds.com/news/toxic-7-useful-materials-certification-disclosure-systems/.

36. "Cradle to Cradle Certified 2021," *Cradle to Cradle Certified Product Standard*, accessed on June 1, 2023, https://cdn.c2ccertified.org/resources/certification/standard/STD_C2C_Certified_V4.0_FINAL_031621.pdf.

37. Mary, J. Brown, "What Is Organic Food, And Is It More Nutritious Than Non-Organic Food?," *Healthline*, September 16, 2021, https://www.healthline.com/nutrition/what-is-organic-food.

38. "The Simple Choice for Energy Efficiency," *Energy Star*, accessed on February 23, 2022, http://www.energystar.gov.

39. Ray Anderson, dir., "The Business Case for Sustainability," *Natural Step Online*, July 7, 2011, https://www.youtube.com/watch?v=9qrQKA0xMko.

40. Suzanne Benn, "Integrating Human and Ecological Sustainability," paper presented at the 2002 Australasian Evaluation Society International Conference, October/November, 2002, Wollongong, Australia, https://www.aes.asn.au/images/images-old/stories/files/conferences/2002/papers/Benn.pdf. The paper is modified from a chapter written by Benn for Dexter C. Dunphy, Andrew Griffiths, and Suzanne Benn, *Organizational Change for Corporate Sustainability: A Guide for Leaders and Change Agents of the Future* (London: Routledge, 2003).

41. Ibid.

42. Ibid.

43. Ibid.

44. "What Is a Circular Economy?," Ellen MacArthur Foundation, accessed on February 23, 2022, https://www.ellenmacarthurfoundation.org/circular-economy/concept.

45. "Ohio BPS Network," *Canton Chamber*, accessed on February 23, https://www.cantonchamber.org/Content/uploads/OhioBPSNetwork.pdf.

46. F. Sadaqat, "By-Product Synergy," *USBCSD*, last modified April 9, 2015, https://usbcsd.org/news-articles/category/By-Product+Synergy.

47. "Materials Marketplace," *Ohio Environmental Protection Agency*, accessed on February 23, 2022, https://ohio.materialsmarketplace.org/.

48. "The World's Leading Industrial Symbiosis," *Kalundborg Symbiosis*, accessed on February 23, 2022, http://www.symbiosis.dk/en/.

49. "Tokyo 2020 Highlights the Possibilities for a Circular Economy," *International Olympic Committee*, 2019, accessed on February 23, 2022, https://olympics.com/ioc/news/tokyo-2020-highlights-the-possibilities-for-a-circular-economy.

50. "Our Approach," *Owens Corning*, accessed on February 23, 2022, https://www.owenscorning.com/en-us/corporate/sustainability/our-approach.

51. R. E. Quinn and A. V. Thakor, "Creating a Purpose-Driven Organization," *Harvard Business Review*, July/August 2018, https://hbr.org/2018/07/creating-a-purpose-driven-organization.

52. "Cummins Water Works," *Cummins*, accessed on February 23, 2022, https://www.cummins.com/company/global-impact/cummins-water-works.

53. "The Truth behind the Trend of Impact Investing," *Berkeley Economic Review*, accessed on February 23, 2022, https://econreview.berkeley.edu/the-truth-behind-the-trend-of-impact-investing/.

54. "Product Stewardship Institute, Inc.," US State EPR Laws, *Product Stewardship Institute*, accessed on February 23, 2022, https://www.productstewardship.us/page/State_EPR_Laws_Map.

55. Committee on Assessing and Valuing the Services of Aquatic and Related Terrestrial Ecosystems, Water Science and Technology Board, Division on Earth and Life Studies, & National Research Council, *Valuing Ecosystem Services: Toward Better Environmental Decision-Making*, 2005, National Academies Press, https://www.nap.edu/catalog/11139/valuing-ecosystem-services-toward-better-environmental-decision-making.

56. M. B. Ahluwalia, "Internal Carbon Pricing," *Center for Climate and Energy Solutions*, accessed on February 23, 2022, https://www.c2es.org/content/internal-carbon-pricing/https://econreview.berkeley.edu/the-truth-behind-the-trend-of-impact-investing/.

57. Makower, *State of Green Business 2021*.

58. Nadya Zhexembayeva, *The Chief Reinvention Officer Handbook: How to Thrive in Chaos* (n.p.: Ideapress, 2020).

# Chapter 2

# Sustainable Development in the Fashion Industry

# Chapter Introduction and Learning Objectives

In this chapter we will look at the definition of sustainability and SDGs in the fashion industry context. This chapter builds on the discussion in chapter 1 and explores how the SDGs are linked with environmental, economic, and social performance in the fashion industry. More specifically, in this chapter we will look at "how our clothes affect global issues such as poverty, inequality, forced, bonded, and child labor, and other human abuses."[1] Students "will also explore how our clothing impacts the planet's health and ecosystems, analyzing issues such as global warming, microplastic pollution in our oceans, and the loss of forests and biodiversity."[2] Case studies presented in this section are for the purpose of illuminating the multilayered sustainability problems in our industry, showcasing why fashion practices are often interlinked with human rights abuses, worker poverty, inequality, and environmental degradation. In the "Student Voices" section of this chapter, the perspectives of students are shared on the SDG topics. The contribution of the students in this section is significantly important because students are positioned here as storytellers and collaborators who advocate for sustainability-driven change in our industry.

This chapter has the following learning objectives:

- Describe sustainability in the context of the fashion industry.
- Discuss Triple Bottom Line (TBL) sustainability.
- Apply TBL to the fashion industry context.
- Define Sustainable Development Goals.

## Key Terms

| | |
|---|---|
| economic sustainability pillar | Registration, Evaluation, Authorization, |
| environmental sustainability pillar | and Restriction of Chemicals |
| greenhouse gas emissions | renewable vs. nonrenewable resources |
| living wage | social license to operate |
| manufacturing restricted | sustainable development |
|   substances list | triple bottom line |
| minimum wage | sustainable |

# Overview of Sustainability

The meaning of sustainability varies widely depending on the group defining it. Sustainability is often defined in general terms relating to the ability to maintain something indefinitely. However, that viewpoint is not all-encompassing because sustainability is not about simply maintaining the status quo. Rather, sustainability requires a market shift and a business shift. Let me explain why. Consider the issue of climate change, for example. Climate change affects everything from weather conditions to world water systems, from global and local economies to overall human health. Likewise, climate change affects individual businesses as well. Nowadays, companies are realizing that raw material costs and energy costs are increasing while governments are setting policies to reduce greenhouse gas emissions. Because climate change and policies to reduce greenhouse gas emissions directly affect energy prices, national income, health, and agriculture, we can argue that climate change is causing an impending market shift. Hence, if we consider climate change as a factor that alters existing market conditions and creates new ones, we can further argue that market shifts create winners and losers and that businesses must innovate to survive.[3] Thus, sustainability is not simply about maintaining the status quo—staying in business while making no effort to change; it is about making a shift in the way an organization does business.

Perhaps the most widely accepted definitions and characteristics of **sustainable development** comes from two sources. The first is the Brundtland Commission's report *Our Common Future* from the World Commission on Environment and Development, which states, "Sustainable development is a development that meets the needs of the present without compromising the ability of future generations to meet their own needs."[4] This statement indicates the importance of two key concepts:

1. the concept of *needs*—especially the basic or essential needs (e.g., air, water, shelter, food, etc.)—that humans need in order to live; and
2. the concept of *limitations* (e.g., environmental and social limits to economic progress).

The Brundtland Report further concludes that "the goals of economic and social development must be defined in terms of sustainability in all countries—developed or developing, market-oriented or centrally planned. Interpretations will vary but must share certain general features and must flow from a consensus on the basic concept of sustainable development and on a broad strategic framework for achieving it."[5]

Sustainability economist Herman Daly uses three principles to define sustainability more precisely, and these principles represent another common source used for interpreting the concept of sustainability. Those principles are known as Herman Daly's Three Rules:

1. Using **renewable resources** sustainably means that the rate of consumption of these resources should not exceed the rate at which they can be renewed. For example, ground water and soil should be used wisely and preserved for futured generations.
2. Using **nonrenewable resources** sustainably means that the rate of consumption of these resources should not exceed the rate at which renewable substitutes can replace them.
3. A sustainable emissions rate for pollution and waste is such that it should not exceed the rate at which natural ecological systems can neutralize and render the pollution and waste harmless.[6]

Although the principles given above have been criticized as being too abstract and too difficult to translate in operational terms, we can see that they all emphasize the importance of responsibility and future-oriented long-term goals.

## Triple Bottom Line Sustainability

The term **triple bottom line (TBL) sustainability** refers to the social, environmental, and economic bottom line of a business. As noted in chapter 1, author and entrepreneur John Elkington coined the term triple bottom line in 1994, in hopes of transforming the financial accounting-focused business system.[7] Elkington's TBL framework says that businesses should focus as much attention on social and environmental issues as they do on profit and financial issues. As a result, gradually since late nineteen-nineties, sustainability has become a key agenda for businesses, whether the motivation is a sincere heart to preserve humans and the environment or is profit-centered. As discussed in chapter 1, the social, environmental, and economic bottom line are also referred to as people, planet, and profit (the 3 Ps). The TBL view of business is grounded on Elkington's idea that businesses do not have the single goal of adding economic value. Rather, adding economic value involves an extended goal set of environmental and social values as well.[8] Further creating a socially, environmentally, and economically sustainable world ultimately requires synergy throughout an organization in which the social, environmental, and economic sustainability pillars are holistically indistinguishable.

In world history, however, harmony between the social, environmental, and economic sustainability pillars has hardly been achievable. Throughout the nineteenth and twentieth centuries, Western society experienced rapid economic growth, the focus being profitability and financial stability. In the middle of the twentieth century, an international environmental movement began. Experts warned that the nonstop cycle of industrial growth was associated with environmental and social damage, including but not limited to environmental destruction, war, and poverty. The rapid global decline of natural resources has forced many businesses to finally acknowledge the importance of sustainable development. Consequently, a global trend of sustainability emerged in the early 2000s, leading businesses across various industries to reshape their operational strategies. In this atmosphere, the sustainability movement has become recognized as a dramatic but necessary business shift where corporate performance moving forward would require the "coexistence of social (people), environmental (planet) and economic (profit) partnerships."[9] As a result, the 3Ps or TBL benchmarks have guided many businesses in the twenty-first century to do as little or as much as they can in order to achieve their desired level of sustainability performance.

## The Social Sustainability Pillar

The social sustainability pillar refers to social standards to which businesses are expected to conform. First, I must clarify that although sustainability is most frequently assumed to be about the environment, it is most basically a social problem. Optimally, the sustainability dynamic can be visually represented if the earth's system is shown as consisting of three concentric circles, where the economy exists within the social sphere, which furthermore exists within the environmental sphere. Such a viewpoint helps to clarify that for communities lacking essential economic resources, attempting to apply long-term multigenerational thinking to sustainability is very challenging and improbable since businesses have to address various social problems, including, for example, hunger and violence on a daily life basis.

Second, I would like to add that the social sustainability pillar ties back in to another important concept, that of the **social license to operate**.[10] The social license to operate, or the social license to run a business, is a corporate right that can be built and earned throughout the time a company proves to take good care of its employees, stakeholders, and the community where a company operates directly (e.g., in the case of the location of retail stores and business headquarters) or indirectly (e.g., in the case of the location of factories, sourcing, processing, and production facilities). If a company is recognized as a responsible corporate citizen, we can conclude that it holds a social license to operate.[11]

Next, it is worth mentioning that the social standards to which businesses are expected to conform are rising over time; this is particularly true when businesses operate within the global supply chain. Let me give you just a couple of quick arguments to support this statement. Today, most fashion retail businesses make use of a very fragmented and global supply chain. A significant portion of the apparel products offered in today's marketplace either have more than one country of origin or are made of raw materials such as fibers and textiles that have more than one country of origin.[12] Therefore, fashion companies must be fully aware of how their supply chains are structured and where their various suppliers are located. Since child labor and unregulated working conditions are outlawed in many nations, retailers need to know whether workers in supplier factories are paid fairly, or whether by some chance child labor is going into the end product. Many large retailers have seriously damaged their public image and almost lost their social license to operate when, for example, tragedies like the Bangladesh factory collapse have revealed neglected and unaccounted social risks in sourcing products from hidden or subcontracted supply chains and/or from lowest cost suppliers.[13]

In conclusion, in order to gain a public trust and preserve their social license to operate, businesses must evaluate and reevaluate social sustainability issues, which include but are not limited to human rights issues, equity issues, and social injustice.

- *Human rights issues:* The United Nations' (1948) Universal Declaration of Human Rights (UDHR) was the first attempt to codify into international law a basic set of rights to which all humans are entitled. More than 170 nations have affirmed their commitment to upholding these rights. For workers, these rights include the following: safe working conditions, "freedom of association and right to collective bargaining, the elimination of compulsory labor, the abolition of child labor, and elimination of discrimination" at the workplace.[14] This body of international law and principles provides a reference point for what constitutes basic human rights. For more details, please see the *ILO Declaration on Fundamental Principles and Rights at Work and Its Follow-up.*[15]

- *Equity issues:* The question of equity addresses the disparity between insider and outsider groups. Differences of sexual orientation, religion, and economic status create insider and outsider groups that fail to communicate on issues of common ground. Although some progress has been made in addressing discrimination, the need to belong represents a key social sustainability issue. Challenges surrounding discrimination are found on a national and international level, with the rich getting richer, the poor getting poorer, and the vast middle tending to disappear. Businesses and local communities also must tackle equity and diversity challenges. As it happens, those organizations that embrace diversity are stronger and more resilient.[16]

- *Social justice issues:* Important components of social justice include but are not limited to the following: general social progress; elimination of poverty and income inequality; ensuring the fulfillment of basic nutritional needs; achieving equal rights for all genders, including youths and women; fostering an understanding of and a respect for our planet, for fisheries, for forests, and for access to clean water; promoting conservation of natural resources and the sustainable

management of these resources; promoting increased disaster prepar-
edness; encouraging respect for all cultures and races; promoting the
adoption of transparent governance structures and processes that allow
for inclusive measures of redress; and promoting accountability to one
another and to oneself.[17]

## Human Rights in the Fashion Supply Chain: Defining Fair Living Wage for Garment Workers

The UN Universal Declaration of Human Rights (Article 23) recognizes a
fair **living wage** as a basic human right whereby everyone "who works has
the right to just and favorable remuneration ensuring for the worker and the
worker's family an existence with human dignity and supplemented by other
means of social protection."[18]

According to the International Labor Organization (ILO), a United
Nations agency whose mandate is to advance social and economic justice
through setting international labor standards, a **minimum wage** is the
"minimum amount of remuneration that an employer is required to pay
wage earners for the work performed during a given period."[19] The ILO
further describes minimum wages as important policy tools; today more
than 90 percent of ILO member states have adopted minimum wages across
industry sectors.[20] The ILO recognizes that minimum wages are particularly
important in the global garment sector, since this is a highly competitive, labor-intensive sector in which collective bargaining over wages is
relatively uncommon. Recognizing the importance of workers' wages, the
ILO is invested in the promotion of fair wage policies with the intention
to ensure a responsible share of the generated profits.[21] The data collected
by associate professor of fashion and apparel studies Dr. Sheng Lu shows
that "the monthly minimum wages for garment workers vary significantly
across the world's countries, ranging from as low as USD $26 in Ethiopia"
to $1,734 in the UK in 2019. It is also worth noting that the minimum world
average wage in 2019 was USD $470/month.[22] Information on monthly
minimal wages in the garment sector is displayed in Table 2.

**Table 2** Monthly minimum wages for garment workers in 2019*

| Country | Monthly Wages (USD) | Country | Monthly Wages (USD) |
|---------|---------------------|---------|---------------------|
| Ethiopia | $2 | Mauritius | $240 |
| Sri Lanka | $55 | Brazil | $246 |
| Bangladesh | $63 | Morocco | $266 |
| Pakistan | $111 | Colombia | $275 |
| Egypt | $122 | Peru | $279 |
| Mexico | $127 | Jordan | $310 |
| Kenya | $136 | Turkey | $352 |
| Vietnam | $151 | Guatemala | $357 |
| India | $168 | Romania | $484 |
| Nicaragua | $173 | Spain | $991 |
| Cambodia | $176 | US | $1,160 |
| Indonesia | $181 | Canada | $1, 518 |
| Philippines | $200 | France | $1,554 |
| China | $217 | UK | $1,734 |

*Table is adapted from Sheng Lu, "Minimum Wage Level for Garment Workers in the World (Updated in December 2020)," Dec. 4, 2020, https://shenglufashion.com/2020/12/04/minimum-wage-level-for-garment-workers-in-the-world-updated-in-december-2020/.

Dr. Lu suggests that the minimum wage should be always interpreted in the local context comparing the costs of living in a community/region with compensation levels. Thus he reminds us that "according to the International Labor Organization (ILO), a living wage is defined as the theoretical income level that an individual must earn to pay for basic essentials such as shelter, food, and water in the country where a person resides." From that perspective, Dr. Lu concludes, a "high minimum wage in absolute terms does not always guarantee a high standard of living, and vice versa."[23] For example, a typical US livable compensation measure is the wage rate per hour enough that one wage earner can afford a two-bedroom apartment while paying no more than 30 percent of their gross income (before taxes) for total housing costs. This further means that although, as shown in Table 2, "the United States offers one of the world's highest minimum wages for garment workers

(USD $1,160/month), that minimum wage level was only about 70% of the living wage (USD $1,660/month) in 2018-2019. In comparison, garment workers in Indonesia earned a much lower nominal minimum wage of USD $181/month. That wage level, however, was much higher than the reported USD $103/month living wage over the same period."[24]

Because there is in many cases a great difference between the minimum wage and the living wage, international activist groups such as the Clean Clothes Campaign[25] and Labour Behind the Label[26] continue to report that the fashion industry exploits millions of garment workers as a source of cheap labor. For example, according to the findings of the Garment Worker Center, workers will not earn a minimum wage, despite working sixty, sometimes seventy hours per week because they typically receive between two and six cents per garment.[27]

Garment workers are routinely subjected to unsafe, unsanitary, and poorly ventilated work environments where they are likely to develop physical ailments as a consequence of the fast pace of their work. Ensuring a salary or minimum wage for these garment workers would help to alleviate some of the ailments commonly sustained because their pay is directly based on the number of garments they work on.[28]

Livia Firth, creative director of Eco Age and UN leader of change, warns that although fashion companies often comply with the minimum wage, this does not necessarily mean that the living standards of workers and their families are secured. She estimates that fewer than 2 percent of garment workers globally earn a living wage.[29] This further implies that the remaining "98% of workers in the fashion industry are being held in systematic poverty and are not able to meet their basic human needs."[30] The NGO Fashion Revolution adds that approximately 75 percent of exploited workers in the garment industry are women between 18 and 24 years old.[31] As a part of the solution to this problem, the Clean Clothes Campaign, in association with Asian Floor Wage Alliance, recommends that minimal wages should be equal to living wages, since only a living wage would secure a decent living for garment workers. They further recommend that the living wage should be calculated using a more comprehensive methodology accounting, for example, for the following factors: food, rent, health care, savings, education, clothing, and transportation. In the Tailored Wages 2019 Report, the Clean Clothes Campaign declared that a living wage in the garment sector should be regarded as a wage paid that is "sufficient to meet the basic needs of a worker and the worker's family and to provide some discretionary income."[32] Specifically, as noted in the same report, this wage must

- Apply to all employed workers
- Apply to work completed in a standard week of forty, and not more than forty-eight hours
- Represent the basic net salary, which means salary after all applicable taxes, bonuses, and overtime are deducted
- Cover the essential needs of a worker and worker's family members; for example "for Asia this can be defined as 3 consumption units, where an adult = 1 and a child = 0.5. For other regions, a calculation to define a family is needed to reflect differing family sizes and expenditure patterns"
- "Include an additional 10% of the costs for basic needs as discretionary income"[33]

## Case study 1: Lowest wage challenge

Fashion brands ABLE and Nisolo joined together to launch #LowestWage-Challenge to raise consumer awareness about the low wages the garment workers who make their favorite clothes receive and to challenge these consumers to consider if these wages are enough to meet the workers' basic human needs and live a life of dignity.[34] ABLE and Nisolo urged all competitors in the fashion industry to join forces to help shift the fashion industry in the direction of sustainability. On their website they identified five major ways in which brands are actively denying paying living wages:

1. Instead of paying a living wage, brands will often say that they pay the legal minimum wage while ignoring the fact that minimum wages in many countries of manufacturing origin in the fashion

industry consist of only half of what would normally be considered a fair living wage.[35]

2. Despite research showing a cost of only 1–4 percent more per
   garment for brands to ensure living wages to workers across supply
   chains, many brands will often claim that living wages are simply
   too costly.[36]

3. Brands transfer responsibility to local manufacturers, declaring that
   manufacturers in the local factory are responsible to pay garment
   workers a living wage.[37]

4. In some cases, brands make the claim the workers themselves are
   responsible for the creation of unions and to require and protect
   living wages through the process of collective bargaining. The problem, however, is that in reality workers are scared to question the
   wages as they might lose their jobs. Therefore, the process of collective bargaining is often obstructed in this industry sector.[38]

5. Brands will frequently claim that it is too difficult to calculate the
   living wage, and this argument is often used as an excuse to avoid
   paying a living wage.[39] However, garment workers can be asked
   about their living expenses which would help brands establish
   optimal living wage figures. Also, brands can use tools such as
   WageIndicator to calculate living wage.[40]

**Discussion Questions:** What surprised you about wages in the garment
sector? How can the data about minimal wages across world nations be
used? What are some of the possible implications of the changing wage
systems in the garment sector?

# The Environmental Sustainability Pillar

The environmental sustainability pillar refers to the effective management
of physical and finite resources so that they can be conserved for the future.
In the fashion media, sustainability is often oversimplified, mischaracterized,
and deceptively promoted by various brand campaigns or labels, like
"environmentally friendly fashion" or "the green chic," regardless of the
brand's production ethics or material footprint,[41] such that these promotions
can create uncertainty and confuse consumers, who may often report that the

meaning of sustainability for them becomes unclear, as may the true social and environmental consequences of fashion production and consumption more generally.[42] As a result, "sustainability is commonly understood as a purely environmental issue, despite the reality that scarcity of natural resources and the ongoing climate crisis directly effects the lives of individual people, regions, and communities and is better understood as an equally important social problem."[43]

This is partly happening because it is easier for businesses to identify, measure, and quantify environmental factors, including, for example, the energy and water that go into the production process, and therefore those factors are most commonly reported publicly. To improve our understanding of environmental sustainability, there follows a closer examination of major environmental issues in the context of the fashion industry. In this chapter I will also elaborate some of the ways in which the fashion industry can reduce its negative environmental impacts. From the environmental standpoint, the primary concern of sustainability is the responsible use of finite resources as they have limited capacity and must be preserved for the future, hence it is suggested that all human and industrial activities start functioning in a way that do not threaten the health of the biosystems (e.g., nature, living organisms).[44] Some of the most critical environmental impacts in the fashion industry include greenhouse gas (GHG) emissions, the continued use of nonrenewable resources, waste issues, and diminishing biodiversity. These negative environmental impacts create a chain reaction that leads to climate change, global warming, water problems, decline of natural capital, toxins in the environment, and air pollution.

**GHG emissions**. The earth has a balance of atmospheric gases that absorb and release infrared radiation. This balance allows the earth to remain at the required temperature for water to be liquid, plants to grow, and creatures to live in comfort. Scientists believe that the very small concentration of natural GHGs in the upper atmosphere has made life as we know it possible by warming the earth's surface. GHGs naturally occurring in our atmosphere include water vapor ($H_2O$), nitrous oxide ($N_2O$), methane ($CH_4$), and ozone ($O_3$).[45] Each of these GHGs can warm the planet to a different degree. The global warming potential (GWP) represents a measure that was developed "to allow comparisons of the global warming impacts of different gases."[46] For example, the GWP of methane is greater than the GWP of carbon dioxide. Specifically, "emissions of one million metric tons of methane is equivalent to emissions of 28 million metric tons (approx.) of carbon dioxide."[47]

With GHGs on the rise, so also are extreme weather events and temperature fluctuations. According to the latest available NASA report on global climate change, nineteen of the twenty hottest years in human history, since record keeping began in the 1800s, have occurred since 2000 (the exception being 1998). According to NASA "the year 2020 tied with 2016 for the hottest year on record since record-keeping began in 1880."[48]

*Unsustainable use of natural sources.* In addition to the impacts on weather events and temperature, climate change has created a number of additional sustainability-related issues affecting natural sources, including but not limited to its effects on fresh water, soil, plants, fish, animals, fibers, and fuel, resulting in a substantial and largely irreversible loss in biodiversity on earth. Scientists estimate that "approximately 60% of the ecosystem's services are being degraded or are being used unsustainably," especially during the last fifty years.[49] These ecosystem services, according to the USDA, include the following: food, clean water, fuel, timber, soil formation, and nutrient cycling.[50] Consequently, the Global Footprint Network estimates that humanity now uses the equivalent of 1.6 planets to provide the resources we use and absorb our waste and estimates that under a "business-as-usual" scenario, two earths will be required to support humanity by 2030.[51]

One of the most critical environmental issues is unsustainable water usage. Unsustainable water usage has become a global issue as a result of the degrading of land-based freshwater systems and ocean water systems as well as overall poor ecosystem health. Global water withdrawals approximately tripled from 1950 to 2010. The UN projects that by 2030, 2.8 billion people may be living in countries or regions with absolute water scarcity.[52]

Another major environmental concern is air pollution. "Air pollution refers to the release of pollutants into the air—pollutants which are detrimental to human health and the planet as a whole."[53] These pollutants are typically assessed in terms of six "criteria pollutants" that threaten human health: nitrogen dioxide, ozone, lead, particulates, carbon monoxide, and sulfur dioxide.[54] In the United States, the Clean Air Act (CAA), represents the federal law established in 1970, which authorizes the US Environmental Protection Agency (EPA) to monitor, control, and regulate air pollution.[55] The World Health Organization (WHO) warns that "approximately seven million people worldwide die from air population every year."[56] WHO data also shows that "9 out of 10 people breathe air containing high levels of pollutants that exceeds the WHO's guideline limits for pollutants, with those living in low- and middle-income countries suffering the most."[57] Specifically, the WHO reports that "more than 80% of people living in urban areas that monitor air pollution are exposed to air quality levels that exceed WHO limits. While all regions of the world are affected . . . 96% of cities in low- and middle-income countries and 56% of cities in high-income countries, with more than 100,000 inhabitants do not meet WHO air quality guidelines."[58]

Toxins represent another serious sustainability issue with potential to permanently damage the natural environment. Approximately two thousand new chemicals, at a rate of roughly six per day, are introduced into the United States each year.[59] "An estimated 140,000 chemicals are on the EU market, which is a reasonable proxy for a global estimate of the number."[60] According to the UN report on global chemicals, the problem with toxins is that from all the emerging chemicals on the global market, only a fraction has been thoroughly evaluated.[61] However, negative effects of emerging chemicals need more testing so that their impact on humans can be promptly evaluated. For example, according to the UN, many studies have documented high levels of persistent "organic pollutants in wildlife, including aquatic mammals, polar bears, and fish-eating birds."[62] Worryingly, research conducted on humans shows that "a mother can pass as much as 33% of her chemical body burden to her child."[63] In the United States, "232 toxic chemicals were found in umbilical blood from newborns."[64]

## Hazardous Chemicals and Their Usage in the Fashion Industry: Environmental Toxins and Public Health

Chemicals used in fashion production deliver valuable features (e.g., color, softness, wrinkle-free, flame and crease resistance, or water repellent properties). However, some chemicals are dangerous, as they cause harm to humans and the natural environment. Scientists estimate that approximately eight thousand synthetic chemicals, including carcinogens and hormone disruptors, are currently used to produce fashion goods.[65] Not only do these chemicals pose health hazards to the garment workers who work with them, particularly when working without using protective equipment, but many of the chemicals also end up in freshwater systems. It is argued that approximately 20 percent of industrial water pollution comes from textile and clothing production.[66] Green America, a nonprofit organization, further warns that "wastewater containing the chemicals and dyes used in manufacturing textiles end up in local water sources; in some fashion manufacturing countries, local water sources are so polluted by chemicals that they can no longer sustain wildlife."[67] This problem is the most prevalent in the production sites where locals can guess what the new color-wise trend of the season is based on what color the local river is.[68] To address the widespread use of hazardous chemicals in clothing production across the fashion supply chain (and countries including China, Indonesia, and Mexico), Greenpeace launched the first global detox campaign. This campaign was so influential that it helped with the "detoxication" of clothing production at the supply chain level. Fashion brands were seriously challenged to embrace taking full responsibility for the impact their manufacturing supply chains have on the environment, and they were invited to commit to achieving a total hazardous chemical discharge of zero (initially) by 2020.[69] In the process of planned detoxication, fashion brands that signed the Detox Commitment were required to create the **manufacturing restricted substances list, or MRSL**, with the intention to back those listed chemicals in their manufacturing. To support detoxification in the fashion industry, multistakeholder, nongovernment organization Zero Discharge of Hazard Chemical (ZDHC) was founded; their progress can be followed on their official website.[70]

In 2012 Greenpeace expanded its research efforts to include not only chemical testing of wastewater samples found in nearby garment factories but also the testing of finished apparel products. As a result, multiple types of chemical testing have been conducted, and finished apparel products have been found to contain traces of chemicals that have been banned or regulated for minimal usage. Specifically, testing of 141 garments from 20 major fashion brands sold in 29 countries showed that *all* had hazardous chemicals of some sort.[71] Depending on the type of hazardous chemical, the amount present in a product, and the type of exposure (e.g., skin penetration, inhalation, ingestion), those substances can be carcinogenic and disrupt hormone activity in consumers who wear toxic garments and/or in the production workers who made them. Given these results, it is clear that toxins used in the fashion industry represent a widespread and pervasive problem, a serious public health issue that still awaits resolution. Children, pregnant women, factory workers, and inhabitants of contaminated textile and apparel production communities are particularly vulnerable populations who might be directly exposed to hazardous chemicals through the wearing and manufacturing of products. Alternatively, they may have been unintentionally exposed to residual materials from production since traces of toxic and carcinogenic compounds can be found in wastewater, soil, and air. Drinking contaminated water and inhaling toxic chemicals have adverse negative effects on humans' health, causing reproductive toxicology, asthma, eczema, dermatitis, cancer, lung disease, brain damage and death.[72]

*Chemical management regulatory laws.* There are certain barriers that impede chemical compound tracing and comprehensive ingredient disclosures in the fashion industry. They include but are not limited to unstandardized international regulations and difficulty in the tracing of restricted chemicals. One of the most comprehensive chemical management regulatory laws is the **Registration, Evaluation, Authorization and Restriction of Chemicals, or REACH**, a European Union regulation dating from 2006. "REACH . . . aims to improve the protection of human health and the environment through the better and earlier identification of the intrinsic properties of chemical substances. This is done through the four processes of REACH, namely the registration, evaluation, authorization, and restriction of chemicals. REACH also aims to enhance the innovation and competitiveness of the European chemical industry."[73] According to the requirements of this regulation, manufacturers and importers are requested to trace chemical substances in their products to ensure safe handling and prevent chemical hazards. REACH also recommends the substitution of the hazard chemicals (referred to as "substances of very high concern") with available and less hazard alternatives. REACH regulates "chemical substances in industrial processes but also those used in our day-to-day lives, for example, in cleaning products and paints as well as in articles such as clothes, furniture, and electrical appliances. Therefore, the regulation has an impact on most companies across the EU."[74] REACH is, furthermore, well aligned with all initiatives taken by the Zero Discharges of Hazardous Chemicals (ZDHC) Foundation. For example, according to REACH and the ZDHC Foundation, all fashion brands are expected not only to have but also to publish publicly a restricted chemical list for consumer goods, known as the RSL. The list is often used as a chemical checklist when testing finished products for the presence of restricted substances.[75] Essentially, all finished consumer products, including clothing and footwear, should undergo chemical testing as part of a structured due-diligence testing program to ensure compliance with regulations and with the company's RSL.[76] Furthermore, fashion brands are also expected to have and to publish another list, known as the manufacturing restricted substances list, or MRSL, showing how they manage chemicals in their supply chain. "MRSL testing analyzes the chemical formulations which are used to manufacture raw materials that go into the production of consumer goods. MRSL testing identifies the amount of each restricted substance on the MRSL that is present in a single chemical formulation, and there are often several chemical formulations that are used to manufacture raw materials which in turn need to be tested to the acceptable limits on the MRSL. MRSL testing is carried out by brands, retailers, and manufacturers as part of a structured due diligence testing program, which is available as part of the BLC Chem-MAP® Program."[77]

## Case study 2: Which fashion brands are becoming toxin free?

Do you know that some of our favorite fashion items may put our health at risk? "Unlike the nutrition facts written on the back of packages of our favorite foods, clothing doesn't come with a conveniently itemized list of ingredients. Instead, the 8,000 chemicals used in fashion are kept undisclosed and hidden within the most styles."[78] Here is the list of chemicals that are commonly used in the fashion industry although it is known that they have negative impact on public health:

- *"Azo dyes* are one of the most commonly used dyes, comprising of 60–70% of dyes in use. Azo dyes can release a compound that is a known carcinogen."[79] Some dyes use pigments that contain mercury, which can be harmful for the skin and damage organs. Azo dyes can cause skin allergies and dermatitis.
- *"Brominated and chlorinated flame retardants* are used to help fire-proof clothing and are commonly found in children's clothing. Flame retardants can cause thyroid disruption, memory and learning problems, delayed mental and physical development, lower IQ, premature puberty, and reduced fertility."[80]
- *"Formaldehyde* is used to keep clothes wrinkle-free and shrink-free and is a known respiratory irritant and carcinogen."[81]
- *Heavy metals* are found in dyes and leather tanning, and depending on the type of heavy metal, they can cause nervous system damage, cause kidney damage, and/or be carcinogenic.
- *Perflourinated chemicals* are used to make clothing waterproof and stainproof" and "can affect liver health and disrupt hormonal functions."[82]
- *"Nonylphenol Ethoxylates (NPEs)* are a large class of common ingredients found in many chemical formulations used to produce apparel and footwear materials. They are widely used as surfactants or emulsifiers in detergents, scouring agents, dye-dispersing agents, printing pastes, spinning oils, and wetting agents."[83] NPEs are recognized as endocrine disrupters.
- *Phthalates* are endocrine disrupters that have been used to produce fashion items that incorporate plastic and in decorative printing.[84]

Although this list is not inclusive of all problematic chemicals used in fashion production, these are commonly used. In order to investigate toxic chemicals used in clothing production, in 2012, Greenpeace tested 141 garments from the fashion brands displayed in table 2 to identify some of the chemicals of concern listed above.

**Table 3** The number of samples in which NPEs, phthalates, and cancer-causing amines released by certain azo dyes were identified*

| Brand | Number of items tested | Number of items tested positive NPEs (percentage) | Number of items tested positive for phthalates, above 0.5% by weight | Number of items tested positive for cancer-causing amines released by certain azo dyes |
|---|---|---|---|---|
| Giorgio Armani | 9 | 5 (56%) | 1 | |
| Benetton | 9 | 3 (33%) | | |
| Blazek | 4 | 2 (50%) | | |
| C&A | 6 | 5 (83%) | | |
| c | 8 | 7 (88%) | | |
| Diesel | 9 | 3 (33%) | | |
| Esprit | 9 | 6 (67%) | | |
| Gap | 9 | 7 (78%) | | |
| H&M | 6 | 2 (33%) | | |
| Jack Jones | 5 | 3 (60%) | | |
| Levi's | 11 | 7 (64%) | | |
| Mango | 10 | 6 (60%) | | |
| M&S | 6 | 4 (67%) | | |
| Meters bon we | 4 | 3 (75%) | | |
| Only | 4 | 4 (100%) | | |
| Tommy Hilfiger | 9 | 6 (67%) | 2 | |
| Vancl | 4 | 4 (100%) | | |
| Vero Moda | 5 | 4 (80%) | | |
| Victoria's Secret | 4 | 2 (50%) | 1 | |
| Zara | 10 | 6 (60%) | | 2 |

*Table is reproduced from "Toxic Threads: The Big Fashion Stitch-Up", Greenpeace (2012), accessed on June 22, 2023, https://www.greenpeace.org/static/planet4-international-stateless/2012/11/317d2d47-toxicthreads01.pdf.

In 2013 Greenpeace continued testing, this time focusing on twenty-seven products from children's collections offered by luxury fashion brands including Dior, Dolce & Gabbana, Giorgio Armani, Hermes, Louis Vuitton, Marc Jacobs, Trussardi, and Versace. As with the testing done in 2012, "accredited laboratories carried out the tests. Sixteen of the products bought by Greenpeace tested positive for one or more banned chemicals, including NPEs, phthalates, and polyfluorinated chemicals. Residues were found in products from all of the brands studied except for Trussardi. The highest concentration of chemicals was found in a Louis Vuitton ballerina shoe and in a Versace jacket."[85] For complete results see the online Greenpeace report *A Little Story About a Fashionable Lie*.[86] After publishing this report, Greenpeace requested major fashion brands to detox their production and commit to zero discharge of chemicals by 2020. Burberry made its detox commitment shortly after these events, but brands such as Versace, Armani, and Louis Vuitton responded to the Greenpeace allegations by saying their products comply with international environment and safety standards.[87] Because it is an urgent task for the fashion industry to remove toxic chemicals from clothing, shoes, and accessories, is it now time to examine which fashion brands are becoming toxin free?

**Discussion Questions:** In more recent years, Greenpeace has claimed that many fashion brands across the mass market, luxury, and premium sectors have accepted their roles as "detox leaders" by starting the process of getting rid of hazardous chemicals in their supply chains and in their final products because the only safe level for hazardous chemicals is zero.[88] Discuss more recent Greenpeace detox campaign findings. Which fashion brands are becoming toxic free? Suggest chemical management improvements for your favorite brands. Identify chemicals of concern that are still commonly used. Have you noticed that sustainable fashion brands often promote alternative or natural dying and processing methods?

# The Economic Sustainability Pillar

The **economic sustainability pillar** requires businesses to align with shareholders' interests but also with stakeholders' values and expectations. It refers to "a broad array of issues, from trade and investment, employment growth, private sector development, tax policy, public-private partnerships, trade and employment policies, national and international finance."[89] At the corporate level, the economic pillar is sometimes referred to as the "corporate governance pillar," meaning that businesses have to align with shareholders' interests but also with stakeholders' values and expectations.[90] Regarding corporate governance, it is important to mention that businesses are expected to use accurate and transparent accounting and reporting methods and that each business is responsible for its performance.

In their book *Embedded Sustainability: The Next Big Competitive Advantage*, Chris Laszlo and Nadya Zhexembayeva declared that three big trends in the global marketplace are reshaping the business landscape. The big three trends according to the authors include declining natural resources (a phenomenon described in the environmental sustainability section), radical transparency (businesses are expected to share transparently corporate and supply chain information), and increasing consumer expectation. Because of these trends, they believe it is not possible to keep going further with the same old mantra of profit at any cost to society.[91] We are entering the era of sustainable value, and that means that value must be created for both shareholders and stakeholders. As a matter of fact, sustainable value creation represents the most promising path forward for business.

Other sustainability supporters believe that "the neoliberal economic system that has dominated the world has reached its limits in such a way that it cannot contribute to further economic growth and prosperity." As a matter of the fact, social tensions have escalated around the world's nations, "with the poor getting poorer and the rich getting richer."[92] In addition, the decline of natural resources is alarming. Thus, operating in a finite world poses great challenges, making it critically imperative that organizations take action and pursue new directions. Understanding the significance of sustainability practices is important for any manager or business leader. There are several important strategies that represent a solid foundation for establishing a responsible business. These strategies include accounting for externalities, having a long-term plan, stimulating circular business models, and supporting sustainable consumption.

*Accounting for externalities.* According to the economist Milton Friedman, externalities are "non-intentional effects of activities carried on for other purposes," meaning that all industrial and business activities carry benefits for some groups, while imposing corresponding negative impacts on the others.[93] Essentially, this means that all products we can find on the market are underpriced. For this reason, Lester Russel Brown, founder of the Earth Policy Institute, said the following in his book *World on the Edge: How to Prevent Environmental and Economic Collapse*: "The key to restructuring the economy is to get the market to tell the truth through full-cost pricing. . . . If the world is to move onto a sustainable path, we need economists who will calculate indirect costs and work with political leaders to incorporate them into market prices by restructuring taxes."[94] In other words, "For energy, this means putting a tax on carbon to reflect the full cost of burning fossil fuels and offsetting it with a reduction in the tax on income."[95] Similar practices would apply to garments as well. For the fashion industry, factoring these externalities into the costs of doing business is probably the most important correction necessary in current fashion market systems. In 2019 the UK Parliament published a report called *Fixing Fashion: Clothing Consumption and Sustainability* urging fashion retailers to account for environmental and social costs when calculating the prices of our garments. In the report it was noted that fast fashion brands especially "chase a cheap needle around the planet," meaning they outsource clothing from countries with low pay, where garment workers are not protected by trade unions, and where environmental laws are weak.[96] As a result, low prices for clothes that can be found on the global fashion market do not account for externalities. Instead, the clothing we buy has many hidden costs that do not affect consumers through the fast fashion pricing systems, and that need to be urgently reformed.[97]

*Having a long term plan.* Sustainability requires businesses to manage for long-term value creation. Companies such as Unilever and Amazon succeeded by focusing on long-term goals rather than on short-term priorities. Research published by the McKinsey Global Institute in cooperation with FCLT Global found that companies that operate with a true long-term business mindset have consistently outperformed their industry peers since 2001 across almost every financial measure that matters. The problem, however, is that businesses often focus on short-term profitable priorities while neglecting the importance of "embedding sustainability in their strategic planning and capital investment decisions."[98] According to the McKinsey Global Institute report above mentioned, a majority of international sustainable business experts see pressure for short-term financial results as a major barrier to businesses becoming more sustainable. Thus, businesses need to prioritize a long-term perspective in order to make decisions based on their future impacts. Unless businesses are ready to manage their interests for the long term, there will be nothing left to provide for our future generations.

*Stimulating circular business models.* The concept of a circular economy strongly relies on cradle-to-cradle thinking, embracing changes to economic systems (e.g., infrastructure, incentives, and designs for materials reuse) that maximize material reuse, with accompanying energy and water savings throughout the life cycle of the products. Examples of circular economy elements include byproduct business networks where each business can use others' wastes. In that way there is no waste in the traditional sense, but one business's output may be used as an input for the next business's production. There are good examples of the byproduct network across industry sectors. To name one, Vegea is a company that produces alternative leather from wine waste. They are collaborating with Italian wineries, and through the process of valorization of wine waste, they collect grape skins, stalks, and seeds discarded during wine production. Those materials are then used to create so-called wine leather that is used mostly in the production of luxurious fashion bags, shoes, and packaging, although wine leather has increasing applications in other industries, including home furnishing, the automotive industry, and transportation.[99] For more information about the circular economy, explore the Ellen MacArthur Foundation website.[100] Chapter 4 of this book will also talk more about business circularity, discussing various waste management strategies in greater detail.

*Supporting sustainable consumption.* The UN defines sustainable consumption as a system where consumers use products responsibly to meet their basic needs so that future generations will be able to meet their needs as well.[101] In order for a society to move toward sustainable consumption patterns, all businesses, governments, and individuals need to take action. For example, consumers may select to live sustainably and downsize their own consumption. Companies can focus on the creation of circular, less polluting products while eliminating or minimizing their waste. Governments can, and should, strongly support sustainable businesses through financial incentives.

Chapter 6 of this book will focus on discussing specific roles various groups of stakeholders have in the process of sustainable development.

## Case study 3: How the fashion industry can react to reduce its greenhouse gas emissions

In 2020 McKinsey and Company published its *Fashion on Climate* report, urging fashion industry players to act faster to reduce their greenhouse gas emissions. McKinsey research "shows that the global fashion industry produced around 2.1 billion tons of GHG emissions in 2018, equaling 4% of total global emissions. . . . This is equivalent to the combined annual GHG emissions of France, Germany, and the United Kingdom!" The results of this study showed that around "70% of the fashion industry's emissions came from upstream activities" (i.e., supply chain activities including fiber production, preparation, and processing). "The remaining 30% were associated with downstream retail operations" (transport, packaging, distribution, etc.), the use phase (clothing maintenance), and end-of-use activities (clothing disposal).[102] McKinsey and team recommend the following three strategies for fashion retailers to help them reduce their GHG footprints:

1. *Reduce GHG emissions from supply chain operations*. Based on data McKinsey collected, manufactures and fiber producers could accomplish up to 60 percent of the accelerated abatement target through the decarbonization of material production.[103] This would require them to downsize manufacturing quantities, reduce manufacturing and processing waste, and transition from fossil fuels to renewable sources.

2. *Reduce emissions from their own operations*. Fashion brands could reduce their GHG emissions by up to 20 percent if they improved their own business practices.[104] Optimally, this would include both efficient packaging systems and other waste reduction strategies (not only in the retail store but also in the corporate headquarters). For example, it would be important to collect and reuse damaged products or to minimize product returns. Brands also need to explore available mechanisms to resell, recycle, or creatively reuse unsold merchandize.

3. *Encourage sustainable consumption.* Fashion brands need to rethink their current businesses in order to adopt a more conscious approach to fashion consumption. Some of the ways in which fashion brands may promote sustainable consumption include clothing rental, product repair, and repurposing or creative reusing of damaged and unsold product inventory.[105] Also, brands are expected to educate their consumers on how to responsibly wash and dry their clothes, as well as on how and where to repair them or dispose of them safely.

In the fashion industry, attaining sustainability has become imperative partly because environmental and economic regulations are becoming stricter, but also due to increasing expectations from investors, consumers, and other stakeholder groups. The Fashion Industry Charter for Climate Action was launched in 2018 under the auspices of UN Climate Change, declaring its vision for net-zero emissions in this sector by 2050.[106] Consequently, many fashion brands have responded to stakeholder pressures, explaining how they are reducing GHG emissions throughout their operations. The H&M brand even made a bold commitment to having a "Climate Positive value chain" by 2040.[107] However, it remains unclear how the company actually plans to achieve this goal. With increasing demands for companies to measure and report carbon emissions, it is of urgent importance that companies move away from bold marketing-focused commitments and adopt science-based approaches to assessing, measuring, and monitoring their emissions. While reducing GHG emissions has become one of the top business imperatives, changes made by brands and their suppliers could have a knock-on effect of encouraging sustainable consumer behaviors.

**Student Activity:** In order to find out more about GHG reduction strategies used among fashion brands, students are asked to select a group of brands across industry sectors (e.g., finding a good balance among apparel and footwear luxury and mass market brands) and investigate their official websites and/or sustainability reports. After gathering enough information about individual company efforts, students are to discuss, compare, and interrogate their findings.

## Sustainable Development Goals (SDGs)

The **Sustainable Development Goals (SDGs)**, also known as the global goals, "were adopted by all United Nations member states in 2015 as a universal call to action to end poverty, protect the planet, and ensure that all people enjoy peace and prosperity by 2030." As the United Nations indicate, the seventeen SDGs are integrated; that is, they "recognize that action in one area will affect outcomes in others and that development must balance social, economic, and environmental sustainability. Through the pledge to leave no one behind, countries have committed to fast-track progress for those furthest behind first. That is why the SDGs are designed to bring the world to several life-changing 'zeros,' including zero poverty, zero hunger, zero AIDS, and zero discrimination against women and girls."[108] In table 4 below you can find listed the seventeen Sustainable Development Goals, along with an explanation of how each of these goals should be practically implemented.

**Table 4** Sustainable Development Goals*

| *SDG* | *Expectations* |
|---|---|
| SDG 1. No Poverty | End poverty in all its forms everywhere. Enhance practices and policies that create shared value with workers and suppliers; help to create equal labor practices, in particular to poor and vulnerable workers; and foster equal rights to economic resources and access to basic services. |
| SDG 2. Zero Hunger | Avoid practices and policies that lead to any form of malnutrition. Enhance practices and policies that end hunger and ensure access to safe, nutritious, and sufficient food for workers in vulnerable situations, including company workers and workers in the company's supply chain. |
| SDG 3. Good Health and well-being | Enhance labor practices and policies that improve well-being and prevent death and mortality among the company's workers and across the company's supply chain. Reduce diseases, injuries, and accidents. |

*(Continues)*

**Table 4** Continued

| SDG | Expectations |
|---|---|
| SDG 4. Quality Education | Ensure inclusive and equitable quality education and promote lifelong learning. Enhance practices and policies that ensure primary and secondary education to the company's workers and across the company's value chain, improving workers' skills and capabilities. Ensure equal access for all women and men to inclusive equitable quality and affordable technical, vocational, and tertiary education, promoting lifelong learning opportunities for workers. |
| SDG 5. Gender Equality | Enhance labor practices and policies that eliminate all forms of violence against women and girls, ensure women have equal rights to economic resources, and promote equal and inclusive labor opportunities across the company's workforce and across the company's value chain. |
| SDG 6. Clean water and sanitation | Avoid practices and policies that lead to pollution of clean water and those that do not foster sanitation for all. Enhance practices and policies that ensure the availability and use of clean water and sanitation. |
| SDG 7. Affordable and clean energy | Enhance practices and policies that ensure access to affordable, reliable, renewable, and modern energy. |
| SDG 8. Decent work and economic growth | Avoid labor practices and policies that lead to indecent work practices' being imposed on company workers and across the company's supply chain. |
| SDG 9. Industry, innovation, and infrastructure | Avoid practices and policies that lead to non-sustainable industrialization and lack of innovation. |
| SDG 10. Reduce Inequalities | Avoid practices and policies that increase inequality within and among countries. |
| SDG 11. Sustainable cities and communities | Avoid practices and policies that result in lack of access to affordable housing and basic services. |
| SDG 12. Responsible consumption and production | Enhance practices and policies that foster the efficient and long-term sustainable use of natural resources and reduce negative environmental impacts. |

(*Continues*)

**Table 4** Continued

| SDG | Expectations |
|---|---|
| SDG 13. Climate Action | Enhance practices and policies that mitigate climate change. |
| SDG 14. Life below Water | Enhance practices and policies that foster the conservation and sustainable use of the oceans, seas, marine resources, and water ecosystems. |
| SDG 15. Life on Land | Enhance practices and policies that foster the sustainable use of terrestrial ecosystems, improve biodiversity, and combat desertification. |
| SDG 16. Peace, justice and strong institutions | Enhance practices and policies to prevent conflict, violence, and abuse of workers and of children. Promote peaceful and inclusive societies for sustainable development, and provide access to justice for workers and children. |
| SDG 17. Partnership for the Goals | Avoid unilateral practices and policies that do not support or foster the SDGs. Foster collaborative and multistakeholder practices and policies to strengthen the means of implementation of the SDGs. |

*Table is recreated and quotes from Sofia Garcia-Torres, Marta Rey-Garcia, and Laura Albareda-Vivo, "Effective Disclosure in the Fast-Fashion Industry: From Sustainability Reporting to Action," *Sustainability* 9, no. 12 (2017): 2256.

*How can sustainable development in the fashion industry be achieved*? The United Nations Alliance for Sustainable Fashion is an initiative of certain United Nations agencies (e.g., UN Global Compact, UN Development Program-UNDP) and allied organizations (e.g., the International Labor Organization, the World Bank Group-Connect for Climate) designed to contribute to the Sustainable Development Goals through partnership and strategically coordinated actions in the fashion sector.[109] The fashion sector as defined by this alliance includes producers of apparel, footwear, accessories, and leather products, and the scope of activities entails all processes that this industry entails, including materials sourcing, production, distribution, retail, consumption, and disposal of fashion products. Alliance members believe that the fashion industry sector plays a key role in transitioning toward a sustainable future. According to the 2022 statistics, the global fashion industry generated revenue of $1.74 trillion, and the market is expected to grow by 2.84% annually in next four years.[110] Because of its size and global reach, this sector has evident unsustainable social, environmental, and economic impacts, and those impacts must be reduced or eliminated the so that the sector can continue to grow sustainably.

## Case study 4: Re/make and their views on how the SDGs relate to the fashion industry

Re/make is an NGO that unites fashion designers, women rights advocates, environmentalists, and social activists who are on a mission to promote sustainable development in the fashion industry and change practices of the industry that are harmful to people and the planet. Famous for their advocacy, social media campaigns, movies, and educational tools, this initiative actively promotes the most urgent issues in need of remediation by the fashion sector. The following sections elaborate Re/make's description of SDGs and related issues in the context of the fashion industry. More information can be found on their official website.[111]

The Re/make team believes that female empowerment in the context of the fashion industry should be considered as one of the most critical initiatives in need of closer attention. According to their team, to achieve SDG 5, gender equality should be prioritized as one of the main industry targets. "Fashion industry workers are mostly female. 80% of garment industry workers are female, and one in six individuals who are employed in the corporate side of the fashion business is female. Furthermore, 85% of graduating students in fashion-related majors in America are female. On the consumption side as well, women evidently spend a higher percent of their earnings on fashion products than their male counterparts." Hence, the Re/make team argues, women continue to be the backbone of this industry although industry practices continues to be controlled by men.[112] This is true on both the corporate side and on the supply chain side, where senior management positions are often dominated by males. For more materials on this topic, please see Re/make's *Made In* documentary series, in which female industry workers share their experience of low wages, sexual assault, short term contracts, and pregnancy penalization as rampant and continuing issues.[113]

Other critical fashion industry issues according to the Re/make team include SDG 8, work and economic growth, and SDG 10, inequalities.[114] The Re/make team urges the public to understand the wealth disparity suffered by female garment factory workers, all while retail profits continue to be tremendous. For this reason they urge fashion brands to bridge this gap and provide a fair wage for female garment workers.

Last but not less important, the Re/make team emphasizes the necessity that retailers ensure responsible and equal partnerships (SDG 17) with communities with which they work. This particularly applies to workers in their supply chain, who deserve improved quality of life without exploitation. Fair wages, documented hours, maker training education (SDG 4), and well-being programs (SDG 3) are essential.[115]

**Student Activity:** Explore Re/make's website and their elaboration of the SDGs that should be particularly targeted within the fashion industry. Then explore your favorite brand website and learn about the SDGs that the company find the most important. Discuss with your peers which SDGs are commonly targeted and why.

# Student Voices: Fashion for SDGs

In the Student Voices section of this chapter, you can read the perspectives of other students on how they are interpreting SDGs that they have observed for the brand of their choice. To ensure the validity of the information, students obtained it directly from the company websites and industry sources. (The following work was created by students enrolled in UNT MDSE 4560 Sustainable Strategies course in Spring 2020.)

*Student I: SDGs of the Eileen Fisher brand*
Interestingly, there are few SDGs that Eileen Fisher does *not* participate in. According to her website, Fisher is committed to promoting sustainability,

conservation, and human rights in all areas of her company and supply chains. Below are the SDGs that I found Eileen Fisher participating in:

SDG 3: Good Health and Well Being. Eileen Fisher has been actively involved in preventing forced labor since 1997 and has committed to the SA8000 Standard. Fisher is also actively involved in *Harvard SHINE*, a three-year LA based research project aimed to shift retail practices to have a positive impact on worker well-being.

SDG 5: Gender Equality. Fisher hosts *Women Together*, a program that, according to their website, is designed for us to share our voices, draw on one another's strength and compassion, and uplift and encourage each other.

SDG 6/SDG 7: Clean Water and Sanitation/Affordable and Clean Energy. Fisher uses an innovative dye process called the Bluesign certified dying process.

SDG 8: Decent Work and Economic Growth. Fisher invests in communities in India, Japan, and Peru - providing workers decent jobs, training, and other resources that empower workers to thrive without the need for aid.

SDG 12: Responsible Consumption and Production. They have moved away from the traditional take-make-waste model of production and developed a circular system that encompasses every factor of production: from design to manufacturing, transportation to consumption, usage to repairing, and recycling.

SDG 13: Climate Action. They use ethical land management practices and animal welfare initiatives to allow wool-providing sheep to live a natural life, grazing and adding nutrients back into the soil.

SDG 15: Life on Land. Fisher requires their suppliers to confirm that their raw materials are ethically harvested—and that they do not come from areas that have been recently converted from natural forest ecosystems.

SDG 17: Partnership for the Goals. Eileen Fisher requires commitments and contracts across their manufacturing and supply chain to hold suppliers accountable to all the SDGs they practice.

*Student II: SDGs of Levi Strauss and Co.*
Levi's has noticeably created changes to their brand to make it more sustainable. Their mantra is Buy Better-Wear Longer. They are currently using Cottonized Hemp, an alternative to cotton that is made to feel like

cotton. Hemp is actually a far more sustainable material. They are also using different technology and other production techniques to make sure that they are creating less waste in the process.

SDG 3: Health and Well-being—They offer a free medical premium for anyone who participates in their well-being program. This also includes eligibility on the first day of work for life insurance and disability benefits. Levi's stands with their employees when times get hard and works hard to help their workers take care of themselves.

SDG 5: Gender Equality—Levi's employee population is made up of 58% Females and 42% Males globally. Women make up a great deal of their work population in corporate and retail. In spite of this, women are not selected in high numbers for leadership positions.

SDG 6, SDG 9, SDG 12: Clean Water, Innovation, and Responsible Consumption and Production—Levi's is taking being strides to be a waterless manufacturing company. While making those strides, they have created new ways to use cleaner and less water. They do this with Water<Less technology, so far finding 20 ways to create the same finishes without using massive amounts of water. Their Water<Less technology is in collaboration with Water Scarcity. Water Scarcity tracks water footprints and controls clean water waste and usage.

SDG 9 (continued): Innovation—Working hard to improve water footprint, in 2019 Levi's created *Cottonized* Hemp jeans in their WellThread line to lessen their environmental footprint. This line is produced with fewer chemicals and less water using rain-fed hemp fiber that requires less water and pesticides to cultivate compared to cotton.

SDG 7 and SDG 13: Affordable and Clean Energy and Climate Control-Like many other companies, Levi's is working hard to be sustainable to the end. Their goal for 2025 is to be sourcing 100% renewable energy. This 2025 goal includes a 90% reduction in greenhouse gases and a 40% reduction in GHG Emissions in the Supply Chain (producing cleaner textiles).

SDG 16: Peace, Justice and Strong Institutions-Levi's follow laws from the start of hiring through the entire working career. These laws are Equal Opportunity Law, EEO Supplement Law, and Pay Transparency Nondiscrimination Provision.

Out of the 17 SDGs, Levi's has met 9. They did not meet SDGs 1, 2, 8, 10, 11, 14, 15, or 17. Although Levi's has not met all SDGs, I believe they will soon. Working to create safer places to live and work, producing sustainable clothing, promoting employee health and well-being, fighting for the rights of all, and making better choices are things they're doing and will continue to do.

## Chapter Summary

In the second chapter, we reviewed the most common definition of sustainability as well as the notion, meaning, and examples of Sustainable Development Goals (SDGs) in the context of the fashion industry. To examine links between the SDGs and environmental, economic, and social performance in the fashion industry, we reviewed some of the most critical issues that our industry is facing nowadays, including exploitation of basic workers' rights, environmental pollution, and the presence of toxic chemicals in our clothing. This chapter contains four case studies. The first one explores whether our favorite brands pay fashion manufacturing workers a living wage. The second case study discusses the issues of toxic chemicals that are used in clothing manufacturing. The third case study investigates how the fashion industry can react to reduce its greenhouse gas emissions, and the fourth one explores activism beyond the Re/make global advocacy group that is organizing and fighting for fair pay and climate justice in the clothing industry. Lastly, but not less important, the Student Voices section of this chapter shares the perspectives of students who explored the SDGs topics in the context of two brands: Eileen Fisher and Levi Strauss and Co. In this section, students are positioned as storytellers and advocates for sustainability driven change in our industry.

## References

1. "Fashion's Future: The Sustainable Development Goals," online course from Fashion Revolution, accessed February 22, 2023, https://www.futurelearn.com/courses/fashion-s-future-and-the-un-sustainable-development-goals-?mc_cid=49260b7390&mc_eid=c1d7badd41.
2. Ibid.
3. Chris Laszlo and Nadya Zhexembayeva, "Embedded Sustainability: A Strategy for Market Leaders," *European Financial Review* 15 (2011): 37–49.

4. Brundtland Commission, *Our Common Future: The World Commission on Environment and Development*, United Nations, 1987, accessed on June 25, 2022, https://sustainabledevelopment.un.org/content/documents/5987our-common-future.pdf.

5. Ibid.

6. Herman E. Daly, *Ecological Economics and Sustainable Development* (Cheltenham, UK: Edward Elgar Publishing, 2007).

7. J. Elkington, "Towards the Sustainable Corporation: Win-Win-Win Business Strategies for Sustainable Development," *California Management Review* 36, no. 2 (Jan. 1994), 90–100, http://dx.doi.org/10.2307/41165746.

8. Ibid.

9. Iva Jestratijevic and Nancy A. Rudd, "Six Forms of Sustainable Fashion," *Latest Trends in Textile and Fashion Designing* 2, no. 4 (Aug. 2018): 220–22, http://dx.doi.org/10.32474/LTTFD.2018.02.000145.

10. Leeora Black, *The Social License to Operate: Your Management Framework for Complex Times* (n.p., Routledge, 2017).

11. Will Kenton, "Social License to Operate (SLO): Definition and Standards," *Investopedia*, last modified September 26, 2023, https://www.investopedia.com/terms/s/social-license-slo.asp.

12. Jung E. Ha-Brookshire, "Country of Parts, Country of Manufacturing, and Country of Origin: Consumer Purchase Preferences and the Impact Of Perceived Prices," *Clothing and Textiles Research Journal* 30, no. 1 (2012): 19–34.

13. Iva, Jestratijevic, Nancy A. Rudd, and James Uanhoro, "Transparency of Sustainability Disclosures among Luxury and Mass-Market Fashion Brands," *Journal of Global Fashion Marketing* 11, no. 2 (2020): 99–116.

14. *ILO Declaration on Fundamental Principles and Rights at Work and Its Follow-up*, ILO, accessed on June 23, 2023, https://www.ilo.org/wcmsp5/groups/public/---ed_norm/---declaration/documents/normativeinstrument/wcms_716594.pdf.

15. Ibid.

16. Seamoon Yoon, "Why Diversity within Organization Matters," *World Economic Forum*, last modified November 18, 2021, https://www.weforum.org/agenda/2021/11/why-diversity-within-your-organization-matters/.

17. Committee of World Food Security, *Principles for Responsible Investment in Agriculture and Food Systems*, Oct. 15, 2014, https://www.fao.org/3/au866e/au866e.pdf.

18. *Universal Declaration of Human Rights 2021*, UN.org, accessed on May 30, 2023, https://www.un.org/sites/un2.un.org/files/2021/03/udhr.pdf.

19. "Chap. 1: What Is a Minimum Wage, 1.1 Definition and Purpose," *International Labor Organization (ILO)*, accessed on May 30, 2023, https://www.ilo.org/global/topics/wages/minimum-wages/definition/WCMS_439072/lang--en/index.htm.

20. ILO, *Global Wage Report 2020–21: Wages and Minimum Wages in the Time of COVID-19*, 2021, accessed on February 21, 2023, https://www.ilo.org/wcmsp5/groups/public/---dgreports/---dcomm/---publ/documents/publication/wcms_762534.pdf.

21. ILO, *Promoting Decent Work in Garment Sector Supply Chains*, accessed on April 2, 2019, https://www.ilo.org/wcmsp5/groups/public/---ed_protect/---pro-trav/---travail/documents/projectdocumentation/wcms_681644.pdf.

22. Sheng Lu, "Minimum Wage Level for Garment Workers in the World (Updated in December 2020)," December 4, 2020, https://shenglufashion.com/2020/12/04/minimum-wage-level-for-garment-workers-in-the-world-up-dated-in-december-2020/.

23. Ibid.

24. Ibid.

25. "Clean Clothes Campaign," *Clean Clothes Campaign*, accessed on May 4, 2023, https://cleanclothes.org/.

26. "Labour Behind the Label," *Labour Behind the Label*, accessed on May 31, 2023, https://labourbehindthelabel.org/.

27. "Garment Worker Center," *Garment Worker Center*, accessed on April 18, 2023, https://garmentworkercenter.org/resources/.

28. Ibid.

29. "Living Wage," *Eco-age*, accessed on April 19, 2023, https://eco-age.com/?s=living+wage.

30. "The Lowest Wage in Our Supply Chain," *Nisolo*, accessed June 10, 2023, https://nisolo.com/blogs/stride-sustainability/the-lowest-wage-in-our-supply-chain.

31. "FAQs: Fashion Transparency Index 2017," *Fashion Revolution*, accessed June 20, 2023, https://www.fashionrevolution.org/faqs-fashion-transparency-index-2017/.

32. "Tailored wages 2019," *Clean Clothes Campaign*, accessed June 22, 2023, https://archive.cleanclothes.org/resources/publications/tailored-wages-2019-the-state-of-pay-in-the-global-garment-industry.

33. Ibid.

34. "Lowest Wage Challenge," *Lowest Wage Challenge*, accessed on June 22, 2023, https://www.lowestwagechallenge.com/about-us.

35. Nisolo, "Lowest Wage in Our Supply Chain."

36. Lowest Wage Challenge, "Lowest wage challenge."

37. Ibid.

38. Ibid.

39. Ibid.

40. "Wage Indicator," *Wage Indicator*, accessed on April 10, 2022, https://wageindicator.org/.

41. Kate Fletcher, *Sustainable Fashion and Textiles: Design Journeys* (London: Routledge, 2013).

42. Jestratijevic and Rudd, "Six Forms of Sustainable Fashion."

43. Ibid, 220.

44. Andrew Crane, Dirk Matten, Sarah Glozer, and Laura J. Spence, *Business Ethics: Managing Corporate Citizenship and Sustainability in the Age of Globalization* (Oxford: Oxford University Press, 2019).

45. "What Is the Greenhouse Effect?," *NASA: Global Climate Change*, accessed on July 24, 2023, https://climate.nasa.gov/faq/19/what-is-the-greenhouse-effect/#:~:text=Greenhouse%20gases%20include%20carbon%20dioxide,effect%20helps%20stabilize%20Earth's%20atmosphere.

46. "Understanding Global Warming Potentials," *EPA*, accessed on May 24, 2023, https://www.epa.gov/ghgemissions/understanding-global-warming-potentials.

47. "Carbon Literacy," *Cynnalcymru*, accessed on May 24, 2023, https://cynnalcymru.com/topic-category/carbon-literacy/?cn-reloaded=1

48. "Global Temperature," *NASA: Global Climate Change*, accessed on July 31, 2023, https://climate.nasa.gov/vital-signs/global-temperature/.

49. Holzman, David, "Accounting for Nature's Benefits: The Dollar Value of Ecosystem services," Environmental Health Perspectives 120, no. 4 (April 1, 2012): a152–57, https://ehp.niehs.nih.gov/doi/10.1289/ehp.120-a152.

50. "Ecosystem Services," *USDA*, accessed on May 24, 2023, https://www.fs.usda.gov/ccrc/topics/ecosystem-services.

51. Global Footprint Network, *Living Planet Report 2008*, accessed on January 10, 2021, https://www.footprintnetwork.org/content/images/uploads/Pre-reading_English.pdf.

52. "Water: At the Center of the Climate Crisis," *UN*, accessed on May 17, 2023, https://www.un.org/en/climatechange/science/climate-issues/water.

53. "Air Pollution: Everything You Need to Know," NRDC, updated October 31, 2023, https://www.nrdc.org/stories/air-pollution-everything-you-need-know#whatis.

54. "Air Pollutants," *EPA*, accessed on August 2, 2023, https://www.epa.gov/criteria-air-pollutants.

55. "Clean Air Act," *EPA*, accessed on August 2, 2023, https://www.epa.gov/clean-air-act-overview/evolution-clean-air-act.

56. "Air Pollution," *WHO*, accessed on June 12, 2023, https://www.who.int/health-topics/air-pollution#tab=tab_1.

57. "9 Out of 10 People Worldwide Breathe Polluted Air, But More Countries Are Taking Actions," *WHO*, May 2, 2018, https://www.who.int/news/item/02-05-2018-9-out-of-10-people-worldwide-breathe-polluted-air-but-more-countries-are-taking-action.

58. "Air Pollution Levels Rising in Many of World's Poorest Cities," *WHO*, last modified December 5, 2016, https://www.who.int/news/item/12-05-2016-air-pollution-levels-rising-in-many-of-the-world-s-poorest-cities.

59. "Human and Ecological Risk Office: Chemicals of Emerging Concern," *DTSC*, accessed on April 19, 2022, https://dtsc.ca.gov/emerging-chemicals-of-concern/.

60. UNEP, *Global Chemicals Outlook*, accessed on December 12, 2022, https://www.scribd.com/document/126709501/Global-Chemicals-Outlook-full-r.

61. Ibid.

62. "Persistent Organic Pollutants," *Government of Canada*, accessed on August 10, 2023, https://www.rcaanc-cirnac.gc.ca/eng/1663276089948/1663276147794.

63. "Rotterdam Convention," *Sustainable Development*, accessed on August 10, 2023, https://sustainabledevelopment.un.org/index.php?page=view&type=30022&nr=132&menu=3170.

64. "Pollution in Minority Newborns," *EWG*, accessed on July 20, 2023, https://www.ewg.org/research/pollution-minority-newborns.

65. "Toxic Textiles FAQs," *Green America*, accessed on July 8, 2023, https://www.greenamerica.org/toxic-textiles-faqs.

66. "Water pollution Due to Textile Industry," *Textile Value Chain*, Sept. 11, 2020, https://textilevaluechain.in/news-insights/water-pollution-due-to-textile-industry/.

67. "What Is the Problem?," *Green America*, accessed on May 28, 2023, https://greenamerica.org/show-ga-blog?nid=15137.

68. Ibid.

69. Greenpeace, *Destination Zero: Seven Years of Detoxing the Clothing Industry*, accessed on June 2, 2022, https://www.greenpeace.org/static/planet4-international-stateless/2018/07/destination_zero_report_july_2018.pdf.

70. "About," *Roadmap to Zero*, accessed on April 10, 2023, https://www.roadmap-tozero.com/about.

71. Greenpeace, *Toxic Threads: The Big Fashion Stitch-Up*, October 2012, https://www.greenpeace.org/static/planet4-international-stateless/2012/11/317d2d47-toxicthreads01.pdf.

72. Cristina M. Villanueva, Manolis Kogevinas, Sylvaine Cordier, Michael R. Templeton, Roel Vermeulen, John R. Nuckols, Mark J. Nieuwenhuijsen, and Patrick Levallois, "Assessing Exposure and Health Consequences of Chemicals in Drinking Water: Current State of Knowledge and Research Needs," *Environmental Health Perspectives* 122, no. 3 (2014): 213–21; Kanwal Rehman, Fiza Fatima, Iqra Waheed, and Muhammad Sajid Hamid Akash, "Prevalence of Exposure of Heavy Metals and Their Impact on Health Consequences," *Journal of Cellular Biochemistry* 119, no. 1 (2018): 157–84.

73. "REACH Regulation," *European Commission*, accessed on September 15, 2022, https://ec.europa.eu/environment/chemicals/reach/reach_en.htm.

74. "Registration, Evaluation, Authorisation and Restriction of Chemicals (REACH)," *Edie*, accessed on June 3, 2023, https://www.edie.net/definition/registration-evaluation-authorisation-and-restriction-of-chemicals-reach/.

75. "MRSL and RSL: What Is the Difference and When to Carry Out MRSL Testing?," *Chem-Map*, February 26, 2018, https://www.chem-map.com/chemical_news/mrsl-rsl-differences-testing-chemicals/.

76. "RSL & MRSL," *Textile Focus*, December 24, 2020, https://textilefocus.com/rsl-mrsl/.

77. Chem-Map, "MRSL and RSL."

78. "Clothing and Textile Information," *Conscious Challenge*, June 5, 2019, https://www.theconsciouschallenge.org/ecologicalfootprintbibleoverview/clothing-textile-information.

79. Green America, "Toxic Textiles FAQs."

80. Ibid.

81. Ibid.

82. Ibid.

83. "Mighty Good: Nonylphenol Ethoxylates (NPEs) Fact Sheet," *Low Tox Life*, accessed on February 10, 2023, https://www.lowtoxlife.com/wpcontent/uploads/2016/07/NonylphenolEthoxylatesNPEOsfactsheet.pdf.

84. Conscious Challenge, "Clothing and Textile Information."

85. "Greenpeace Doing Their Own Hazardous Chemicals Testing on Fashion Footwear and Clothing," *FDRA*, accessed on August 1, 2023, https://fdra.org/latest-news/greenpeace-doing-their-own-hazardous-chemicals-testing-on-fashion-footwear-and-clothing/.

86. Greenpeace, *A Little Story about a Fashionable Lie: Hazardous Chemicals in Luxury Branded Clothing for Children*, accessed on May 2, 2022, https://www.greenpeace.org/static/planet4-international-stateless/2014/02/0a4ad7fa-a-fashionable-lie.pdf

87. FDRA, "Greenpeace Doing Their Own Hazardous Chemicals Testing."

88. Greenpeace, *Little Story about a Fashionable Lie*.

89. Maha Elia, "Design for Circular Economy" (master's thesis, University of Windsor, 2019). https://scholar.uwindsor.ca/cgi/viewcontent.cgi?amp=&article=9215&context=etd.

90. "G20/OECD Principles of Corporate Governance", OECD Publishing, Paris, accessed on April 2, 20222, http://dx.doi.org/10.1787/9789264236882-en

91. Chris Laszlo and Nadya Zhexembayeva, *Embedded Sustainability: The Next Big Competitive Advantage* (London: Taylor and Francis), 2017.

92. "Economic Sustainability," *Alternative*, accessed on August 10, 2022, https://alternativet.dk/en/politics/party-programme/economic-sustainability.

93. Pierre Lemieux, "Government Externalities and the Friedman Criterion," last modified on July 10, 2022, https://www.econlib.org/government-externalities-and-the-friedman-criterion/.

94. Lester Brown, *World on the Edge: How to Prevent Environmental and Economic Collapse* (New York: W. W. Norton, 2011), 183–84, https://www.earth-policy.org/images/uploads/book_files/wotebook.pdf.

95. Ibid, 184.

96. House of Commons, Environmental Audit Committee, *Fixing Fashion: Clothing Consumption and Sustainability*, February 19, 2019, p. 3, https://publications.parliament.uk/pa/cm201719/cmselect/cmenvaud/1952/1952.pdf.

97. John Guest, "The Economics of the Fast Fashion," September 16, 2021, https://pearsonblog.campaignserver.co.uk/the-economics-of-fast-fashion/.

98. Dominic Barton, James Manyika, and Sarah Keohane Williamson, "Finally, Evidence That Managing for the Long Term Pays Off," *Harvard Business Review*, February 9, 2017, https://hbr.org/2017/02/finally-proof-that-managing-for-the-long-term-pays-off.

99. "Vegea," Vegea Company, accessed on January 29, 2023, https://www.vegea-company.com/.

100. "Ellen Macarthur Foundation," *Ellen Macarthur Foundation*, accessed on January 29, 2023, https://ellenmacarthurfoundation.org/.

101. "Sustainable Consumption and Production Policies," UNEP, accessed on January 29, 2023, https://www.unep.org/explore-topics/resource-efficiency/what-we-do/sustainable-consumption-and-production-policies.

102. McKinsey & Company, *Fashion on Climate: How the Fashion Industry Can Urgently Act to Reduce Its Greenhouse Gas Emissions*, 2020, accessed on May 24, 2023, https://www.readkong.com/page/climate-fashion-on-how-the-fashion-industry-can-urgently-3977307.

103. Ibid.

104. Ibid.

105. Ibid.

106. "Milestone Fashion Industry Charter for Climate Action Launched," UN, last modified December 2018, https://www.un.org/sustainabledevelopment/blog/2018/12/milestone-fashion-industry-charter-for-climate-action-launched/.

107. Melissa Schwartz, "H&M Leads the Way for Sustainable Fast Fashion," accessed on May 10, 2023, https://d3.harvard.edu/platform-rctom/submission/hm-leads-the-way-for-sustainable-fast-fashion/#.

108. "United Nations Sustainable Development Goals," *UNRIC*, accessed on June 20, 2023, https://unric.org/en/united-nations-sustainable-development-goals/.

109. "Fashion Alliance," *United Nation Alliance for Sustainable Fashion*, accessed on January 10, 2023, https://unfashionalliance.org/.

110. "Apparel Worldwide," *Statista*, accessed on June 29, 2023, https://www.statista.com/outlook/cmo/apparel/worldwide.

111. "How the United Nations SDGs Relate to the Fashion Industry," *Remake*, 2020, accessed on July 13, 2023, https://remake.world/stories/news/how-the-united-nations-sdgs-relate-to-the-fashion-industry/.

112. Ibid.

113. Example of Remake movies can be seen at "Films: Made in America," *Remake*, August 7, 2020, https://remake.world/stories/made-in/made-in-america/. Other similar movies can be found at "Stories," *Remake*, https://remake.world/category/stories/.

114. Remake, "How the United Nations SDGs Relate to the Fashion Industry."

115. Ibid.

# Chapter 3

# Sustainability in the Fashion Business: Core Principles and Assessments

- Chapter Introduction and Learning Objectives
- The Fashion Industry Supply Chain and Global Interdependence
- Sustainability Drivers
- Intergovernmental Principles
- Legislature
- Nongovernmental Organizations (NGOs)
- Interest Groups
- Why and How Do Businesses Practice Sustainability?
- Sustainable Business Practice
- Sustainable Business Assessment
- Materiality Assessment
- Life Cycle Assessment (LCA)
- Social Life Cycle Assessment (S-LCA)
- Supplier Scorecard Assessments
- Sustainable Business Certifications
- Chapter Summary
- References

# Chapter Introduction and Learning Objectives

In this chapter we will explore the core sustainability principles and assessments used to appraise fashion businesses. The purpose of this chapter is to clarify why sustainability presents the most significant issue currently confronted by fashion businesses. As sustainability becomes a key component of successful decision-making processes, fashion businesses must respond by making decisions that showcase their dedication to sustainable business activity. Consequently, this chapter frames how sustainability-oriented companies can assess their products and their corporate and supply chain practices according to the industry-relevant sustainability standards. Case studies presented in this chapter showcase that sustainability represents a valuable lens for the business practitioner to navigate necessary and needed changes in the fashion industry.

This chapter has the following learning objectives:

- Explore the core sustainability principles and assessments used to appraise fashion business.
- Consider drivers to sustainable corporate behavior.
- Analyze case studies to evaluate the various strategies employed in the development of a sustainable business.
- Understand how to conduct core sustainability assessments.

**Key Terms**

| | |
|---|---|
| B-Corp certification | life-cycle assessments |
| embedded vs. bolted-on sustainability | materiality assessments |
| Higg Index | social life-cycle assessments |
| key performance indicators | supplier scorecard assessments |

# The Fashion Industry Supply Chain and Global Interdependence

"Most apparel products travel through various parts of the world and through many hands before reaching store shelves."[1] Garment production starts with the sourcing of raw materials, followed by the fabric production, and then through spinning, knitting, weaving, and other processes that prepare the item for the final assembly stage. In such a long process, suppliers in the countries carrying out the final assembly stage of taking the fabric and making it into clothes might not be the same as the suppliers in the country from which the fabric was initially sourced.[2] To simplify the supply chain complexity somewhat, we can say that, broadly speaking,

> three main supply chain segments are often recognized as a part of sequential production phases, where suppliers are divided among the tier-one (finalization), tier-two (input production and processing), and tier-three (raw material cultivation) stages. Both mass-market and luxury brands operate across complex supply chains. In 2016, H&M Group reported having an estimated one million supply chain workers, employed by approximately 820 suppliers and 1,900 factories. Inditex (Zara), in the same year, reported partnerships in 50 countries with 1,725 tier-one suppliers and 6,298 other facilities. In the luxury sector, Burberry and Prada were among the first brands to announce production delocalization, from countries of brand heritage (in their case the UK and Italy) to countries with lower production costs. In 2010, Prada disclosed a supply network that included 480 manufacturing facilities in China, Turkey, Vietnam, and Romania. In 2015, the luxury giant Gucci reported audits on 659 international suppliers.[3]

The fragmentation of the fashion industry is well documented in the scientific literature. For example, in 2013, the worldwide apparel import trade amounted to US $481 billion. "The leading apparel importer was the United States with US $91 billion, followed by Germany (US $35.5 billion), Japan (US $33.6 billion), France (US $23.4 billion), and the United Kingdom (US $22.8 billion). In the same year, the world apparel export trade came to US $460 billion, and China was the leading apparel exporter, with US $177.4 billion. Italy (US $23.7 billion), Bangladesh (US $23.5 billion), and Hong Kong (US $21.9 billion) were the next leading apparel exporters." More recent apparel trade statistics "indicate that developed countries such as the US, Germany, Japan, France, and the UK are engaged in apparel import activities, while exporting countries such as China, Italy, Bangladesh, and Hong Kong are involved in apparel export activities." While "in the early 1960s, most developed countries were engaged in apparel exports, today they are now the world's leading apparel importers" because production has been relocated to the developing countries, where the labor cost is lower.[4] Because fashion production is fragmented around the world, it is clear that most of the apparel items of global market have more than one country of origin. However, tracing all locations where garments were produced in various stages is hardly possible. Thus, consumers still have very little information on origin of the garments they consume.[5]

The complexity, fragmentation, and invisibility of the global fashion supply chain was sharply brought into question after several incidents occurred in this sector in recent history. For example, in 2013 the Rana Plaza garment factory collapsed in Bangladesh and killed at least 1,132 garment workers.[6] After the tragedy brands could not determine whether they were sourcing from that particular factory despite their clothing labels being found in the rubble.[7] However, brands dismissed allegations of responsibility for the tragedy, transferring responsibility to their contractors. Moreover, brands claimed that they did not track their supply chains, meaning that they were not responsible for their suppliers' actions or for the effects of those actions. Even worse, this event showed that in some cases, due to supply chain fragmentation and supplier subcontracting, brands did not even know who their suppliers were.[8] Therefore, this incident proves that continuing to recent times, the fashion industry has faced a tug-of-war between corporate social responsibility and profitability.

Globalization and the market power of multinational apparel companies and retailers has allowed them to push their production processes into low-income countries that hire predominantly female workers who are often either unskilled or semiskilled, due to the constant demand for less costly methods of manufacturing as the apparel industry has become highly competitive. Because of this disconnect between the apparel companies and their production chain, the companies have stayed focused on retailing, product selling, and promotion for the sake of profit creation while they "export their environmental and social problems to developing countries."[9] This division of roles was made easier by the disjointed and weak labor legislation in the developing nations, which did not have legal or structural means to deal with these growing environmental and social issues in their countries and whose laws were often considered inadequate, outdated, or insufficiently enforced by local governments.[10]

After the Rana Plaza tragedy however, many positive changes took place in the fashion industry due to the combined pressure from different stakeholders that were driving business and legislative change. "Over 200 fashion brands and retailers joined forces to collaboratively develop two historic parallel agreements, the Accord on Fire and Building Safety in Bangladesh and the Alliance for Bangladesh Worker Safety. The Accord is the first modern legally binding agreement between global brands and retailers and trade unions that represented garment workers. It was governed by a steering committee with equal representation from apparel companies and trade unions, with a neutral chair provided by the International Labor Organization (ILO)."[11]

According to Fashion Revolution organization reports, the Bangladesh Accord had a highly significant impact across other developing countries that comprise the global supply chain. More specifically, Fashion Revolution estimates that since its inception in 2013, the Bangladesh Accord has helped to detect more than 145,000 safety violations in Bangladesh factories under the accord. Regarding those violations, 93% of the safety issues identified were remedied. "The Accord's grievance mechanism has also proven effective in resolving over 700 safety complaints from factory workers and their representatives, while more than 1,300 joint labor-management factory level safety committees have been set up to regularly monitor safety measurements."[12] This example shows that in cases where binding agreement exists among brands, retailers, and manufactures, it is possible to hold all parties accountable and responsible for their actions. For this reason, there is a greater need for other countries that are heavily involved in apparel production to be covered by similar kinds of programs.

## Sustainability Drivers

In early the 1980s, Edward Freeman launched stakeholder theory, arguing that companies need to create value not only for shareholders but also for various stakeholders, including customers, suppliers, employees, and financiers.[13] For this reason we can argue that the primary sustainability drivers represent demands that various stakeholders might have. Theoretically, managing stakeholders' needs requires companies to attend to at least minimal stakeholder interests in order to satisfy them.[14] Practically, however, stakeholder theory warns that establishing a business's reputation as sustainable means not only satisfying minimal stakeholder needs (e.g., accepting required environmental or social policy in order to make business compliant) but also creating higher values (e.g., proactive acceptance of environmental and social policies to improve safety and quality of life for workers in the sourcing community). I should also mention that higher value creation is a process, and as such it requires a strategic plan for establishing and maintaining satisfactory stakeholder relationships.[15] For example, establishing responsible sourcing practices from artisanal communities requires a long-term perspective where businesses anticipate and adapt to changes in artisanal communities in both the present and the future. Those changes include but are not limited to changing governmental regulations and trade politics as well as potential changes in human, natural, and financial capital. In such a scenario, businesses must take into account and address multiple stakeholder needs, not just one at the exclusion of others. Further, businesses must understand the social, environmental, and economic impacts their activities have on the local community in order to limit any negative impacts, and they must ensure that adequate resources are available for future generations.

Here I will introduce some of the most prominent sustainability drivers as they relate to different stakeholder categories.

## Intergovernmental Principles

*The United Nations Global Compact (UNGC).* The UNGC initiative was developed in 1997 in the form of a nonbinding pact that aims to encourage businesses to adopt sustainable polices and report on their implementation. Currently, with over 12,000 organizations based in more than 160 countries, the UNGC represents the largest corporate sustainability initiative in the world.[16] Because sustainability principles form the foundation upon which company-specific business principles and standards can be formed, the UNGC established foundational principles to guide companies that aim to meet fundamental responsibilities in the following areas:

- human rights
- labor

- environment
- anti-corruption

Within these four areas, the UNGC has established ten principles "derived from the Universal Declaration of Human Rights, the International Labor Organization's Declaration on Fundamental Principles and Rights at Work, the Rio Declaration on Environment and Development, and the United Nations Convention Against Corruption."[17] These principles are broken down into four areas:

- *Human rights*
  - Principle 1: "Businesses should support and respect the protection of internationally proclaimed human rights"
  - Principle 2: Businesses should ensure "that they are not complicit in human rights abuses"
- *Labor*
  - Principle 3: "Businesses should uphold the freedom of association and the effective recognition of the right to collective bargaining"
  - Principle 4: Businesses should uphold "the elimination of all forms of forced and compulsory labor"
  - Principle 5: Businesses should uphold "the effective abolition of child labor"
  - Principle 6: Businesses should uphold the "elimination of discrimination in respect to employment and occupation"
- *Environment*
  - Principle 7: "Businesses should support a precautionary approach to environmental challenges"
  - Principle 8: Businesses should "undertake initiatives to promote greater environmental responsibility"
  - Principle 9: Businesses should "encourage the development and diffusion of environmentally friendly technologies"
- *Anti-corruption*
  - Principle 10: "Businesses should work against corruption in all its forms, including extortion and bribery"[18]

The UNGC states that "companies with operations and supply chains extending around the world need to understand locations far from their headquarters and view sustainability through a local lens."[19] For this purpose, the UNGC created the Global Compact Local Networks to advance the ten principles at the country level. The Global Compact Local Networks "help companies understand what responsible business means within different national, cultural, and linguistic contexts and facilitate outreach, learning, policy dialogue, collective action, and partnerships. Through networks, companies can make local connections—with other businesses and stakeholders from NGOs, government, and academia—and receive guidance to put their sustainability commitments into action."[20]

The UNGC emphasizes that businesses should adhere to the ten principles within both corporate and supply chain operations to avoid:

- *"Legal risks*: It is increasingly becoming illegal in a company's home country for the company to engage in corrupt practices in other countries.
- *Reputational risks*: Companies whose policies and practices fail to meet high ethical standards or that are exposed to serious reputational risks.
- *Financial costs*: According to the UN Development Programme, in 2014, corruption was estimated to cost some countries up to 17% of their GDP.
- *Erosion of internal trust:* Unethical corporate behavior negatively affects the overall ethical culture of the company" and decreases the trust of its employees.[21]

*Rio Declaration principles.* The Rio Declaration principles represent the outcome of the Rio 1992 Earth Summit. The Rio Declaration on Environment and Development provides definitions for twenty-seven governing principles that form a strong foundation for responsible and sustainable business development around the world.[22] Those principles outline the responsibility of nations to pursue sustainable development that equitably meets the environmental and developmental needs of present and future generations. For example, nations where businesses operate are expected to prevent overproduction, overconsumption, and incarnation of unsold products;

coordinate safe waste disposal; collaborate to eradicate poverty; and improve workers' rights and salaries. Furthermore, businesses that pollute at higher levels must pay higher taxes for environmental degradation. Several European nations, for example, established carbon taxes aiming to create behavioral change through economic policy. As a result, businesses in those countries are motivated to shift from using high polluting carbon sources, such as coal, to using preferred low carbon sources, such as solar power. In 2021 Sweden had the highest carbon tax rates, followed by Switzerland, Liechtenstein, and Finland.[23]

*The UN Guiding Principles on Business and Human Rights framework.* The UN Guiding Principles on Business and Human Rights framework was developed in 2011, when the UN Human Rights Council introduced the Guiding Principles on Business and Human Rights to guide implementation of the UN's Protect, Respect, and Remedy framework.[24] The foundational principles for business enterprises include a responsibility to respect human rights as expressed in the Declaration on Fundamental Principles and Rights at Work put forward by the International Labor Organization (ILO). The foundational principles require companies to carry out due diligence for human rights, which includes assessing actual and potential human rights impacts, taking actions upon the findings, and transparently communicating how impacts are addressed. According to the UN Guiding Principles on Business and Human Rights framework, fashion brands must identify "salient human rights" that are applicable to their own supply chain network, provide definitions and specify the relevance of the issues that are identified, and discuss emerging issues continuously.[25]

## Legislature

*The California Supply Chain Transparency Act.* The California Supply Chain Transparency Act was launched in California in 2012. This act requires manufacturers and retailers (including fashion retailers) running businesses in California to publicly disclose the efforts they make in order to prevent human trafficking and slavery in the supply chain. "A company must meet certain criteria to be subject to the law. It must (a) identify itself as a retail seller or manufacturer in its tax returns; (b) satisfy the legal requirements for 'doing business' in California; and (c) have annual worldwide gross receipts exceeding $100,000,000. The law requires companies subject to the law to disclose information regarding their efforts to eradicate human trafficking and slavery within their supply chains on their website or, if a company does not have a website, through written disclosures." This act is important for the fashion industry since it covers all

- "retail sellers or manufacturers
- entities doing business in the state of California
- with annual worldwide gross receipts in excess of $100,000,000."[26]

According to the State of California Department of Justice, businesses that are subject to this law are required to disclose their initiatives in five areas: verification, audits, certification, internal accountability, and training. Specifically, in its supply chain disclosure, a company must disclose to what extent, if any, it

1. Engages in verification of product supply chains to evaluate and address risks of human trafficking and slavery. The disclosure shall specify if the verification was not conducted by a third party.
2. Conducts audits of suppliers to evaluate supplier compliance with company standards for trafficking and slavery in supply chains. The disclosure shall specify if the verification was not an independent, unannounced audit.
3. Requires direct suppliers to certify that materials incorporated into the product comply with the laws of the country or countries in which they are doing business regarding slavery and human trafficking.
4. Maintains internal accountability standards and procedures for employees or contractors failing to meet company standards regarding slavery and trafficking.
5. Provides company employees and management who have direct responsibility for supply chain management training on human trafficking and slavery, particularly with respect to mitigating risks within the supply chains of products.[27]

*The Modern Slavery Act (2015).* The modern Slavery Act (2015) is an act of the Parliament of the United Kingdom designed to combat modern slavery in the production value chain.[28] According to "the Modern Slavery Act (2015), organizations conducting business in the United Kingdom with worldwide revenues of at least £36 million are required to publish a transparency statement describing the steps they have taken in the last financial year to ensure their business and supply chains are free from modern slavery and human trafficking. This obligation applies to financial years ending on or after 31 March 2016, and transparency statements should be published as soon as reasonably practicable after, and ideally within six months of, the financial year end."[29]

What does modern slavery mean? According to Anti-Slavery International, an international NGO, modern slavery comes in different forms including:

> 1) forced labor: any work or services which people are forced to do against their will under the threat of some form of punishment, 2) bonded labor: the world's most widespread form of slavery, in which people borrow money they cannot repay and are required to work to pay off the debt, after which they lose control over the conditions of both their employment and the debt, 3) human trafficking: the transporting, recruiting or harboring people for the purpose of exploitation, using violence, threats, or coercion and 4) child slavery: different from child labor, child slavery occurs when a child is exploited for someone else's gain. It can include child trafficking, the use of child soldiers, child marriage, and child domestic slavery.[30]

According to the Walk Free Foundation, this act is important since the global fashion industry remains one of the biggest drivers of modern slavery, with more than one hundred billion pounds worth of garments potentially involving the use of modern slavery imported into the G20 countries every year.[31]

In table 5, I use Walk Free Foundation reports to describe some of the products of the fashion and textile and home-décor industries that have been identified as at the most risk of involving modern slavery.[32]

**Table 5** Examples of modern slavery cases in fashion, textiles, and home décor industries*

| Country, | Product | Modern slavery case |
|---|---|---|
| Uzbekistan | Cotton | Uzbekistan has been under scrutiny for a long time for forced labor in its annual cotton harvest. In 2017, a monitoring report published by the International Labor Organization (ILO) stated that systematic use of child labor in Uzbekistan's cotton harvest had come to an end, and that at that time cotton pickers were recruited voluntarily. However, other research published by Human Rights Watch (HRW) found that more than one million people including children, students, and workers in the public sector were being mobilized to pick the cotton under the threat of penalty. |
| Kazakhstan | Cotton | A UN organization has collected evidence that the cotton sector in that country has become a destination for low-skilled migrant workers from Uzbekistan, Kyrgyzstan, and Tajikistan who are abused and work in poor and hazardous working conditions, often dealing with delayed payment and blackmailed through confiscated personal identity documents. |
| Tajikistan | Cotton | The International Organization for Migration (IOM) conducted studies in 2012, 2013, and 2015 assessing exploitation during the cotton harvest through surveys and interviews with adults and children. Findings showed that in later years the percentage of forcibly mobilized children and adults decreased although frequent labor violations including not being paid for work or not having a written contract still continued. |
| Brazil | Garments | A 2013 report states that migrant workers from poorer Latin American countries (Bolivia, Peru, Haiti) are exploited in the textile sector in Sao Paulo. An Aljazeera investigative journalist discovered numerous sweatshops in the Bras neighborhood in the central area of Sao Paulo. |

*(Continues)*

**Table 5** Continued

| Country, | Product | Modern slavery case |
|---|---|---|
| China | Garments | Various reports provide evidence that between 2007 and 2017, workers in the garment sector in Southeastern China were forced to produce shoes for international brands while being verbally and physically abused. |
| India | Garments | The textile industry in Tamil Nadu, India has been reported to be exploiting young women workers in the spinning and textile units under what is called the "Sumangali Scheme." Reports state that women from lower castes in remote regions are specifically targeted and they are brought under false promises to work in camp labor where their movement is restricted and pay is withheld until the fixed-term contract completion. They reported working 60 hours per week. The research was conducted by Solidaridad and Fair Labor Association. |
| Vietnam | Garments | The Vietnam-based charity Blue Dragon Children's Foundation found 14 children working under exploitative conditions. The foundation believes that besides exploitation in the garment industry, external child-trafficking is another problem on the government's agenda. |
| India | Carpets | A 2014 report created by Harvard University's Center for Health and Human Rights identified more than 5,000 cases of forced labor, including child labor and bonded labor, in India's handmade carpet industry. |
| Pakistan | Carpets | Studies conducted in 2017 in provinces of Sindh, Punjab, and Baluchistan found that bonded child labor existed in Pakistan's carpet industry and that children working in carpet-weaving were often working in unsafe working conditions due to exposure to hazard chemicals with notable consequences to their health. |

*Table quotes from "The Global Slavery Index 2018: Walk Free Foundation," Respect International, accessed on May 31, 2023, https://respect.international/wp-content/uploads/2018/07/The-Global-Slavery-Index-2018-Walk-Free-Foundation.pdf.

*The Accord on Fire and Building Safety in Bangladesh.* This act represents a formal agreement between fashion brands and the IndustriALL Global Union, the UNI Global Union, and eight of their Bangladeshi affiliated unions to work toward a safe and healthy garment and textile industry in Bangladesh. It was "signed in the immediate aftermath to the Rana Plaza building collapse. Over 220 companies signed the five-year Accord, and by May 2018, the work of the Accord had contributed to significantly safer workplaces for millions of Bangladeshi garment workers. To maintain and expand the progress achieved under the 2013 Accord, over 190 brands and retailers have signed the 2018 Transition Accord with the global unions, a renewed agreement which took effect on June 1, 2018." Key features of the accord include "safety inspections, and remediation programs, disclosure of inspection reports and corrective action plans, safety training programs, safety and health complaint mechanisms, and optional listing of home textile, fabric, and knit accessories suppliers."[33]

## Nongovernmental Organizations (NGOs)

"A nongovernmental organization (NGO) is not a private company and does not have formal affiliation with any government. NGOs are interest groups that are often trying to influence business behavior either directly by persuasion or protest or indirectly by being influential in shaping public policy. There are many NGOs influencing the operating context for sustainable businesses."[34] Here I will list some examples of the most influential NGOs that support sustainable development in the fashion and other affiliated industries.

Ceres collaborates with businesses, governments, and policymakers to create sustainable solutions. For example, Ceres created the Global Reporting Initiative (GRI) proposing framework that companies might use to report their sustainability efforts. In 2018 Ceres published the apparel and footwear sector analysis, and the key findings of Ceres analysis are presented in the case study in this chapter.

The Sustainable Apparel Coalition unites international fashion brands, manufacturers, retailers, governments, and educators to create sustainable solutions in fashion industry. One of the biggest accomplishments is creation of the **Higg Index**, "The standardized measurement of value chain sustainability" available to all fashion industry participants. The Higg tools are available on the official website where you can find more details about Higg Brand, Higg Product, and Higg Facility measurements.[35]

## Interest Groups

There are various interest groups that influence public policy and lobby international governments in order to support sustainable development. Those interest groups include "trade and business associations, labor unions, professional organizations, environmental organizations, advocacy groups, and charities."[36] For the purpose of this book, I will review here some of the groups that are very influential within the context of the global fashion industry; please understand that the list given in table 6 is not exhaustive.

**Table 6** Selected interest groups that support sustainable development in the fashion industry*

| Interest Group | Description |
| --- | --- |
| Textile Exchange | Textile Exchange is a global non-profit that works to drive industry transformation in sustainable fibers, integrity and standards, and responsible supply networks. |
| Redress | Redress is an environmental charity with a mission to reduce and transform textile waste to catalyze a circular economy and reduce the fashion industry's water, chemical, and carbon footprints. |
| Clean Clothes Campaign | Clean Clothes Campaign is a global alliance dedicated to improving working conditions and empowering workers in the global garment and sportswear industries. |
| Labour Behind the Label | Labour Behind the Label is the UK platform of the Clean Clothes Campaign, which campaigns for garment workers' rights worldwide. |
| Good on You | Good on You is an app used to discover ethical brands and see how the user's favorites measure up. |

*(Continues)*

**Table 6** Continued

| Interest Group | Description |
|---|---|
| International Labor Organization | The only tripartite U.N. agency, since 1919 the International Labor Organization has brought together governments, employers, and workers to set labor standards and develop policies while promoting decent work for all. |
| Greenpeace | Since 2011 Greenpeace has been calling on major brands to eliminate the use and release of harmful chemicals from their production chain through committing to detoxification. Greenpeace also works to rewind habits of unsustainable consumption and production so that we can live within our planetary limits. |
| IndustriALL Global Union | IndustriALL represents 50 million workers in 140 countries across many sectors, including textiles, garments, leather, and footwear; it fights for better working conditions and trade union rights around the world. |
| Global Fashion Exchange | Global Fashion Exchange (GFX) is an international platform promoting sustainability in the fashion industry through inspiring forums, educational content, and circularity initiatives. |
| Fair Wear Foundation | Fair Wear Foundation is a non-profit organization that works with brands, factories, trade unions, NGOs, and governments to verify and improve workplace conditions for garment workers in 11 production countries. |
| Ethical Trading Initiative | The Ethical Trading Initiative (ETI) is a leading alliance of companies, trade unions, and NGOs that work together to tackle the many complex questions about what steps companies should take to trade ethically and how to make a positive difference in workers' lives. |
| Ellen MacArthur Foundation | The Ellen MacArthur Foundation works with business, government, and academia to build a framework for an economy that is restorative and regenerative by design. |

(*Continues*)

**Table 6** Continued

| Interest Group | Description |
|---|---|
| Anti-Slavery International | Anti-Slavery International is a lobby for global recognition and alleviation of modern slavery in all its forms. |
| Environmental Justice Foundation | The Environmental Justice Foundation is working to secure a world where natural habitats and environments can sustain and be sustained by the communities that depend upon them for their basic needs and livelihoods. |
| Fashion Revolution | Founded in the wake of the Rana Plaza disaster in 2013, Fashion Revolution has become the world's largest fashion activism movement, mobilizing citizens, industry, and policymakers through research, education, and advocacy work. |
| Remake | Remake is a community of millennial and Gen Z women who pledge to wear their values and put an end to fast fashion. |
| Fairtrade Foundation | Fairtrade Foundation's mission is to connect disadvantaged farmers and workers with consumers, promote fairer trading conditions, and empower farmers and workers to combat poverty." |
| Solidaridad Network | Solidaridad works to create sustainable supply chains from the producer to the consumer and to enable producers in developing countries to get a better price for better products while preserving their environment. |
| War on Want | War on Want campaigns for human rights and against the root causes of global poverty, inequality, and injustice. |
| Ethical Fashion report by Baptist World Aid | Baptist World Aid is a Christian non-profit organization that creates annual Ethical Fashion report called The Truth Behind the Barcode. |

*Table quotes comes from "Key Organizations," Fashion Revolution, accessed on July 29, 2023, https://www.fashionrevolution.org/key-organisations/.

## Case study 5: Footwear and apparel sector analysis- corporate progress on the Ceres road map for sustainability

Ceres analysis "takes a closer look at whether and how 15 publicly traded U.S. footwear and apparel companies are establishing, implementing, and disclosing sustainable business strategies that drive improved performance across critical material impact areas, such as climate change, water scarcity, and human rights."[37] The companies included in the evaluation are Foot Locker, Gap Inc., Hanes Brands, L Brands, Lululemon Athletica, Michael Kors, NIKE Inc, PVH Corp, Ralph Lauren, Ross, Tapestry (formerly known as Coach), TJX Companies, Under Armour, Urban Outfitters, and VF Corp.

A deeper look at the footwear and apparel sector shows that the "limited visibility of global supply chains remains a key challenge for companies that are looking to ensure responsible manufacturing of their products. The environmental and social impacts related to sourcing (and product manufacturing) remain the most significant sustainability risks for these companies." Reports state that in the case of the investigated companies,

> as much as 88 percent of the carbon footprint is embedded in upstream activities. At the same time, the water-intensive nature of obtaining raw materials—as well as dyeing, laundering, and finishing textiles—is creating a business imperative for closely monitoring these resources in water-scarce regions of countries like China and India. While high-profile human rights violations, such as the use of forced labor in harvesting cotton in Uzbekistan and the Rana Plaza building collapse in Bangladesh, have prompted many of the above-mentioned companies to enhance supplier engagement and auditing, the continued reliance on low-cost, low-skill, and outsourced labor creates serious obstacles for companies striving to improve supplier transparency and performance.[38]

Thus, reports state that although there is evidence that companies in the fashion industry are establishing recommended polices, there is little evidence about how those policies are implemented into daily supply chain operations. Table 7 summarizes key findings.

**Table 7**  Footwear and apparel sector analysis key findings*

| Disadvantages | Advantages |
| --- | --- |
| 27% of investigated footwear and apparel companies embrace governance for sustainability as a core part of doing business—but the great majority have yet to formalize and incentivize oversight and accountability. | Footwear and apparel companies demonstrate slow but steady progress toward improved water stewardship. |
| Only 20% of investigated companies directly engage investors on sustainability. | The footwear and apparel sector outperforms its peers in tackling climate change but lacks clear and time-bound targets to drive improvements. |
| 0% of companies link executive compensation to sustainability performance metrics. | 80% of investigated companies have commitments to reducing GHG emissions |
| Strategies for reducing emissions must focus not only on direct operations but also on sourcing, manufacturing, and the materials themselves. | 20% of investigated companies set quantitative, time-bound targets to increase renewable energy procurement |

*Table quotes from Ceres, *Turning Point Sector Analysis: Footwear and Apparel A deeper look at sector performance within Corporate Progress on the Ceres Roadmap for Sustainability*, 2018, https://www.ceres.org/resources/reports/turning-point-corporate-progress-ceres-roadmap-sustainability.

Based on the report's findings, Ceres provides the following recommendations for steps that footwear and apparel companies can take to improve their sustainability performance:

- *"Link executive compensation to sustainability performance metrics.* Tying executive compensation to sustainability metrics (e.g., GHG reduction targets) would show that becoming a sustainable corporation is a business imperative. Most of the footwear and apparel sector assigns senior-level executives responsibility for sustainability performance. Linking compensation, not just for executives but for all employees, to environmental and social metrics will support sustainability performance."

- *"Proactively engage investors on sustainability risks and opportu-nities*. Investors increasingly integrate ESG factors into company assessments and seek comparable quantitative data to understand both short- and long-term social and environmental risks. Elevating ESG performance information within investor-directed communications will help investors better understand both the company's approach to risk mitigation and its vision for long-term value creation."

- *"Set science-based GHG emissions reduction goals*. To help limit global warming to below 2 degrees Celsius, companies will need to set time-bound, quantifiable, science-based targets for reduc-ing GHG emissions."[39] It is critical to reduce GHG emissions and prioritize usage of renewable energy both in direct operations and throughout the value chains.

- *"Set context-based water targets that prioritize areas and operations involving the greatest risk to water*. Water represents a key natu-ral resource for the companies in the footwear and apparel sector. For this reason, water management strategies must be established and supported by time-bound targets. Water risk assessments must be conducted for companies to focus conservation efforts on the watersheds at most risk."[40] Context-based water targets need to be established as well.

- *"Identify salient human rights impacts*. A company's salient human rights issues are related to those human rights that its activities or business relationships place most at risk."[41] For this reason, compa-nies should conduct **materiality assessments** to assess

    first the severity and scale of risks to people or rights-holders that result from its business activities, as well as its ability to manage those risks. The choice should not be whether to exam-ine issues and impacts through either the lens of salience or that of materiality; instead, companies should use both lenses. The identification of salient human rights can illuminate over-lap between issues that pose risks to people and those that pose risks to the business and can ensure that critical human rights issues are not overlooked by helping to prioritize those impacts and determine how to allocate resources to address them most effectively. [42]

**Student Activity:** Go online and explore current sustainability efforts of any one of the fifteen footwear and apparel companies covered by the Ceres 2018 report. Discuss the current sustainability efforts for the selected brand. Based on the knowledge you gained in this chapter, provide suggestions for further sustainability improvements.

# Why and How Do Businesses Practice Sustainability?

Browse through the internet looking at business portals (including fashion businesses), and you will see that businesses are becoming more and more focused on social issues and issues of environmental sustainability. Topics ranging from climate change to water and energy savings, $CO_2$ emissions, antidiscrimination, child labor, workers' rights, and social equity are appearing daily. *Fortune* magazine declared that the business of the twenty-first century is "green business,"[43] and I ultimately agree with this perspective: it is clear that business reality today, as compared to the business reality of the past, has been dramatically reshaped.

For example, if we look back through the major part of the twentieth century, we can see that corporations were generally considered as entities responsible solely for wealth accumulation. The American poet Ambrose Bierce once cynically described corporations as entities that have a single goal: to obtain individual profit without any obligation to have social responsibility.[44] Even in 1970, the Nobel Prize winner economist Milton Friedman said that a business has "one and only one social responsibility—to use its resources and engage in activities designed to increase its profits."[45] Such viewpoints make it clear that for a very long time, companies were perceived as entities creating only one kind of value—value of a financial or fiscal nature. In other words, businesses were expected to create profit to satisfy the interests of their shareholders. In the 1960s and 1970s, those traditional views on the purpose of business were challenged. Debates over corporate social responsibility took place, and nongovernmental entities such as Greenpeace and Friends of the Earth were established with the purpose to question corporate responsibilities. In 1979 Archie Carroll developed the well-established four-part model of corporate responsibility, which recognized four interrelated responsibilities that every business has: economic, legal, ethical, and philanthropic. These four responsibilities were visually represented as layers in a pyramid, and Carrol argued that a corporation that is socially responsible must meet all four principles at the same time.[46] Here each responsibility is briefly defined:

- *Economic responsibility.* According to Carroll, businesses are set up in society with the purpose of functioning as economic units. Therefore, in order to stay in business, companies must secure a reasonable return on their investments, and they have to pay employees who want safe and fairly paid jobs. For these reasons, the satisfaction of economic requirements is essential for all corporations.
- *Legal responsibility.* Legal responsibility demands all businesses to obey the law and be legally compliant.
- *Ethical responsibility.* "This type of responsibility obliges corporations to do what is right, just, and fair even when they are not compelled to do so by the legal framework." Carroll argues that ethical responsibilities consist of what is generally *expected* by society over and above a business' economic and legal expectations.
- *Philanthropic responsibility.* The Greek word "philanthropy" means love for humanity, and this aspect of social responsibility addresses a great variety of issues, including things such as charitable donations, support for local communities and schools, or the sponsoring of philanthropic events. "According to Carroll (1991), philanthropic responsibilities are therefore merely *desired* of corporations without being expected or required, making them "less important than the other three categories."[47]

Carroll, along with other corporate social responsibility thinkers such as Wood[48] and Frederick,[49] further defined four strategies of social responsiveness, suggesting that a company can be

- *Reactive*: when a company denies responsibility for social issues, transferring responsibility to government, NGOs, or other parties.
- *Defensive*: when a company admits responsibility but avoids fulfilling it, doing the very least that seems to be required.

- *Accommodative*: when a company accepts responsibility and does what is demanded of it in order to adhere to certain standards.
- *Proactive*: when a company seeks to go above and beyond industry norms and anticipates future expectations by doing more than is expected.

Although the main benefit of the four part model of corporate responsibility was its inclusion of the various social responsibilities in the business context, the major limitation of this model was a lack of solutions when two or more responsibilities were in conflict. This limitation was overcome to some degree with the development of stakeholder theory by Edward Freeman in the 1980s, which we already mentioned in the previous chapter.[50] Stakeholder theory emerged from the study of business ethics, and it represents a core theoretical foundation for today's sustainable business development. Unlike the corporate social responsibility (CSR) approach, which focuses narrowly "on the corporation and its responsibilities, the stakeholder approach starts by looking at various groups to which the business has a responsibility."[51] Probably the most common definition of a stakeholder is the following: A stakeholder is any group or individual that is affected by the achievement of the organization's objectives.[52] Evan and Freeman argue that the simplest way to determine who can be a stakeholder in a specific business context is to ask a question about who has corporate rights (e.g., rights that should not be violated and need to be respected), and then another question about who is affected by the corporate actions (e.g., businesses responsible for the effects of their actions on others).[53]

*Why do stakeholders matter*? Freeman presents two primary arguments to explain why stakeholders matter for any organization.

First, on a merely descriptive level, if one examines the relationship between the company and the various groups to which it is related by all sorts of contracts, it is simply not true to say that the only group with a legitimate interest in the business is shareholders. From a legal perspective, there are many groups apart from shareholders that hold a legitimate "stake" in the business since their interests are affected by the business in some way. There are not only legally binding contracts with suppliers, employees, or customers but also an increasingly dense network of laws and regulations enforced by society that make it a simple matter of fact that a large spectrum of stakeholders have certain rights. The second group of arguments comes from an economic perspective.[54]

In light of new institutional economics, there are further objections to the traditional shareholder or stockholder view. For example, there is the problem of externalities (in this context externality represents a side effect or consequence of an industrial or commercial activity that affects other parties). For instance, if a company releases post-production waste in the form of hazard chemicals in a local river located in a small outsourcing community where their supply chain is located, inhabitants of the community will be directly affected because their soil, water, and air will become polluted, and consequently the health and well-being of the plants, animal species, and humans in that community will be harmed. Therefore, from a stakeholder perspective, this business action would be perceived as irresponsible, such that the business would have to remediate those harms and negative business impacts by cleaning the local water and carrying out all possible mitigations in such a situation. However, from a traditional business standpoint, the obligation to protect the environment and well-being in the outsourcing community is not a responsibility of the business because there is no contractual relationship with the inhabitants in that community. I hope that this extreme but realistic example helps you understand my point that business reality can be radically reshaped if one compares the most important postulates of twentieth- and twenty-first-century business theories.

Therefore, we can conclude that unlike the period prior to 2000, when companies focused on faster, quicker, and cheaper production with little regard to externalities and the negative impacts of the business, through the 2000s, a new era of business in and for a society emerged. Consider issues such as the numerous natural disasters such as Hurricane Harvey and Hurricane Katrina, the Tohoku earthquake and tsunami, the Afghanistan blizzard, the Mozambique floods, the Haiti earthquake, and global health threats (e.g., Ebola, SARS, and COVID-19). Those crises significantly altered the market environment. Starting from the early 2000s, big corporations such as Walmart and Unilever began investing in environmental and social sustainability programs, and other retailers followed suit.[55] Suddenly, it became obvious that increasing expectations by investors, consumers, employees, and government were redefining the ways in which businesses created value.

For example, consumers today do not want just any product; instead, they have increasing expectations that the products they consume are nontoxic, ethically sourced, and sustainably packaged. For this reason, businesses today are challenged to rethink how they make what they make and what kinds of impacts that production has on society and the environment. Barely two decades ago, retailers of the shirt you are wearing considered only the ethical sourcing practices in their supply chain or the toxicity of dyes used to color the shirt. Now, the same retailer must consider which suppliers to select to ensure supply chain ethics, as well as whether the specific dye is toxic or is shortlisted as being hazardous for workers' and consumers' health. For all these reasons, whether business owners like it or not, the fact is that a new reality has challenged businesses to reinvent a new value in order to stay in the market game. Alternatively, if a business does not adapt, it will simply find itself thrown out of the market game! For this reason, we can conclude that sustainability is an overriding reality, and sustainable value is a kind of value that any business today is expected to generate.

*Sustainable value.* Sustainable value, in a nutshell, exists in a dynamic state that occurs when a company responds profitably to the emerging needs of diverse groups, including investors, employees, local communities, NGOs, workers' unions, and consumers. A simple way to think of sustainable value is to think about managerial necessity and the skill required to manage not just one dimension of the business (e.g., profit creation) but rather multiple interest groups and often conflicting needs at the same time. Such an approach requires a major shift in the traditional view of managerial responsibility.

Interestingly, if we consider the earliest responses to the sustainable value proposition within Harvard business review articles and McKinsey authors, we will quickly conclude that sustainable value was most often seen as involving an inevitable trade-off with profits. Indeed, there is still a widespread belief that if something is good for society and the environment, it must be more costly for business. Therefore, it is not uncommon to hear the argument that "sustainability can come only with a hefty price tag."[56]

(In this book, I am arguing against that viewpoint). In reality, sustainable value is not as much about new value creation as it is about resilience[57] and risk mitigation.[58]

There are two types of risks that sustainable value helps a business avoid. The first is the negative sustainability impacts of the business (e.g., the social risks of child labor can be minimized with operational procedures to avoid the use of child labor in the first place). The second kind of risk is that of fighting the negative consequences that follow immediately after the emergence of negative business impacts (in terms of the previous example, that would mean taking actions to investigate child labor issues in the supply chain and compensate or penalize the parties involved, manage reputational harm, avoid consumer rejection, etc.). For this reason, it is important for a manager, who has to manage potentially costly liabilities, to think about sustainable value creation.

Next, creating sustainable value helps to improve business efficiency. Cutting the quantity of water, energy, waste, and input materials in fact helps companies eliminate unnecessary costs. Sustainable value is also about new market creation because growing ecological and social needs bring new opportunities. For this reason, companies are motivated to enter these new markets either by adopting existing knowhow or through radical innovation. Sustainable value is also about product and service differentiation, as new products and services offer extra benefits and, therefore, are expected to cost somewhat more. For this reason, it is crucially important that businesses establish credible information about sustainable product attributes.

Last but not least important, sustainable value helps to protect and enhance brand image. Being seen as doing good for the environment and the planet while making a profit can be a powerful tool to attract new talented employees, investors, and suppliers of choice. However, companies cannot survive if they make claims that are not true and verifiable. For this reason, we can conclude that companies can either gain or lose market share based on stakeholder perceptions of positive or negative business impacts.

There are two main approaches for businesses to engage in sustainability endeavors. Informally, we can say the first approach is preferable, while the second and more frequently adopted one is more problematic. The preferred approach was mentioned in chapter one as the embedded approach; let me briefly explain that approach.

*Embedded sustainability.* A sustainable business is a business that embeds sustainability in its corporate core. This means that the company incorporates environmental, social, and economic value in its DNA with no trade-offs in terms of product quality.[59] Embedded sustainability creates sustainable value, and that value is at the company's heart. The same sustainable value pertains throughout the value chain, and all employees are engaged in sustainability endeavors. Sustainability is not something that certain individuals are doing in a "scapegoat" department; rather, sustainability is everyone's job. Competitors are seen as collaborators and a potential source of gain. Similarly, all business relationships are transformative, and stakeholders, such as suppliers, NGOs, government, policymakers, and consumers, are engaged to help build transformative and systematic change that everyone can benefit from. Last, but not least important, companies are more invested in sustainability performance then in communications advertising their sustainability.

*Bolted-on sustainability.* The second and unfortunately more common (but misguided) approach is often described as the "bolted-on" approach. This term means that companies "bolt on" sustainability to the corporate core, despite their best intentions. In other words, companies often advertise green initiatives or philanthropic endeavors, inadvertently highlighting the unsustainability of their core business activities.[60] This practice is evidently spreading among fast fashion brands that extensively advertise green products, despite the growing number of younger consumers who understand that cheap prices come with hidden costs. If H&M, for example, advertises a line of green or so-called conscience garments, what are its other products? One way to recognize that a business is not truly sustainable but that its sustainability is bolted on is to consider the following questions: Does the business promote sustainability as an additional and not a core strategy of its operations? Does the business have any legitimate sustainability business (e.g., B-Corp) or product certificate (e.g., GOT, GRS, etc.)?

Does the business transparently disclose information about the sourcing practices, suppliers, and social and environmental policies in its supply chain? Does the company have a separate department responsible for sustainability performance, or is sustainability everyone's job? Even if you think you know all answers to those questions, carefully investigate the official website and available sustainability reports for the company and try to understand their philosophy. Unfortunately, many businesses still self-produce and self-enforce sustainability narratives, bringing little or no value to people or the environment.

Key features of the bolted-on sustainability approach include:

- The approach is focused primarily on shareholder value
- Sustainability represents not the core but added business value
- Sustainability is not central to the company but remains at the margins
- Sustainable activities are limited to the corporate headquarters (in other words, they do not translate to the supply chain or to the sourcing community)
- Greenwashing, or heavy advertising of sustainability efforts with limited evidence, is employed.[61]

In summary, we can conclude that unlike CSR initiatives that consider stakeholder value to be at the expense of shareholders, embedded sustainability offers various opportunities to create enduring profits for the business. However, embedding sustainability in the corporate DNA involves a radically different way of thinking, doing, and transforming business. For this reason, there are many pathways to creating a sustainable business, whether this involves strengthening the business's position in the market or discovering and winning new markets that emerge. Depending on the company's goals, there are numerous approaches to design pathways that lead to the coveted destination. To explore the reasons why business leaders pursue sustainability, a series of independent surveys was conducted by the Boston Consulting Group and Massachusetts Institute of Technology (MIT), McKinsey and Company, and the UN Global Compact. For this purpose, the CEOs of the largest multinational companies were surveyed; the results of those surveys are displayed in table 8.

**Table 8** Why do business leaders pursue sustainability?*

| Greatest benefits from addressing sustainability issues | Top reasons for addressing sustainability issues | Factors driving action on sustainability |
|---|---|---|
| Brand image – 35% | Corporate reputation – 36% | Brand, trust, reputation – 72% |
| Cost savings – 12% | Alignment with business goals – 21% | Revenue growth or cost reduction – 44% |
| Competitive advantage – 10% | Improving efficiency/lowering cost – 19% | Consumer demand – 39% |
| Employee retention – 10% | Meeting customer expectations – 19% | Employee engagement/recruiting – 31% |
| Offering innovation – 10% | Strengthening company positioning – 17% | Government regulation risk – 24% |
| New sources of revenue – 8% | Leadership's personal interest – 14% | Investor/shareholder pressure – 12% |
| Risk management – 7% | Attracting/retaining employees – 11% | |
| Stakeholder relations – 6% | Pressure from NGOs – 3% | |

*\* Results in this table are combined based on the information I received from above mentioned survey in the process of book preparation.*

In conclusion, we can see that corporations commonly pursue sustainability not only for economic reasons (e.g., cost efficiency, revenue, and business growth) but also to strengthen relationships with their stakeholders and shareholders. From that standpoint it becomes clear that pursuing sustainability for these corporations means creating dynamic sustainable value by balancing competing interests through a process of negotiation and compromise. In other words, pursuing sustainability requires a company to profitably meet the needs of all parties that have a stake in it (including shareholders, employees, local communities, NGOs, customers, etc.) so that all these parties can benefit from the business's success. From a moralist theoretical perspective, we can also say that the main goal of a business is not only to make a profit but also to make a profit so that the corporation can do something more or better for the society; therefore, creation of sustainable value is frequently described as a moral issue.[62]

## Sustainable Business Practices

Sustainability principles are sets of fundamental ground rules for achieving sustainability. There is no single "right" framework or set of principles to help businesses practice sustainability. However, there are useful frameworks and principles to guide the application of sustainability thinking across a wide variety of situations and contexts. For these reasons the sustainability professionals in any company need to be conversant with commonly used sustainability frameworks and principles and able to apply and adapt appropriate frameworks and principles depending upon the situation and context. The Natural Step is an international NGO founded in 1989 in Sweden with the goal of facilitating sustainable business transformation.[63] This organization has developed a useful framework for sustainable business development called the Hierarchical Framework for Strategic Sustainable Development, or FSSD.[64] The framework contains five levels: system, success, strategy, action, and tools. I will briefly review them here.

The first level of the framework is called *system*, and it requires companies to apply systems thinking while being aware that all individuals, organizations, communities, and nations exist in both the society and the biosphere. The problem is that the application of systems thinking will reveal the essential problems of today's unsustainable society. Indeed, industrial society is designed in such a way that negative impacts are bound to increase globally. For example, humans keep extracting natural substances such as water from the earth at a greater rate than nature can replenish them, human activities emit chemicals at a faster rate than nature can absorb them, and human activities are degrading natural systems; consequently, there is a global depletion in natural resources. Therefore, businesses must be cognizant that all the natural resources a company needs to run its operation efficiently will eventually decline (this applies to water, forests, fisheries, fossil fuels, etc.). In order to balance the natural decline of the resources in the biosphere and growing need for these resources for running their business, sustainable companies must learn how to operate within the laws of nature that govern the system. Luckily, innovative businesses are trying to stay on the cutting edge of developing solutions to profit with sustainability, and examples of innovative technologies are already visible around us (e.g., electric cars, solar energy, renewable business solutions, water power, etc.).

The second level of the framework is called *success*. At this level, after building an awareness of how the biosystem and the society systems function, sustainability professionals must plan business strategies that will help them gain success within the system's limits. Two key principles in the planning stage are dematerialization and substitution. The principle of dematerialization requires businesses to minimize the resources they use to create their products. Alternatively, businesses are encouraged to completely dematerialize their operations; for example, instead of focusing on new production, they can rent what has already been produced. Similarly, they can repurpose and resell items that have not been sold for the regular price. Those kinds of initiatives are evident in the clothing retail sector, where we witness the increased popularity of clothing resale and rental businesses as well as the creative reuse of textiles and garments (e.g., textile quilts, patchwork collections, textile shopping bags, etc.). Next, the principle of substitution requires businesses to prioritize the usage of renewable resources gained through fair practices instead of using limited or rare resources (e.g., using recyclable material or biodegradable materials instead of blended materials, using natural dyes instead of synthetics, use of faux fur and faux leather instead of genuine materials, etc.).

The third level of the framework is *strategy*. At the strategy level, it is advised that companies consider "back casting from the basic principles." If the basic principles mean that corporations traditionally made strategic plans based on the forecasting from current circumstances, back casting from the basic principles requires companies to be flexible enough to understand that there is a gap between the existing state and the vision state. Therefore, it is preferable to consider concrete but flexible steps that are stepping stones in the right direction.

The fourth level of the framework is *actions*. Once the strategic planning process is complete, a company begins to take concrete actions.

The fifth level of the framework is *tools*. Here it is important for businesses to understand that regardless of the sustainability approach, various tools are available for sustainability assessments and monitoring programs. For example, tools include but are not limited to materiality assessments, life cycle assessments, and social life cycle assessments, and other assessments that will be described in more detail in the following section.[65]

## Sustainable Business Assessments

Why is sustainability assessment important for a business? Assessment results provide important information that serves the needs of different stakeholders. For example, information collected during assessment is important for senior management of the company, helping them ensure they are capturing opportunities and avoiding sustainability risks. Sustainability assessments also help to engage employees who tend to be more productive when they learn that their company is committed to a good cause. Research shows that in sustainability-oriented corporations, employees are more loyal and engaged. Sustainability assessment is also critical for building and mainlining trustworthy relationships with suppliers. Suppliers who are committed to sustainability earn more points on buyers' supplier rankings. Investors and insurance companies also prefer low-risk partners. Governments also ask companies to report their sustainability performance. Customers increasingly opt for sustainable products and services. NGOs support proactive companies that are devoted to environmental and social issues. Raters and rankers increasingly assess sustainability matrixes when ranking businesses across industry sectors.

Because sustainability assessment is critical for business success, various assessment methods have been developed. The first task is to determine which sustainable factors to consider. In recent years, as explained in previous chapters, we have often considered so-called ESG issues within three areas: the environmental, social, and governance areas. How a company addresses those issues will be reflected in their stance and strategy on climate change mitigation or their approach to preventing child or forced labor. There are a number of **key performance indicators (KPIs)** that should be considered.[66] For example, *environmental* KPIs should be implemented in every production step, from sourcing and manufacturing to retailing and waste management. In this regard a business can be evaluated on aspects including water consumption, energy consumption, waste management, greenhouse gas emissions, pollution prevention, biodiversity, material circularity, and environmental compliance. For example, a textile business can be evaluated on the basis of how it addresses environmental issues by using circular materials, improving processing and dyeing practices, and preventing waste generation.

*Social* KPIs can be assessed though investigation of a company's internal or direct network (management and employees) as well as through its extended business network, including its supply chain, customers, and the wider community. Social KPIs are assessed through human rights policies and practices, including, for example, safety management procedures, labor standards, workplace treatment, and security. When the treatment of customers and the broader community are assessed, factors such as safety, privacy, responsibility, and empowerment come into play.

*Governance* KPIs are important to consider because they showcase a business's transparency and its relationships with investors, its board of directors, and various stakeholders (e.g., suppliers, NGOs, customers, etc.). Transparency in this area is critical to show who in the company is responsible for sustainability performance as well as how corruption and bribery are prevented in order to insure fairness.

Most often companies communicate their KPIs within their official websites, mission and vision statements, and annual reports ,including corporate social responsibility and sustainability reports. There are a number of assessment tools and techniques that companies use to ensure sustainable development; here I will review four assessment tools commonly used among fashion companies: materiality assessments, life cycle assessments, social life cycle assessments, and supplier assessments.

## Materiality Assessments

The common role of **materiality assessment** is risk identification. Materiality assessment represents a strategy used to identify the most material or "silent issues" that should be publicly reported and that can be improved in future business operations. "The process of identifying these issues involves reaching out to internal stakeholders (employees, suppliers, customers) and external stakeholders (communities, various NGOs, etc.) to ask for their input."[67] Here are some key lessons regarding the conducting of materiality assessments.

The initial step in conducting a materiality assessment is to achieve a "clear understanding of the information a company or business owner is looking for." The next step is understanding that materiality assessments always have a dual goal: to inform both sustainability reporting (a largely backward-looking task) and to inform future business strategies (a largely forward-looking task).[68] It is worth mentioning that sometimes the topics prioritized by the employees and other stakeholders may differ. For example, organizations aligned with the Global Reporting Initiative want to prioritize disclosure of the most critical issues (i.e., ones that have the biggest impacts). Therefore, employees, NGOs, and investors can help by answering materiality assessment questions.

The ultimate outcome of the materiality assessment is the visual map of the findings or materiality matrix. According to *GreenBiz*, the three most common strategies for materiality matrix construction are 1) the GRI old school approach, 2) the new GRI approach, and 3) the strategy matrix. The GRI old school approach is focused on material topics that have a direct or indirect impact on the business. The new GRI approach was created to simplify the old approach which consisted of three plots. In this approach two plots reflect stakeholder interests versus the internal interests of the company, and materials issues are ranked on the scale from the most significant to the least significant. The third solution for materiality matrix creation is the strategy matrix, "which does not visualize the materiality issues requested by the GRI but instead is focused on the impacts that the business has, particularly the ones that business may control." The strategy matrix can be shown on one plot, for example, one in which Y displays issues that company can impact (low ability to impact vs. high ability to impact) and X displays the impact the issue has on the business (low business impact to high business impact).[70]

## Life Cycle Assessment (LCA)

A **life-cycle assessment (LCA)** is a methodology used to measure the environmental impact of garment production starting from raw material extraction through fiber processing, manufacture, distribution, use, disposal, and recycling. The LCA experts suggest that the total environmental impact of any product should be considered during the planning and preproduction processes. Actually, it is suggested that the product planning and product design phases should account for negative impacts of the production, usage, and disposal as well. For example, it is much more efficient to prevent negative impacts in the first phase (at the product design stage) than to adapt solutions after the product is already manufactured, when it is possible to apply solely end-of-pipe solutions (e.g., last possible strategies to minimize negative impacts). For this reason, LCAs should be conducted at the design stage so that the negative impact of each garment production can be evaluated accordingly. Alice Payne in the article "The Life-Cycle of the Fashion Garment" explains that the life of any fashion garment begins at the fiber level, which is known also as a "cradle" level, moving through to textile production, the garment design process, manufacture, distribution, retail, the use phase and eventual disposal—known as the "grave" level. Further, Paine notes that, as suggested with cradle-to-cradle design, manufacturing waste should be eliminated as a concept, and the production loop should be closed.[71]

In such a way, the traditional cradle-to-grave system should be replaced with cradle-to-cradle solutions where sources are used and reused.[72] There are at least eight steps that should be assessed during LCAs; the key features of the process will be briefly reviewed here:

1. *The first step in the LCA is to carefully select the optimal fiber.* When planning the creation of a sustainable garment, designers must evaluate problematic aspects of the fiber(s) they intended to use. For example, "Polyester is made from a petro-chemical, a non-renewable source, but its processing uses less water than is required to grow organic cotton. Bamboo is a renewable resource, but the processing of bamboo into fiber requires a lot of energy."[73] While new natural fibers such as hemp, lotus fiber, banana, or pineapple fibers are becoming more popular nowadays, it is important to carefully assess their advantages and disadvantages and the end-of-life opportunities involved.

2. *The second step in the LCA focuses on textile production, including various processes such as spinning, weaving, dyeing, and finishing.*[74]

Innovation in this phase is particularly important due to the extensive negative impacts that are inherent to all material processing operations. Today we are witnessing that many of the major fashion brands are testing or using natural dyeing and waterless dyeing techniques. (Kate Fletcher did a great job explaining these new methods in the book titled *Sustainable Fashion And Textiles: Design Journeys.*[75])

3. *The third step in the LCA is design.* The design phase of the garment life cycle is critical for designing for sustainability.[76] As previously said, at the product design stage, impact of the garment production should be carefully assessed. If the designer is interested in applying sustainable approaches, this phase represents the right moment to plan innovation. For example, a designer might plan how the garment might be repurposed or recycled after its usage (see how some brands promote product repurposing and using it as a tote or apron).

4. *The fourth step in the LCA is production or manufacturing.*[77] In this phase the assessor of the manufacturing process should consider where and how the garment will be produced (e.g., locally or abroad). Sometimes producing garments locally means being able to inspect more frequently how the garments are produced and how the workers are treated. This might not be the case with long, global, and fragmented supply chain in which retailers often do not know by whom where, and under what conditions their garments are produced.

5. *The fifth step in the LCA is product distribution.* Experts argue that transportation costs represent a serious challenge for the fashion industry.[78] For American brands, for example, domestic manufacture is rarely a viable option due to the lack of manufacturing infrastructure. Hence, most of the textiles, products, and product parts are manufactured all over the globe, and costs of transportation, imports, and packaging can be very high.

6. *The sixth step in the life-cycle assessment is retail.* In planning an optimal strategy for sustainability, retailers might use different ways to engage consumers whether through product co-design or through

innovative service systems.[79] For example, some brands offer services that include in-store garment alteration and repair, as well as garment upcycling and creative use.[80] Here it is also worth mentioning numerous physical and online resale options for new, upcycled, and unsold products (e.g., Ebay, Etsy).

7. *The seventh step in the LCA is the usage phase of the product.* This phase is often overlooked, although it is very important to plan in the design stage how the garment will be repaired, laundered, and maintained.[81]

8. *The last but not least important step in the LCA is planning the end-of-life, considering disposal, reuse and cradle-to-cradle alternatives.*[82] In the United States alone, the volume of textiles that end up in landfills has doubled in the last twenty years. The EPA estimates that around 17 million tons of textiles were discarded in 2018. This figure accounts for 5.8% of total solid waste generated in the same year. The reality, however, is that most (if not all) of that textile can be recycled.[83] Therefore, it is critical to think about garment end-of-life before garments are discarded. Similarly, it is critical to rethink the collection mechanisms for unwanted clothes. For example, fashion brands nowadays offer take-back programs where customers are offered incentives to bring their unwanted clothing back to a store so that brands can redistribute it. Eileen Fisher, for instance launched project Renew with a goal to offer second life to unwanted garments that are resold.[84]

## Case study 6: Levi's and the first life cycle assessment in the fashion industry

Levi's is the first fashion brand that conducted an LCA, as they wanted to better understand the life cycle impact of a core set of their products. In this case study, we will examine how the Levi's team conducted an LCA for one pair of Levi's 501 jeans. In the report published in 2015, the Levi's team announced they had conducted the LCA in order to measure and possibly reduce negative environmental impacts of their production.

First, they determined the functional unit to be a pair of Levi's 501 jeans, which among all their products are produced in the highest volume. Functional attributes included "5 fabrics and 8 finishes (low to high complexity)"[85] for a pair of jeans produced in the 2012 production year. As described in the report, they included the following stages:

- "cotton production
- fabric production
- garment manufacturing
- packaging
- sundries
- transportation & distribution
- consumer care
- end of life."[86]

In the cotton production stage, they focused only on the markets where they source their cotton, including the United States, India, Pakistan, Brazil, China, Australia, the United Kingdom, and France. They also included their largest consumer markets: the United States, the United Kingdom, France, and China. Data for the report were sourced from internal sources, eleven supplier factories, and six fabric mills. Several impact categories were analyzed:

- "Climate change (the global warming potential of greenhouse gases released into the environment – unit/ kg $CO_2$-e)
- Water intake (fresh water taken from the environment) – unit/liter
- Water consumption (net freshwater taken from the environment minus water returned to the same watershed at the same quality) – unit/liter
- Eutrophication (oxygen depletion as a result of nitrogen and phosphorous deposit into freshwater or marine environments) – g $PO_4$-e
- Land Occupation – Total land occupied to support the product system assessed – unit/ $m^2$ -yr.
- Abiotic Depletion – A measure of the depletion of non-renewable resources that includes fossil energy, metals, and minerals, unit/mg Sb-e.[87]

**Table 9** Impact phases and impacts of the highest significance*

| Impact Phases | Sourcing or Production stage | Impact Significance |
|---|---|---|
| raw material production | natural fibers<br>synthetic fibers<br>recycled fibers<br>metals<br>livestock derived materials | High impacts. "Water Consumption: Fiber production, predominantly that of cotton, contributes greatly to water consumption." |
| Intermediate production | extrusions<br>fabric assembly<br>pre-spinning & spinning<br>weaving & dyeing<br>finishing & sundries<br>production (molding and forming) | High impacts. "Notable contributions related to climate change impact and non-renewable energy consumption." |
| Apparel production | garment assembly<br>cutting, sewing<br>gluing, welding, seam taping<br>garment finishing<br>garment dyeing | Lower impacts compared to previous stages. |
| Chemical production and energy carriers | fossil and renewable fuel extraction and usage, monomers, process chemicals, dyes, detergents, finishing chemicals,<br>electricity, steam, hot water,<br>fertilizers, pesticides and other agricultural chemicals, paper, and plastic production for packaging | High impacts. |
| Transport phase | transport and distribution of<br>waste in all phases | Low impacts. |

*(Continues)*

**Table 9**  Continued

| Impact Phases | Sourcing or Production stage | Impact Significance |
|---|---|---|
| Use phase | wearing washing drying ironing repairing | High impacts. Significant differences between consumers in different regions: "in China, consumers wash jeans in cold water and air dry; America shows the highest water intake and use of non-renewable energy due to the most frequent washes." |
| End of life phase | landfill incineration recycling & biodegradation | Low impacts. |

*Table information and quotes from "Full LCA Result," *Levi's*, 2015, accessed on July 30, 2023, https://www.levistrauss.com/wp-content/uploads/2015/03/Full-LCA-Results-Deck-FINAL.pdf.

**Table 10**  The entire life cycle of one pair of Levi's 501 jeans*

| Effect | Equivalence |
|---|---|
| Climate Change: 33.4 kg CO2-e | 69 miles driven by the average US car 246 hours of TV on a plasma big-screen |
| Water Consumed: 3,781 liters... | 3 days' worth of one US household's total water needs |
| Eutrophication: 48.9 g PO4-e | The total amount of phosphorous found in 1,700 tomatoes |
| Land Occupation: 12 m2 /year | Seven people standing with arms outstretched, fingertips touching, would form one side of a square this size |

*Table text is quoted from "Full LCA Result," *Levi's*, 2015, accessed on July 30, 2023, https://www.levistrauss.com/wp-content/uploads/2015/03/Full-LCA-Results-Deck-FINAL.pdf.

Recommendations for impact reduction:

For Levi's

- Influence global supply chain partners to procure Better Cotton Initiative cotton and adopt water recycling and reuse standards
- Water recycling programs
- Improved chemical management programs
- Responsible sourcing initiatives
- Wellthread: A holistic approach to sustainable product design & manufacturing
- Waterless: Jeans made using less water
- Wasteless: Jeans made using recycled plastic bottles

For consumers

- Washing every ten times a product is worn instead of every two times reduces energy use, climate change impact, and water intake by up to 80 percent
- Line dry your jeans
- Donate old jeans
- Repair old jeans

Interesting findings:

- Life cycle stages that had the lowest contribution to environmental impacts include fabric transport, product transport, packaging, production wastes, distribution, retail, and end of life waste.
- Fiber production, predominantly that of cotton, contributes greatly to water consumption and to the eutrophication impact.

**Student Activity:** Students are asked to explore the official website of the Levi's company (or any other denim brand) and their most recent LCA reports. After gathering sufficient information about the most recent LCA findings, students are asked to discuss, compare, and interrogate their findings. Students may track LCA findings and improvements across the years, as well as compare the LCA findings data for Levi's versus competing denim brands.

# Social Life Cycle Assessment (S-LCA)

A **social life cycle assessment (S-LCA)** is a methodology used to assess the social aspects of products and their potential positive and negative impacts along their life cycle, encompassing the extraction and processing of raw materials, manufacturing, distribution, use, reuse, maintenance, recycling, and final disposal. Although the S-LCA can be applied on its own, it complements the (environmental) LCA by looking at social and economic aspects. Unlike LCA assessment methodology, which is becoming more widespread across industry sectors, S-LCA methodology is still in the early stages of its development. S-LCA application is made difficult due to the complexity of measuring social factors. For example, GHG emissions are easily quantifiable and can be reported using numerical data. The same applies to water and energy usage. However, there is difficulty in translating comprehensive qualitative data into quantitative indicators, and for this reason the S-LCA is still being developed in practice.[88]

Further development of S-LCA methodologies, however, is critical for assessing total product impacts because the S-LCA's factors are certainly as important as environmental ones. Thus, it is important to think about how we can measure the social impacts of our garments. Furthermore, how do we collect and interpret the results from every phase of the life cycle together? To provide answers to these questions, I will briefly review the S-LCA process as explained by the United Nations Environment Programme (UNEP). First, it is important to note that the UNEP provides the S-LCA framework, which is aligned with the ISO 14040 and 14044 standards for LCAs. The S-LCA categorizes social impacts into stakeholder categories (e.g., workers, consumers, supply chain, community, etc.) and impact categories.[89] Here, social impacts can be understood as social interactions that are woven in the processes of the production or consumption.

Broadly speaking, impacts can be divided into three categories:

- *corporate behaviors*: positive or negative corporate decisions (such as avoidance or use of child labor)
- *socioeconomic processes*: social impacts as a result of the downstream effects of the macro socioeconomic decisions that often direct micro level corporate politics

- *capitals*: capitals include human, social, and cultural forms, which are often related to the original context.[90]

Next, stakeholders are divided into the appropriate categories, and for each category social factors of importance (defined in accordance with international agreements and conventions) are added in the form of subcategories (see table 11).

**Table 11** Stakeholder categories and social factors of importance*

| Stakeholder category | Subcategory |
|---|---|
| supply chain worker | • freedom of association<br>• collective bargaining<br>• child/forced/bonded labor<br>• fair wages<br>• equal opportunities<br>• antidiscrimination<br>• health and safety<br>• social benefits |
| local community | • access to material resources<br>• access to immaterial resources<br>• delocalization and migration<br>• cultural heritage<br>• safety & health<br>• living conditions<br>• respect for indigenous rights<br>• community engagement<br>• local employment<br>• secure living conditions |
| public | • public commitments to sustainability issues<br>• contribution to economic development<br>• prevention of conflicts<br>• technology development<br>• anti-corruption |
| consumer | • health & safety<br>• consumer engagement<br>• consumer education<br>• consumer privacy<br>• transparency<br>• end of life responsibility |

*(Continues)*

**Table 11** Continued

| Stakeholder category | Subcategory |
|---|---|
| suppliers | • fair competition<br>• promoting social responsibility<br>• supplier relationships<br>• respect for intellectual property rights |

*Table is adapted from Evan Stuart Andrews, *Guidelines for Social Life Cycle Assessment of Products: Social and Socio-Economic LCA Guidelines Complementing Environmental LCA and Life Cycle Costing, Contributing to the Full Assessment of Goods and Services within the Context of Sustainable Development* (Paris: UNEP/Earthprint, 2009).

Once stakeholders and subcategories are identified, it is necessary to set the assessment boundaries and determine what will be included in the S-LCA. The first goal is to specify the function of the functional unit in an S-LCA. For example, this step includes describing the product by its properties and utilities (aesthetics, quality, technicality, ingredients, costs, market segment, alternatives, etc.) and determining the flow for each of the product systems (e.g., identifying product inputs that are required to deliver the quality or maintain the function of the product and identifying production stages—working hours, for instance). The next step is deciding how data will be collected—for example, whether site-specific data are needed for a specific process occurring in a specific location or facility. Often, site-specific data must be collected in person from a specific location and from a specific group of stakeholders. In other cases specific data might be collected online as well. For example, often social factors are assessed through surveys and written information which are collected directly from the employees. Types of data easily collected in such a way include payrolls, working hours, excess hours, and health and safety measures. Such data can be additionally supplemented by data that a certain company shares publicly via websites and corporate reports. Similarly, if data on alternative products are needed, they can be collected in a similar manner by an exploration of close competitors across national and international markets. Finally, after data have been collected from all determined sites, they must be validated and aggregated. The ultimate goal of the S-LCA is to improve social conditions throughout the product life cycle. For this reason, stakeholder participation is expected and highly encouraged.[91]

*Similarities between the LCA and the S-LCA.* The scope of the S-LCA is similar to that of the LCA: the entire life cycle of the product. In both the S-LCA and the LCA, direct impact is assessed, but indirect impacts might also be considered.

*Differences between the LCA and the S-LCA.* The biggest difference between the LCA and the S-LCA is in their primary foci. While the former evaluates environmental impacts, the latter assesses social and socioeconomic impacts.[92] Similarly, while the LCA focuses primarily on collecting quantifiable information related to the product and its processes, the S-LCA collects essentially qualitative information on organizational aspects and business practices along the supply chain.

*Recommendations for best practices in conducting the S-LCA.* It goes without saying that it is recommended that S-LCA assessments be conducted objectively and ethically. Ideally, the S-LCA should be peer reviewed to prevent its misuse. On a more technical side, one of the main issues with the S-LCA is ensuring consistency among the standards assessed. However, we must be aware of the fact that even when the standards are similar, differences among cases will naturally occur. Nevertheless, although numerical data are quite useful— for example, in assessing the wages in the supply chain—additional data are always needed to comprehend the meaning gleaned from the numerical data (for example, assessing whether actual and reported wages are in compliance with minimum wage laws or how well they are aligned with livable wage recommendations). The current limitations of the S-LCA (due to data collection challenges, expenses, and unstandardized assessment criteria) are many.[93] At minimum we can conclude that an S-LCA is challenging to conduct because qualitative data are often subjective and must be handled by capable experts. However, when an S-LCA complements an LCA, it is clear that those assessments provide a more comprehensive picture of the product's life cycle impacts.

## Supplier Scorecard Assessments

Traditional supplier scorecards are used to enable retail businesses to track, quantify, and rank supplier performance. The main benefit of scorecards is that they can break down supplier performance into quantifiable categories. For example, a supplier scorecard tool may include metrics to grade product quality, delivery, cost, and service. Beside the traditional scorecards, which are most used, retailers also increasingly use balanced scorecards. The balanced scorecards were developed in the 1990s by Kaplan and Norton in order "to measure business performance in four key areas: finances, internal processes, customers, and learning."[94] Nowadays, sustainability metrics were added to traditional balanced scorecards so that retailers can track, quantify, and rank suppliers not only according to their traditional metrics (e.g., cost, delivery, quality) but also accounting for their sustainability performance in the measurements. This is how sustainability balanced scorecards (SBSCs) were created. A wide range of factors can be added to the supplier sustainability scorecards assessments (e.g., packaging, transportation, recycling). Retailers can create their SBSCs in a number of ways, but only the most general one will be briefly introduced here.

First, to conduct supplier assessments, the retailer must identify their supply chain members, which includes identifying each supplier entity, their location, contacts, the services provided, and expertise. For example, Nike launched a manufacturing index, publicly disclosing supply chain members on the official website of the company.[95]

Second, retailers must consider which factors to include in the assessments and how those factors can be grouped into broader categories (e.g., quality, cost, and delivery). Going back to the Nike company example, more recently the company has developed various tools to assist them in making sustainable sourcing decisions. For instance, Nike developed the country risk index, with the intention to measure the risk of sourcing from a supplier country.[96]

Third, once retailers know which factors they want to track, the next step is deciding how to grade and rank their suppliers. Sometimes, retailers start with simple evaluations. In such cases they assess whether, for example, a supplier provides products of adequate quality, or whether they deliver orders on time. However, sometimes the factors considered are more nuanced, and the level of satisfaction or dissatisfaction with the supplier performance is graded on a scale (from the least to the most satisfactory). For purposes of efficient ranking, it is also important to define the meaning of each rank. It goes without saying that companies invested in sustainability prioritize sourcing from the highest-ranked suppliers.

For example, the brand H&M ranked their preferred suppliers in two groups: platinum and gold, and these suppliers produce around 60 percent of H&M products. H&M intends to establish a long-term partnership with their platinum and gold suppliers, sometimes planning production capacities up to five years ahead. Additionally, H&M provides various trainings and workshops for suppliers that are their strategic partners. Silver suppliers are second best rated, and with those suppliers H&M plans production capacities up to one year ahead.[97] Suppliers who are ranked as "others" are the newest additions to the supplier teams meaning that the company worked with them less than a year. According to the H&M reports these suppliers are evaluated after an initial testing periods.[98]

## Case study 7: A comparison of sustainability supplier scorecards among apparel retailers

For an evaluation and comparison of the sustainability supplier scorecard assessment tools currently in use among five international apparel retailers, a sample of five international apparel retailers was created: Walmart, Eileen Fisher, Nike, GAP Inc, and H&M. For these brands, eight sustainability supplier scorecard assessment tools were identified. The following score-cards were included in this case study: Walmart—the THESIS Index; Eileen Fisher—the Eco Ethical Scorecard and the Social Product Scorecard; Nike—the Supplier Performance Scorecard; Gap—the Preferred Fibers Scorecard and Toolkit, the Facility and Factory Performance Rating, and the Supplier Scorecard; and H&M—the Sustainable Impact Partnership Program.[99] The names of the companies and scorecards are also displayed in table 12.

**Table 12** Companies and names of sustainability supplier scorecard assessment tools

| Company name | Name of sustainability supplier scorecard assessment tool(s) |
|---|---|
| Walmart (apparel) | THESIS Index |
| Eileen Fisher | Eco-ethical Scorecard |
| | Social Product Scorecard |

(Continues)

**Table 12** Continued

| Company name | Name of sustainability supplier scorecard assessment tool(s) |
|---|---|
| Nike | Supplier Performance Scorecard |
| GAP Inc | Preferred Fibers Scorecard and Toolkit |
| | Facility/Factory Performance Rating |
| | Supplier Scorecard |
| H&M | Sustainable Impact Partnership Program |

Data about the scorecards were retrieved from official websites and sustainability and corporate responsibility reports from the selected companies. This case study had three objectives that guided research tasks:

1. To evaluate and compare sustainability supplier scorecard assessment tools by identifying the main scope of the sustainability supplier scorecard assessment tools.
2. To facilitate an understanding of the way in which supplier performance is assessed by sustainability supplier scorecard assessment tools.
3. To identify and compare commonalities in sustainability supplier scorecard assessment tools.[100]

First, the results of this case study confirmed that the scope of the sustainability supplier scorecard assessment tools varied depending on the retailer and on the types of scorecard assessment tools that were used.

- With Walmart's THESIS index, the company states the goal is to increase sustainable product offerings while maintaining low prices and minimizing the social and environmental impact through collaboration with suppliers. The scope of Walmart's THESIS assessment is primarily economic.
- Eileen Fisher's Eco-ethical Scorecard, as the company states, was established to help improve production and sourcing practices. Similarly, the Social Product Score Tool aims to improve workers' quality of life. The scope of Eileen Fisher's scorecards is social.

- The goal of Nike's Supplier Performance Scorecard is to improve its overall sustainability through supplier collaboration and to identify high-scoring suppliers in order to shift more of the company's business to them. The scope of the scorecards is primarily economic.
- Each of GAP Inc.'s three sustainability supplier scorecard assessment tools has different goals. The Preferred Fiber Scorecard and Toolkit's aim is to assist the company's sourcing team in selecting and sourcing sustainable fiber selection. The scope of the Preferred Fiber Scorecard and Toolkit is both social and environmental. The Facility/Factory Performance Rating aims to improve working conditions by supporting suppliers. The goal of the Supplier Scorecard is to improve sourcing practices related to social issues. The goals of both the Facility/Factory Performance Rating tool and the Supplier Scorecard include support for social sustainability.
- H&M's Sustainable Impact Partnership Program's Scorecards aim to improve the company's social and environmental performance through collaboration with suppliers. The scope of the goal set by H&M is both social and environmental.[101]

Second, supplier performance measurements vary depending on the scorecard assessment tool. For instance, Walmart's THESIS index uses the Sustainability Consortium to set standards for environmental and social impacts. KPIs are used to score suppliers in three categories: category, facility, and supply chain. The index includes a survey with sustainability performance questions specific to the supplier's product category in order to assist in supplier performance evaluation and measurements. The survey itself was not disclosed online.

Eileen Fisher's Eco-ethical Scorecard uses the Social and Environmental Implementation Guide to set standards for suppliers and to provide a code of conduct. Scoring methodologies are shared with the company's suppliers but are not disclosed on its website or in public reports. Eileen Fisher's Social Product Score Tool provides standards for suppliers based on consultation with internal and external stakeholders such as Future Fit and UN foundations as well as with other retailers with similar initiatives such as Patagonia and Levi's. The scoring tool used to score suppliers is SPS 1.5; it is based on social responsibility criteria determined by the Eileen Fisher company.[102]

Nike's Supplier Performance Scorecard standards are based on the results from Nike's social compliance auditing tool, known as the NCAT. Standards are also set through the Culture of Safety program. Suppliers are assessed based on the areas of quality, delivery, cost, sustainability, growth and potential in leadership, operations, innovation, and product creation. A color-coding system is used to categorize suppliers, where silver or gold ratings are given to suppliers who participate in capacity-building programs and sustainability initiatives, a bronze rating is given to suppliers in baseline compliance with Nike's standards, and yellow or red is given to suppliers below baseline compliance.[103]

GAP Inc.'s Preferred Fibers Scorecard and Toolkit standards for suppliers are based on information from the Sustainable Apparel Coalition (SAC) Material Sustainability Index and were developed in partnership with Textile Exchange. The Higg Materials Sustainability Index, developed by SAC, is used to assess the environmental impacts of materials. Each fiber is scored in the following areas: water usage, chemicals used, energy consumption and emissions, land use and biodiversity, social conditions, animal welfare, potential for circularity, improved conditions for women, quality, cost, availability, and traceability.

GAP Inc.'s Facility/Factory Performance Rating is based on analysis from their internal sustainability, global supply chain, and data insights teams. Action plans are developed by the team to build awareness with suppliers, collaborate with all stakeholders, and formalize systems to address issues. GAP Inc.'s Supplier Scorecard is used by sourcing departments to analyze performance, but further information on performance measurement was not disclosed.

H&M's Sustainable Impact Partnership Program (SIPP) is used to evaluate suppliers' compliance with the sustainability commitment as well as to measure suppliers' performance. The factors of SIPP include minimum requirement verification, self-assessment, validation, and capacity building. The SAC's Higg Facility Module is used as the standard for assessment. Suppliers' scores are based on energy use, water use, wastewater, waste management, air emissions, and chemicals.

Third, overall, not many commonalities in sustainability supplier score-cards could be identified among the retailers that were studied. Improving sourcing practices is included as a goal for Eileen Fisher's Eco-ethical Scorecard, Nike's Supplier Performance Scorecard, and GAP Inc.'s Supplier Scorecard. Four of the eight tools we investigated require suppliers to engage in some sort of self-reporting, such as filling out surveys. Three of the eight tools involve supplier audits or onsite checks. Common areas of measurement that were seen across multiple tools include quality, cost, (not specified) social issues, water, emissions, energy, labor standards, chemicals, and sustainability (not specified). Interestingly, no areas of measurement were found to be used among three (or more) scorecard assessment tools, suggesting that those tools have overall more particularities than commonalities.[104]

**Student Activity:** After reading this case study, students are asked to explore the most recent sustainability scorecard assessment tools used by a retailer of their choice. Based on the comparison between various assessment tools and their goals, students are expected to indicate a potential area or areas of improvement for each tool. Students may be invited to discuss the advantages and disadvantages of each tool and to describe and justify improvement priorities.

# Sustainable Business Certifications

In recent years more companies across industry sectors have become certified for their sustainability practices. The reasons for becoming certified are obvious. Business leaders who believe that social and environmental responsibility are as critically important as profit prefer to formalize their sustainability commitments through acquiring third party sustainability certification. Such certifications bring various advantages, but they are significant for two primary reasons. First, official certification demonstrates the business's genuine commitment to sustainability causes. Legitimate third-party business certification, therefore, brings competitive advantage, enhances credibility, and helps businesses stand out from the greenwashing in which many businesses unfortunately partake today. Second, involvement in formal sustainability programs and evaluation mechanisms helps to strengthen corporate strategies and maintain consistency in sustainability priorities, creating corporate culture that values, engages, and rewards all business stakeholders, including employees, suppliers, investors, consumers, community members, and the general public.

The most common certifications for sustainable businesses practices in the fashion industry include the **B-Corp certification**, and I will more closely examine this certification here. "B Corp Certification is an international certification that verifies that companies meet the highest standards of overall social and environmental performance, public transparency, and legal accountability."[105] As reported on the B Corp official website, companies that apply for B-Corp certificate are evaluated by B Lab corporation, which assesses corporate performance across five areas: governance, workers, community, environment, and customers.[106] The process of evaluation is long and rigorous, and both business model and daily activities are considered when estimating the positive impact of the company. It is suggested that all companies interested in applying first complete initial assessment to see if they qualify. Also, this assessment can help them understand which practices they need to improve to qualify for this application in the future.[107] Interestingly, it is hard for larger companies to meet B-Corp certifications, and consequently not many major apparel and footwear retailers are B-Corp certified. Among the well-known brands that are internationally recognized as B-Corp certified are Patagonia, Athleta, Allbirds, Tom's, and Eileen Fisher.[108] Also, there are some smaller circular national fashion businesses that have B-Corp certification. For more information on businesses that are B-Corp certified in each geographic region, you can browse the B-Corp directory found on the official website of the B Corporation.

B Corporations are without doubt seen as leaders in today's sustainable oriented economy. Their importance lies in the fact that B-Corp businesses are purpose-driven. Thus, they are important as they create benefits for all stakeholders and not exclusively for business shareholders. Also, B-Corp businesses are recognized as a source of sustainability leaders as they use business as a force for improvement.[109] This is clearly seen in their declaration of independence, which states

- that B-Corp certified corporations are businesses that must be "the change we seek in the world.
- that all business ought to be conducted as if people and place mattered.
- that, through their products, practices, and profits, businesses should aspire to do no harm and benefit all.

- that B-Corp businesses are expected to understand that they are dependent upon each other and thus responsible for each other and future generations."[110]

Because B Corp believes that business can manage only what it measures, B-Corp assessments are based on comprehensive standards that are assessed using various tools to benchmark business performance. For this reason it is important to understand that B-Corp certification does not merely evaluate a product or service; rather, the certification has a holistic nature, and B Corp evaluates the overall impact of the company that stands behind it. Impact assessments in the B-Corp evaluation process are called B Impact Assessments, and they consist of rigorous assessment of a business's impacts on its employees, customers, supply chain workers, the community, and the broader environment. A B impact report for every B-Corp certified corporation is published on the B Corporation website and is open to the public.[111] B Impact reports are significant resources that drive the sustainability performance of companies, providing them with feedback regarding how they stack up against other companies who are rated in the same category. They also show which practices a business has already improved and which practices it could improve in the future. Let us examine here (table 13) the B Impact assessments for the B-Corp certified brands Patagonia, Athleta, Allbirds, Tom's, and Eileen Fisher.

**Table 13** The B Impact assessments for the B-Corp certified brands Patagonia, Athleta, Allbirds, Tom's, and Eileen Fisher*

| Brand | Category | Impact Score (0-200) | Certification year | Business Core values |
|---|---|---|---|---|
| Patagonia | Apparel | 151.4 | 2011 | Functional, repairable, durable minimalistic products are made in a circular manner. |
| Athleta | Apparel | 84.3 | 2018 | 40% of Athleta apparel is made from recycled and sustainable materials, while the ultimate goal is to reach full recyclability. |

(*Continues*)

**Table 13** Continued

| Brand | Category | Impact Score (0-200) | Certifica-tion year | Business Core values |
|-------|----------|---------------------|---------------------|---------------------|
| Allbirds | Footwear | 89.4 | 2016 | Sustainable footwear is made from natural materials. |
| Tom's | Footwear | 121.5 | 2018 | The company is committed to investing 1/3 of its profits into grassroots goods and the unique needs of the communities. |
| Eileen Fisher | Apparel | 89.1 | 2015 | Circular design, responsible fibers, Bluesign certified dying, and resale options are available. Since 2009 over 1.5 million pieces of clothing have been purchased back from consumers to be resold or repurposed in the Renew program. |

\* This data is reported based on the author's exploration of B impact scores for each brand found in the B-Corp brand directory, accessed on July 1, 2023, https://www.bcorporation.net/en-us/find-a-b-corp/.

Despite the similarity of their names, benefit corporations and B Corporations are not the same. While their goals both result in conducting business to create a more equitable and sustainable global market, benefit corporations are not certified, although they judge qualitatively their performance metrics. Rather than focusing entirely on the shortsighted acquisition of growth and profit, benefit corporations integrate their social, environmental, or economic initiatives into the self-analysis of their performance. Benefit corporations, at their core, signify a difference in leadership and guiding principles compared to traditional companies. For example, benefit corporations are driven by their business purpose and not necessarily by profit generation. In contrast, B Corps are certified by B Lab, a nonprofit third party. This certification is much more stringent compared to the title of benefit corporation, carrying significant weight in the perception of that brand. You can read more about benefit corporations and B-Corp corporations in *An Entrepreneur's Guide to Certified B Corporations and Benefit Corporations,* published by Patagonia and The Yale Center for Business and the Environment.[112]

## Chapter Summary

In the third chapter we explored the core sustainability principles and assessments used to appraise fashion businesses including LCAs, S-LCAs, materiality assessment, and supplier assessment. We analyzed three case studies to evaluate the various strategies employed in the development, legitimization, and promotion of sustainable businesses. The first case study discusses corporate progress on the Ceres Roadmap for Sustainability among footwear and apparel retailers. The second case study reviews Levi's initiatives and approach to creating the first LCA in the fashion industry. The third case study focuses on supply chain assessments and compares sustainability supplier scorecards among five apparel retailers: Walmart, Gap, Eileen Fisher, Nike, and H&M. This chapter also reviews the process to certify businesses for their sustainability efforts, providing examples of the most common certifications in the sector.

## References

1. G. Nimbalker, J. Mawson, H. A. Lee, and C. Cremen, "The Ethical Fashion Report: The Truth Behind the Barcode 2017," *Baptist World Aid Australia,* accessed on September 20, 2022, https://apo.org.au/sites/default/files/resource-files/2017-04/apo-nid75801.pdf.
2. "The Apparel Industry," *Duke,* accessed on September 20, 2022, https://sites.duke.edu/sociol342d_01d_s2017_team-7/2-global-value-chain/.
3. Iva Jestratijevic, Nancy A. Rudd, and James Uanhoro, "Transparency of Sustainability Disclosures among Luxury and Mass-Market Fashion Brands," *Journal of Global Fashion Marketing* 11, no. 2 (2020): 99–116.
4. Jung Ha-Brookshire, "Global Sourcing: New Research and Education Agendas for Apparel Design and Merchandising," *Fashion and Textiles* 2, no. 1 (2015): 1–12.

5.  Iva Jestratijevic and Nancy Rudd, "Sustainable Exclusivity for the Global Marketplace," in ITAA Monograph #12, *The Future of Luxury*, ed. Jana M. Hawley, Nancy Casill, and Kristie McGowan, 2018, https://cdn.ymaws.com/itaaonline.org/resource/resmgr/publications/Monograph12-2018_Future_of_L.pdf.

6.  Zeenath Reza Khan and Gwendolyn Rodrigues, "Human before the Garment: Bangladesh Tragedy Revisited. Ethical Manufacturing or Lack Thereof in Garment Manufacturing Industry," *World* 5, no. 1 (2015): 22–35.

7.  Iva Jestratijevic and Nancy Rudd, Making fashion Transparent: What Consumers Know about the Brands They Admire," in *Bloomsbury Fashion Business Cases*, ed L. Divita and L. D. Burns (London: Bloomsbury), https://doi.org/10.5040/9781474208765.0007.

8.  Jestratijevic, Rudd, and Uanhoro, "Transparency of Sustainability Disclosures."

9.  Janet Hethorn and Connie Ulasewicz, *Sustainable Fashion: Why Now?: A Conversation about Issues, Practices, and Possibilities* (New York: Fairchild Books, 2008).

10. Khan and Rodrigues, "Human before the Garment."

11. "Bangladesh Accord an Urgent Call to Action to Protect Progress," *Fashion Revolution*, accessed on December 1, 2022, https://www.fashionrevolution.org/bangladesh-accord-an-urgent-call-to-action-to-protectprogress/.

12. Ibid.

13. R. Edward Freeman, Jeffrey S. Harrison, Andrew C. Wicks, Bidhan L. Parmar, and Simone De Colle, *Stakeholder Theory: The State of the Art* (Leiden: Cambridge University Press, 2010).

14. Jeffrey S. Harrison, Douglas A. Bosse, and Robert A. Phillips, "Managing for Stakeholders, Stakeholder Utility Functions, and Competitive Advantage," *Strategic Management Journal* 31, no. 1 (2010): 58–74.

15. Chris Laszlo and Nadya Zhexembayeva, "Embedded Sustainability: A Strategy for Market Leaders," *European Financial Review* 15 (2011): 37–49.

16. "Sphera Joins United Nations Global Compact," *Sphera*, accessed on January 31, 2022, https://sphera.com/press-release/sphera-joins-united-nations-global-compact/.

17. "Ten Principles UN Global Compact," *UN Global Compact*, accessed on August 10, 2023, https://www.unglobalcompact.org/what-is-gc/mission/principles.

18. Ibid

19. "Engage Locally," *United Nations Global Compact*, accessed on September 19, 2022, https://unglobalcompact.org/engage-locally.

20. Ibid.

21. "Principle 10," *United Nations Global Compact*, accessed on September 19, 2022, https://unglobalcompact.org/what-is-gc/mission/principles/principle-10.

22. "The Rio Declaration on Environment and Development," published in 1992, accessed on June 19, 2023, https://www.iau-hesd.net/sites/default/files/documents/rio_e.pdf.

23. "Carbon Taxes in Europe 2022," *Tax Foundation*, accessed on May 29, 2023, https://taxfoundation.org/carbon-taxes-in-europe-2022/.

24. *The UN's "Protect, Respect, and Remedy" Framework for Business and Human Rights*, UN, accessed on May 20, 2023, https://media.business-humanrights.org/media/documents/files/reports-and-materials/Ruggie-protect-respect-remedy-framework.pdf.

25. "UN Guiding Principles Reporting Framework," ungreporting.org, accessed on May 20, 2023, UNGuidingPrinciplesReportingFramework_withimplementationguidance_Feb2015.pdf.

26. "California Transparency in Supply Chain Act," OAG, accessed on December 10, 2022, https://oag.ca.gov/SB657.

27. Ibid.

28. "The Modern Slavery Act 2015," Legislation.gov.UK, accessed on June 19, 2023, https://www.legislation.gov.uk/ukpga/2015/30/contents/enacted.

29. "The Modern Slavery Act 2015," *Harvard Law School Forum on Corporate Governance*, accessed on July 19, 2023, https://corpgov.law.harvard.edu/2017/03/10/the-modern-slavery-act-2015-next-steps-for-businesses/.

30. "Fashion Revolution's Statement of the UK Modern Slavery Act and Accountability," *Fashion Revolution*, accessed on June 18, 2023, https://www.fashionrevolution.org/fashionrevolutions-statement-on-the-uk-modern-slavery-act-and-accountability/.

31. "Stitched with Slavery in the Seams," *Walk Free*, accessed on June 28, 2023, https://www.walkfree.org/global-slavery-index/findings/spotlights/stitched-with-slavery-in-the-seams/.

32. "Beyond Compliance in the Garment Industry," *Walk Free*, accessed on June 23, 2023, https://www.walkfree.org/reports/beyond-compliance-in-the-garment-industry/.

33. "Environmental and Social Management Framework," *Idcol*, accessed on June 19, 2023, https://idcol.org/download/Environment%20and%20Social%20Management%20Framework_Textile%20%28English%29.pdf.

34. R. Gittell, M. Magnusson, and M. Merenda, *The Sustainable Business Case Book* (n. p.: Saylor Foundation, 2012), accessed on June 28, 2023, https://archive.org/details/TheSustainableBusinessCaseBook/page/n11/mode/2up.

35. "Higg Index Tools," *Sustainable Apparel Coalition*, accessed June 28, 2023, https://apparelcoalition.org/the-higg-index/.

36. Gittell, Magnusson, and Merenda, *Sustainable Business Case Book*.

37. Ceres, *Turning Point Sector Analysis: Footwear and Apparel A deeper look at sector performance within Corporate Progress on the Ceres Roadmap for Sustainability*, 2018, https://www.ceres.org/resources/reports/turning-point-corporate-progress-ceres-roadmap-sustainability.

38. Ibid.

39. Ibid.

40. Ibid.

41. Ibid.

42. Ibid.

43. "Recognizing Fundamental Changes on the Nature of Capitalism Eco Daily," *Fortune*, accessed on June 29, 2023, https://fortune.com/2021/06/28/recognizing-fundamental-changes-in-the-nature-of-capitalism-ceo-daily/.

44. Ambrose Bierce, "The Devil's Dictionary," *Xroads Virginia*, accessed on June 30, 2023, https://xroads.virginia.edu/~Hyper/Bierce/bierce.html.

45. M. Friedman, "The Social Responsibility of Business Is to Increase Its Profits," *New York Times Magazine*, 1970, 122–26.

46. Archie B. Carroll, "A Three-Dimensional Conceptual Model of Corporate Performance," *Academy of Management Review* 4, no. 4 (1979): 497–505.

47. Judith Hennigfeld, Manfred Pohl, and Nick Tolhurst, eds., *The ICCA Handbook on Corporate Social Responsibility* (West Sussex, UK: John Wiley & Sons, 2006), https://epdf.pub/the-icca-handbook-of-corporate-social-responsibility65800.html.

48. Donna J. Wood, "Corporate Social Performance Revisited," *Academy of Management Review* 16, no. 4 (1991): 691–718.

49. William C. Frederick, "Moving to CSR: What to Pack for the Trip," *Business & Society* 37, no. 1 (1998): 40–59.

50. Ibid.

51. Hennigfeld, Pohl, and Tolhurst, *ICCA Handbook on Corporate Social Responsibility*, 16.

52. David Chandler, "Stakeholder Theory," chap. 3 in *Strategic Corporate Social Responsibility: Sustainable Value Creation* (Thousand Oaks, CA: Sage, 2020), https://www.sagepub.com/sites/default/files/upm-binaries/105382_ch3_258527.pdf.

53. Hennigfeld, Pohl, and Tolhurst, *ICCA Handbook on Corporate Social Responsibility*.

54. Ibid, 18.

55. C. Laszlo and N. Zhexembayeva, *Embedded Sustainability: The Next Competitive Advantage* (London: Taylor and Francis, 2017).

56. Ibid, 61.

57. "Sustainability Is about Value Creation as Much as It Is about Resilience," *Economist Impact*, accessed June 30, 2023, https://impact.economist.com/projects/profiles-of-progress/article/sustainability-is-about-value-creation-as-much-as-it-is-about-resilience/.

58. Laszlo, and Zhexembayeva, *Embedded Sustainability*.

59. Ibid.

60. Ibid.

61. Ibid.

62. Jung Ha-Brookshire, "Toward Moral Responsibility Theories of Corporate Sustainability and Sustainable Supply Chain," *Journal of Business Ethics* 145 (2017): 227–37.

63. "The Natural Step," *Natural Step*, accessed on July 30, 2023, https://thenatu-ralstep.org/.

64. "FSSD framework," *Redamaltea*, accessed on June 30, 2023, https://redamal-tea.es/wp-content/uploads/2017/05/Framework.pdf.

65. Ibid.

66. "KPI Basics," *KPI*, accessed on July 30, 2023, https://kpi.org/KPI-Basics.

67. Mia Overall, "How to Make Your Materiality Assessment Worth the Effort," *GreenBiz*, August 15, 2017, https://www.greenbiz.com/article/how-make-your-materiality-assessment-worth-effort.

68. Ibid.

69. Ibid.

70. Ibid.

71. Alice Payne, "The Life-Cycle of the Fashion Garment and the Role of Austral-ian Mass Market Designers," *International Journal of Environmental, Cultural, Economic and Social Sustainability* 7, no. 3 (2011): 237–46.

72. William McDonough and Michael Braungart's book *Cradle to Cradle: Remak-ing the Way We Make Things* (New York: North Point Press, 2010) explores this philosophy to the greatest detail.

73. Payne, "Life-Cycle Of The Fashion Garment," 240.

74. Ibid.

75. Kate Fletcher, *Sustainable Fashion and Textiles: Design Journeys* (London: Routledge, 2013).

76. Payne, "Life-Cycle Of The Fashion Garment."

77. Ibid.

78. Ibid.

79. Ibid.

80. "13 Ethical Fashion Brands that are going circular," *ECO*, accessed on July 30, 2023, https://www.eco-stylist.com/13-ethical-fashion-brands-that-are-going-circular/.

81. Payne, "Life-Cycle Of The Fashion Garment."

82. Ibid.

83. "Textiles: Material specific data," *EPA*, accessed on July 30, 2023, https://www.epa.gov/facts-and-figures-about-materials-waste-and-recycling/textiles-material-specific-data.

84. Eileen Fisher, "Renew," accessed on July 30, 2023, https://www.eileenfisher-renew.com/.

85. "Full LCA Result," *Levi's*, 2015, accessed on July 30, 2023, https://www.levis-trauss.com/wp-content/uploads/2015/03/Full-LCA-Results-Deck-FINAL.pdf.

86. Ibid.

87. Ibid.

88. Evan Stuart Andrews, *Guidelines for Social Life Cycle Assessment of Products: Social and Socio-Economic LCA Guidelines Complementing Environmental LCA and Life Cycle Costing, Contributing to the Full Assessment of Goods*

*and Services within the Context of Sustainable Development* (Paris: UNEP/ Earthprint, 2009).

89.   Ibid.

90.   Ibid.

91.   Ibid.

92.   Ibid.

93.   Ibid.

94.   Rachel Creighton, Iva Jestratijevic, and Daton Lee, "Sustainability Supplier Scorecard Assessment Tools: A Comparison between Apparel Retailers," *Journal of Global Fashion Marketing* 13, no. 1 (2022): 64.

95.   Ibid.

96.   Ibid.

97.   "Good Practice Guidance: 2018 Living Wage Assessment," *Livingwage*, accessed August 1, 2023, https://www.livingwage.nl/wp-content/uploads/2019/ 09/Good-Practice-Guidance-2018.pdf.

98.   "Supply Chain," *H&M*, accessed on December 25, 2023, https://hmgroup.com/ sustainability/leading-the-change/transparency/supply-chain/.

99.   Creighton, Jestratijevic, and Lee, "Sustainability Supplier Scorecard Assessment Tools," 61–74.

100.  Ibid.

101.  Ibid.

102.  Ibid.

103.  Ibid.

104.  Ibid.

105.  "Why Companies Are Becoming B Corporations and Certified Green Businesses," *Green Business Bureau*, accessed on December 25, 2023, https:// greenbusinessbureau.com/blog/why-companies-are-becoming-b-corps-and-certified-green-businesses/.

106.  "Find a B Corp," *B Corporation*, accessed on August 1, 2023, https://www. bcorporation.net/en-us/find-a-b-corp/.

107.  Green Business Bureau, "Why Companies Are Becoming B Corporations and Certified Green Businesses."

108.  Stephanie B. Escudero, Iva Jestratijevic, Jeremy C. Short, and Marcus T. Wolfe, "B Corp Certification in the Age of Fast Fashion: Using Hierarchical Clustering and Correspondence Factor Analysis to Highlight Social Entrepreneurial Advancement in the Fashion Industry," *Journal of Business Venturing Insights* 20 (2023): e00412.

109.  Ibid.

110.  "What Is a B Corp?," *B Corporation*, accessed on July 1, 2023, https://bcorporation.uk/b-corp-certification/what-is-a-b-corp/.

111.  B Corporation, "Find a B Corp."

112.  Patagonia and The Yale Center for Business and the Environment, *An Entrepreneur's Guide to Certified B Corporations and Benefit Corporations*, accessed on July 1, 2023, https://www.patagonia.com/static/on/demandware.static/-/Library-Sites-PatagoniaShared/default/dw73962ce0/PDF-US/ CBEY_BCORP_Print.pdf.

# Chapter 4

# Fashion Circularity and Waste Management Strategies

- Chapter Introduction and Learning Objectives
- Circularity versus Linearity
- Ten Principles for a Circular Fashion Industry
- Selection of Textiles Based on Their Impacts
- Waste Management Strategies
- Waste Management and Health Issues
- Textile Waste
- Textile Waste Collection Market Overview
- Textile Waste Diversion: Best Practices
- Other Opportunities for Textile Waste Diversion
- Packaging Waste
- Sustainable Packaging Solutions in Use among Fashion Brands
- Sustainability Expert Profile: Dr. Jana Hawley
- Chapter Summary
- References

# Chapter Introduction and Learning Objectives

In this chapter we will discuss textile, apparel, and packaging waste generation in the fashion industry and its impacts on the environment and on human well-being. The intention of the chapter is to provide valuable insights into the applications of the circular economy principles within wasteful and linear fashion industry systems. The focus in this chapter is therefore given to sustainability problems related to textile and apparel consumption processes and to various circular strategies to reduce and reuse fashion industry waste. Special focus of the chapter is to show-case why in a circular economy waste must be reconsidered as a valuable resource for the next production cycle. The sustainability expert whose work is presented in this chapter is Dr. Jana Hawley, dean of the College of Merchandising, Hospitality, and Tourism at the University of North Texas, because she is one of the first researchers in the United States to conduct research on textile recycling and apparel sustainability.

This chapter has following learning objectives:

- Discuss the circular economy principles and their application in fashion business
- Evaluate the different waste management strategies employed in the fashion industry
- Demonstrate the new roles that different forms of waste have in the circular industry system.

## Key Terms

| | |
|---|---|
| by-product networks | extended producer responsibility |
| chemical recycling | linear economy |
| circular economy | mechanical recycling |
| closed-loop system | textile waste management |

# Circularity versus Linearity

For a long time (and even today), our economy has been **linear**. This means that raw materials are used to make a product, and when the product ends its life cycle, it is thrown out as waste. For example, "The conventional life cycle of clothes from a linear perspective would include the following steps: product design, fiber sourcing and production, garment cutting and tailoring (including finishing), transport, storage, sales, consumer use, disposal,"[1] and subsequent landfill disposal or incineration. This viewpoint indicates that product disposal is perceived as the end of the life cycle.[2] However, one of the basic principles of sustainability is that of circularity. The idea is that instead of living in a linear economy (where things and products are produced, quickly used, and disposed of), products can be used, recycled, and reused over and over. Therefore, sustainability promotes principles of a strong circular industry and economy where "waste" is seen as "food" for the next production cycle.[3] The concept of circularity in fashion was influenced by the work of the Ellen MacArthur Foundation.

According to the Ellen MacArthur Foundation, "The term **circular economy** refers to an industrial economy that is restorative by intention; aims to rely on renewable energy; minimizes, tracks, and eliminates the use of toxic chemicals; and eradicates waste through careful design."[4] In other words, as Dr. Ana Brismar suggests, "Circular fashion can be defined as clothes, shoes or accessories that are designed, sourced, produced and provided with the intention to be used and circulated responsibly and effectively in society for as long as possible in their most valuable form, and thereafter returned safely to the biosphere when no longer of human use."[5]

The principle of circularity suggests that all fashion products should be designed in a circular way, meaning durability, biodegradability, or recyclability should be prioritized. Also, whenever possible, local and renewable resources should be used, and products should be used for as long as possible. Products should be maintained through good care, repair, refurbishment, and sharing, among multiple users over time (through rent/lease, secondhand, swap, etc.).[6]

In essence, circular philosophy implies that waste as we know it does not exist but instead should be considered as a resource for another production cycle. Hence, all products should be either biologically or technically compatible. For example, all natural fibers such as cotton, silk, and wool are compatible with biological cycles, meaning they can naturally decompose. In contrast, polyester, nylon, acrylic, metals, and plastics are considered "technical components" and should be recycled in separate flows.[7] To support a circularity principle, new ways of collaborations are needed, and new business models should be set up. For fashion brands this often means expending service offerings to include product repair, rental, or creative reuse. Thus, we can conclude that circular practices bring many opportunities for fashion brands, and some of these opportunities will be reviewed in this chapter.

## Ten Principles for a Circular Fashion Industry

Here I will review the core principles to consider in the creation of circular fashion products. The core principles that are presented here account for the entire fashion product life cycle, starting from its sourcing, and continuing to manufacturing, sale, use, and end of life, and they are presented from a fashion business perspective.

*Principle 1: Fashion products must contain inherent value.* Instead of creating value-free fast fashion objects that are cheap, nondurable, and low in quality, fashion businesses must embrace a new approach to fashion creation. In his book *Emotionally Durable Design*, Jonathan Chapman reported that fashion products are discarded when they do not hold any substitutional meaning and when emotional and experiential connection does not exist between the consumer and the fashion object. To create fashion products that have inherent value, Chapman recommends different pathways. For instance, it is important for products to be high in quality, durable with a good design, and possess maintainable attributes. Marketing narratives should communicate those unique qualities of the product to stimulate conscious consumption of the product based on its inherent qualities.[8]

*Principle 2: Select textiles based on their impacts.* Sustainability issues associated with each fiber involve different trade-offs. Various tools are available to aid fiber comparisons and assessments. The previously discussed LCA is commonly used, instead of assessing the life cycle of the product, to assess the life cycle of specific materials. Another alternative is to assess life cycle phases for each fiber to support, for example, responsible fiber use. There are also comparative studies that assess water use, energy emission, and pesticide use for various fibers. For example, the nonprofit organization Made-by has published a classification of fibers based on their environmental impacts, starting from rank A, which includes most environmentally friendly options, to E (with the least environmentally friendly options). In their rankings they considered six environmental impacts: greenhouse gas emission, water input, energy input, land use, human toxicity, and eco-toxicity.[9]

*Principle 3: Estimate resource efficiency.* It is important that businesses understand that there are limits in natural resources, and it is critical to minimize the waste or overuse of those resources. Businesses must measure resource use, identifying so-called hot spots, or places where opportunities to reduce natural resource usage exist. In more recent years in the fashion industry, many businesses have begun measuring carbon footprints, water footprints, land use, and material use. As a result, some brands have designed products using lightweight materials aiming to provide the same functionality for the products although sources used in their production are minimized, and thus environmental impacts are reduced. Perhaps the best-known example of efficient resource use is Levi's innovative program Waterless Jeans, where designers challenged themselves to produce jeans with the same look and quality although they were made using less water in the finishing stage.[10]

*Principle 4: Source and produce locally.* The textile supply chain in the fashion industry is global rather than local. Transport and supply chain logistics create significant negative impacts, including air and water pollution and energy consumption from transportation activities. It is not uncommon that many sustainability-oriented designers believe that localism offers opportunities to foster change in the direction of sustainability. For example, McDonough and Braungart argue that the best products result from human and material engagement with place.[11] In the last decades of the twentieth century, apparel companies largely moved their manufacturing facilities overseas, which created complex, globally spread supply chains. Consequently, production was separated from retailing, and the profit was created through economy of scale, in which large quantities of goods were produced at low prices. Localism is proposed as an alternative to globalization, and we can even say that localism represents one of the central tenets of sustainability. Its advantages arise from three primary factors: (1) it proposes a revised scale which is always smaller and more local; (2) it prioritizes local community well-being and the health of local ecosystems; (3) and local systems also preserve local tradition, rely on local knowledge, and bring diversity.[12]

*Principle 5: Design for product circularity.* From a linear viewpoint, disposal is perceived as the end of a product's life. However, the circular or cradle-to-cradle philosophy[13] suggests that beyond the first life cycle of the product there is a next life cycle as well. The main principle of the circular philosophy is that each new product that we create must be designed to be compatible with either the biological cycle or the technical-mechanical or industrial cycle. In the biological cycle, the loop is closed naturally, and the products are returned to nature safely to degrade naturally. In the mechanical or industrial cycle, the loop is closed mechanically, through recycling. Although some products are already made in a circular manner, there are still various technological challenges to closing the loop either naturally or mechanically. For example, the key challenge for biodegradable products is to secure 100 percent biodegradability where not only product parts but also full products are made from biodegradable components (including zippers, buttons, and sewing thread). Similarly, an obvious limit to product recyclability is the extensive use of material blends.[14]

*Principle 6: Create safe, nontoxic products.* Textiles are commonly dyed in multiple steps, which involve the dyeing of fibers, yarn, and fabric. The dyeing process is resource-intensive as it uses large amounts of water, energy, and chemicals, along with often-used metal pollutants, including chromium, copper, and zinc. Some alternatives for reducing hazardous dying methods include avoiding dark shades (e.g., navy and black, green, and turquoise), which are difficult to achieve without using a heavy metal such as copper.[15] Various steps have been taken to improve dying methods and to restrict usage of toxic chemicals. Those steps include legal restrictions, which ban usage of heavy metals and any form of hazardous chemicals. Also, improved dyeing methods have become more widespread in recent years. Alternative dying methods are also available. In them, natural dyes are made from plants, animals, and shells, and they may achieve beautiful colors while protecting humans and the environment.[16]

*Principle 7: Offer and promote circular services.* There are numerous ways for retailers to reduce negative business impacts. Switching from exclusively selling products to providing service opportunities brings new and exciting ways in which retailers can meet the consumer's needs. For example, repair services represent an exciting opportunity to offer extended utility of the product. To support this principle, it is recommended that designers consider all available ways to secure the extended life of the product. The new logic they should follow is that consumers seek not only the product but also the functionality that it offers.[17] To secure product durability, Patagonia is promoting products that have mendable attributes. In addition, the retailer is offering repair services for those products, promising to return them back to like-new condition using the same or similar fabric and hardware. Alternatively, businesses might introduce other services into the market that was traditionally dominated by the selling of the products. For example, Mud company believes in "ownerless consumption" in which the company, instead of selling the jeans, is focused on their lease for a monthly pay of approximately ten dollars.[18]

*Principle 8: Promote sustainable clothing usage.* There is research-based evidence that in the Netherlands, for example, the typical garment is worn between 2.4 and 3.1 days between washings.[19] The same research also argues that the most of a garment's environmental impact arises from the process of laundering and drying. This is also supported in Levi's LCA assessment, which found the washing and drying of a pair of jeans is responsible for almost two-thirds of the energy consumed for its production.[20] Therefore, retailers need to encourage consumers to responsibly care for the clothing they possess. For example, just by instructing consumers to wash items less often, the products' overall energy consumption and water usage can be significantly cut. There are other techniques that retailers can use to promote responsible product care. For example, innovation in the area of fabrics and garments that can be laundered less or can be sun dried is important. Repair or repurposing services provided by the retailer also encourage consumers to buy fewer, higher quality items that have repairable attributes.

*Principle 9: Provide sustainable packaging.* "The apparel and footwear industry creates large amounts of packaging waste that filter through the entire value chain. Packaging is used not only to protect, handle, and transport textiles, apparel, and footwear products but also to distribute the final goods to distribution centers, stores, and, ultimately, consumers."[21] For this reason, it is critically important that retailers not only improve their products in a sustainable manner but also rethink sustainable packaging solutions. Because packaging is most often discarded just after the product purchase, businesses may consider reusable or recyclable solutions. For example, goods can be packed in a "fabric wrap that can be reused as a gift bag or scarf."[22] Similarly, packages can be creatively upcycled. For example, children's brand Monday's Child is packaging clothing in recycled cardboard boxes that look like doll houses, which gives them a fun new use after the product is unpacked. Perhaps the easiest and most cost-efficient method to improve packaging is to reduce them in terms of layers, size, and weight. For example, the brand Roxy's launched new strong boxes that can be shipped alone, which helps retailers avoid traditional box-in-a-box shipping.

*Principle 10: Manage waste in a circular manner.* Efficient **textile waste management** strategies provide substantial benefits. At a minimum, they help reduce and redistribute waste, often creating new business opportunities that also generate profit. For example, unsold wearable merchandise might be redistributed and resold (as needed) locally, nationally, or internationally. In the case of wearable items, the products are used for the same purpose. Another approach to efficient textile waste management, when dealing with nonwearables is recycling.[23] In recycling, the products are often used for another purpose. Discarded materials are shredded, and they can be respun into yarns. In the fashion market today, there is a growing interest in recycled yarns, fabrics, and other products. Unsold clothes can also be donated or creatively repurposed to provide those garments a chance to have an extended life. It goes without saying that a new vision for efficient waste management requires new ways of thinking about waste and its potential value, along with the new roles waste may have in a sustainably oriented fashion industry. Last but not least important, I should note that the above ten principles are defined from a business perspective. However, some of these principles are also highly relevant and applicable to consumers as well.[24] For example, Principle 8 is related to sustainable clothing usage, in which consumers may be asked to follow responsible practices for product washing, cleaning, and drying and also to consider using circular services such as clothes mending or creative repair (Principle 7) to prolong the life of clothes they already own. Similarly, Principle 10 recommends some good techniques for textile waste management that are effectively applicable to all consumers (e.g., resell, donate, repurpose, reuse).

## Selection of Textiles Based on Their Impacts

Materials used in the fashion industry represent the starting point for sustainability change. Indeed, most of the books about sustainable fashion have been focused on sustainability issues in textiles, and therefore we will only briefly review this topic here. Broadly speaking, we can say that two fibers, cotton and polyester, have dominated clothing and household textiles markets in the last two decades. We can also say that there are two kinds of textile materials, some that are natural and others that use manufactured or manmade fibers. Natural materials are made from plants (e.g., cotton, help, flax, banana, etc.) and animal resources (e.g., leather, wool, silk, cashmere, mohair). Manufactured fibers are commonly made from natural polymers (e.g., viscose, modal, acetate, triacetate, modal, rubber) and synthetic polymers (e.g., polyester, nylon, acrylic etc.). For a long time, researchers have been debating the sustainability impacts of natural and manmade fibers and assessing resources consumed (e.g., energy, water, chemicals, land, waste, emissions produced, etc.) in the process of their manufacturing. Let us review a summary of recent findings about the advantages and disadvantages entailed in each fiber.

Cotton represents the most frequently used clothing fiber that comes from a renewable source: cellulose. Yet "cotton is also the most pesticide-intensive crop in the world . . . it takes up a large proportion of agricultural land, much of which is needed by local people to grow their own food."[25] Although cotton is a natural fiber, negative environmental and social impacts of cotton production are well documented. For example, two major environmental concerns are chemical use in cotton agriculture, and waste generation, while the major social concern relates to health "issues related to the heavy use of toxic pesticides, especially in countries where regulatory systems are weak or absent."[26]

Organic cotton is grown "without the use of synthetic fertilizers, herbicides, and pesticides. The cotton is grown using natural fertilizers (e.g., manure) and by replacing pesticides with beneficial insects that prey on insects harmful to the plants."[27] In the global market nowadays, various certifications verify that cotton is organic and that it was grown properly. Also, federal regulations strictly prohibit the use of genetically modified seed for organic farming, thus all organic cotton must be sold and promoted following strict federal regulations.[28]

Wool is a natural, renewable fiber obtained from animals, most commonly from sheep. Although natural fiber, wool must be processed using "soap and alkaline solutions to clean the fibers and to remove grease and impurities. Chemicals are also used on wool fabrics to prevent shrinkage, to ensure machine washability, and to provide resistance to moths and stains."[29] Wool can be naturally colored, although acid dyes and chemical substances are commonly used to obtain unique and vivid colors.

Organic wool is "different from conventional wool in at least two major ways: (1) sheep cannot be dipped in insecticides to control external parasites such as ticks and lice, and (2) organic wool farmers are required to ensure that they do not exceed the natural carrying capacity of the land on which their animals graze." Organic wool in the United States must be produced according to strict federal standards that cover "not only management of the livestock according to organic or holistic management principles but also the processing of the raw wool, using newer, more benign processes rather than harmful scouring and descaling chemicals, as well as wastewater treatment from scouring and processing according to the Global Organic Textile Standard (GOTS)."[30]

Rayon is the first manmade fiber produced from regenerated cellulosic fiber. It was also known as "artificial silk" until the name "rayon"
was adopted in 1924. Rayon production has high impact on the environment as "the processing of wood pulp into fiber and its cleaning after
extrusion uses large quantities of harsh chemicals which can contribute
to water and air pollution."[31]

Tencel (with the generic name lyocell) is produced from regenerated
cellulosic fiber, which originates from wood pulp. Scientists argue that
compared to the production of rayon, the production of Tencel poses much
less adverse impacts on the environment.[32] For this reason, Tencel is quite
popular among sustainable-oriented fashion brands. Since it is plant-derived
fiber, Tencel is biodegradable and compostable.[33]

Nylon is among the most widely used synthetic fibers in the United States.
"The manufacture of nylon emits nitrous oxide, a substance partly responsible
for depleting Earth's ozone layer." In the production process. the fiber is also
extensively treated with harsh chemicals, dyes, and bleaching agents.[34]

Polyester is the most popular synthetic fiber, derived from petroleum.
Polyester production is similar to that of nylon, but unlike nylon polyester
can be extensively recycled to reduce waste in landfills. For example, plastic
bottles that are recycled are used to create recycled polyester fiber, which is
significantly less polluting compared to the production of polyester fibers
made from new raw materials.[35]

Leather is another natural, biodegradable, and renewable fiber, obtained
from the skins and hides of a variety of mammals (notably cattle, pigs,
goats, and sheep). However, the leather's production, processing, and dyeing
involves usage of many harsh chemicals. For example, "The skins and hides
are first salted, then cleaned to remove hair, tanned, colored or dyed, and
finally finished to achieve certain appearance or performance properties."
From all mentioned processes in leather production, leather tanning is the
most problematic one, as solutions composed of chromium-based salts and
oils are used to treat the leather.[36]

The extensive application of dyes and hazard chemicals in fashion
production is widely known. All stages that are involved in textiles treatment (e.g., bleaching, sandblasting, dyeing, printing etc.) are including

hazardous chemicals, and for that reason textile production is highly polluting. "The most common bleaching agents include hydrogen peroxide, sodium hypochlorite, sodium chloride, and sulfur dioxide gas. The dyes and chemicals used in the dyeing process create many pollutants, which originate from the dyes themselves (e.g. salt, surfactant, levelers, lubricants, and alkaline substances)." Natural dyes represent a viable renewable and biodegradable solution to less impactful textiles dyeing. Yet scientists estimate that "the textile sector is approximately only 1% due to certain technical and sustainability issues involved in the production and application of these dyes such as their unavailability in ready-to-use standard form, unsuitability for machine use, and limited quantities of nonreproducible shades."[37]

## Waste Management Strategies

Waste can be classified as controlled and non-controlled waste depending on its regulation. Controlled waste is generated from households, commercial and industrial organizations, and its handling and disposal is strictly regulated.[38] Noncontrolled waste commonly results from agriculture, dredging, and mining and for different reasons it is excluded from solid waste regulation.[39] Further, solid textile waste can be classified on the basis of its generation as pre-consumer textile waste, post-consumer textile waste, and industrial textile waste.[40]

Pre-consumer textile waste refers to textile waste that remains after the production process meaning that this waste has produced and discarded by a business. The advantage of this waste is that it can be well defined in terms of content but may or may not be available in large, uniform volumes.[41] This waste can be sold to interested parties for low prices. Since the content is known, this waste has a great potential for reuse and recycling.[42]

Post-consumer textile waste refers to all the clothing and apparel waste that is discarded after consumer-use which typically happens at any point in the garment's life.[43] The potential of this waste is enormous, as it can be reused for the same or different purposes. For example, clothing in good shape can be sold in a secondhand market.[44] Alternatively, it can be shredded and reused.

Industrial textile waste represents the "result of the manufacturing processes and is termed 'dirty waste. This waste has collection and contamination issues and may not be recovered. An example that has created the immense problems to the health and environment is the mounds of solid waste that have been piled up in textile dyeing industries, ready to be disposed of in landfills."[45]

## Waste Management and Health Issues

There are well documented health issues related to waste management. Perhaps the biggest challenges are experienced with residents who live close to the landfill or dumping sites.

As suggested by Subramanian Muthu, "Exposure levels and duration of exposure to substances like cadmium, arsenic, chromium, dioxins, nickel, and polycyclic aromatic hydrocarbons not only produce carcinogenic effects but also have serious implications for the central nervous system, liver, kidney, heart, lungs, skin, and reproduction of the people near the waste sites. Pollutants like sulfur dioxide or $SO_2$ and coarse dust particles (PM10) cause disease and death to vulnerable groups of the society like infants and the elderly, while dioxins and organochlorides are lipid-loving molecules which tend to settle in fat-rich tissues, resulting in serious reproductive or endocrine disorders."[46] For example, during the 1930s and 1940s, large quantities of toxic waste from pesticide production were dumped at Love Canal, New York. By the mid-1970s, the leaching of chemicals was detected in streams, soil, sewers, and air quality in houses that were built around the landfill site in the 1950s, leading to research and reports regarding such areas. Residents in this area reported, in a series of epidemiological studies that were conducted over the years, health issues like nuisance, odor, risk, stress, birth defects, reproductive disorders, congenital malformations, and cancer. The third largest site for waste dumping, the Miron Quarry site in North America, showed incidence of cancers in the liver, kidney, and pancreas correlating to the closeness of the inhabitants to the site. Further, the workforce in the waste sites faces health risks related to gastric and lung cancer and skin problems due to VOCs, bioaerosols, and dust levels.[47] UNEP also reports negative health impacts of dumping at the largest open landfill in Latin America and the Caribbean, where more than 2,700 metric tons of municipal waste is discarded annually.[48]

## Textile Waste

Textiles are one of the largest forms of solid waste categories in the world, and textile waste continues to grow at an alarming rate. For example, notable sources such as the Ellen MacArthur Foundation and WRAP UK estimate that consumer clothing purchases are currently at least four times as frequent as they were in 1980.[49] The rapid increase in clothing purchase explains the corresponding increase in the amounts of textiles that are discarded. For example, the United States Environmental Protection Agency (EPA) data revealed that in 2018, 17 million tons of textiles were deposited into US landfills (see table 14). As noted by the EPA "this figure represents 5.8 percent of total MSW generation that year."[50] Further, it is expected "that annual apparel waste disposal rates will increase by 60% by 2023."[51] Among all discarded textile categories, the largest is "discarded clothing, while other smaller sources include footwear, carpets, sheets, and towels."[52]

In order for us to discuss meaningful ways in which we can reduce the number of textiles in the landfills, or divert them, we will first review post-consumer textile waste facts in greater detail. Referring solely to the United States, the main source of information on post-consumer textile waste is the EPA, along with other state and local government institutions, where information varies considerably depending on the state and the type of for-profit or nonprofit organizations involved. For example, at this point, the most recent publicly available EPA report provides the following information:

- "It is estimated that US consumers dispose of 70 to 80 pounds of textiles each year on average."[53]
- "The recycling rate for all textiles was 14.7 percent in 2018, with 2.5 million tons recycled.
- Within this figure, the EPA estimated that the recycling rate for textiles in the clothing and footwear category was 13% based on information from the American Textile Recycling Service.

**Table 14**  Generation, recycling, composting, combustion with energy recovery, and landfilling of textiles, rubber, and leather materials in MSW, 2018 (in millions of tons, with the percent of generation of each material)*

| Total Wasted Materials | Weight Generated | Weight Recycled | Weight Combusted with Energy Recovery | Weight Landfilled | Recycling as Percent of Generation | Combustion as Percent of Generation | Landfilling as Percent of Generation |
|---|---|---|---|---|---|---|---|
| Textiles | 17.03 | 2.51 | 3.22 | 11.30 | 14.7% | 18.9% | 66.4% |
| Rubber and leather | 9.16 | 1.67 | 2.50 | 4.99 | 18.2% | 27.3% | 54.5% |
| Clothing and footwear | 12.9 | 1.69 | 2.2 | 9.07 | 13% | 17% | 70% |

* Includes waste from residential, commercial, and institutional sources. This table was adopted from EPA, *Advancing Sustainable Materials Management: 2018 Fact Sheet,* accessed on June 30, 2023, https://www.epa.gov/sites/default/files/2021-01/documents/2018_ff_fact_sheet_dec_2020_fnl_508.pdf.

- For comparison, the rate for home furnishing items such as sheets and pillowcases was 15.8 percent in 2018.
- The EPA estimated that 66.4% of textiles go to landfills although at least 95% of post-consumer textile waste can be recycled or reused in a circular manner.
- Consumers in the US believe that cities and municipalities should institute textile recycling programs."[54]

Who is in charge of textile waste in the US? Commonly in most of the world countries, "Textiles are collected by non-profit organizations who use profits generated from collection to support their missions and by for-profit entities who capitalize on collection privately. Both practices are well-established, operating under a revenue-based model rather than a waste management or reduction model."[55] According to the *A Tipping Point: The Canadian Textile Diversion Industry* report, there are six main channels available to collect all textiles:

**Table 15** Six main channels available to collect textile waste*

| Method | Collection |
|---|---|
| Donation Bins | With or without property owner consent |
| Direct Drop-off | At thrift retail or depot locations |
| Curbside | Offered to every home in given areas |
| Residential Door | Offered to selected homes via phone soliciting or flyer drop-offs |
| Drives or Events | At limited times and locations |
| Retail Returns or Take Back | Retailer's overrun, returns, or collections at point of sale |

*This table was adopted from NACTRS, *A Tipping Point: The Canadian Textile Diversion Industry: An In-Depth Look at the Current Industry and the Prospects for the Future,* published in 2019, accessed on June 10, 2023, https://nactr.ca/wp-content/uploads/2022/02/The-Canadian-Textile-Diversion-Industry-April-2019.pdf.

After the waste is collected, it must be audited and categorized. Unfortunately, there are no reliable and steadfast state-specific data available for textile diversion in America. As suggested in the same report, "To create a proper benchmark for textile diversion rates, a standard must be followed for both landfill and curbside textile waste audits." For example, in Canada there is a recommended list of textiles that is arranged by product type and divided into six categories: "clothing, footwear, accessories, household textiles, stuffed toys, and other textiles."[56]

Once the waste is audited, the textile waste processing cycle starts. Processing involves six steps:

1. Textiles are collected and distributed to secondary market warehouses and thrift stores that have facilities for processing them.
2. Once sorted and graded, textiles are resold to rag dealers and clothing graders in bales. Contaminated or soiled textiles are then sent to landfill.
3. All high quality textiles are resold or donated.
4. If textiles do not sell in 4-5 weeks they are removed from the store, and they are offered to clothing graders and rag dealers.
5. Data shows that somewhere between 75%–80% of textiles sold to clothing graders and rag dealers are not fit for resale in Canada

or the US. Thus, that portion of the textiles is prepared for international markets.

6. "Sorted textiles are exported to markets around the world for further re-use or recycling. An estimated 70% of the global population wears 'recovered' clothing."[57]

## Textile Waste Collection Market Overview

In America most cities do not yet have in place necessary infrastructure and resources to manage the intensifying textile waste flows. Research shows that cities and municipal authorities are not directly involved in postconsumer textiles collection for further reuse other than by issuing permits to charities or commercial resellers to conduct these activities, who organize and manage the collection and provide infrastructure.[58]

Commercial resellers are also referred to as for-profit textile collection businesses. In the United States, commercial resellers are commonly private entities in charge of textile waste diversion and redistribution. According to the research published by McCauley and Jestratijevic, the major players in the postconsumer textile waste market in the United States can be categorized into seven categories: material sources, collectors, sorters/aggregators, processors, recyclers, manufacturers, and retailers.[59] Dynamics between these different players in this specific context is described in the article titled "Exploring the Business Case for Textile-to-Textile Recycling Using Post-Consumer Waste in the US: Challenges and Opportunities," which you may use as a further reference to this topic.[60]

*Nonprofit organizations.* In the United States, the Goodwill organization (established in Boston approximately 120 years ago by the early social innovator Reverend Edgar J. Helms) is a leading nonprofit chain that has collected household goods, clothing, shoes, and textiles in wealthier areas and then trained and hired people to repair collected items to resell them in their stores.[61] Today, the organization's headquarters are located in Rockville, Maryland. This organization is invested in community-based programs, including job training opportunities centered around selling donated clothing and household items in more than 3,200 Goodwill stores in North America as well as the online platform shopgoodwill.com. In 2020 alone the organization helped to employ 126,938 people within local Goodwill communities. In recent history, Goodwill has partnered with twelve countries interested in opening Goodwill stores outside of the US and Canada.

The Salvation Army was established in London in 1865 by a preacher, William Booth, who recognized the growing need for affordable merchandise. Booth named his organization the Household Salvage Brigade, and he hired a group of men and women who were collecting unwanted clothing, textiles, and household items.[62] As the demand for used clothing items grew around the world, Salvation Army began expending their missionary work. Today they are the largest provider of secondhand household and clothing materials in the United States, where they helped approximately 32 million people in 2022.[63]

*Re-commerce market.* Re-commerce or the secondary market is the market that sells secondhand goods. A ThredUp report announced that this market is expected to grow 127% by 2026 (reaching around $82 billion in sales), which is three times faster than the overall apparel market. Based on those facts, we can expect that much of the textile waste that is currently generated will in the future be resold through traditional retail methods. In 2022 eighty-eight major global fashion brands (e.g., Patagonia, REI, Lululemon, Levi's, Eileen Fisher, Taylor Stich, the North Face, Tommy Hilfiger, and others) started offering secondhand items to their customers as they start seeing re-commerce as a part of their omnichannel strategy. However, ThredUp also reports that "retailers are barely scratching the surface of secondhand resale's potential impacts" as "secondhand apparel makes up <1% of the total apparel volume sold by retailers who have launched resale shops."[64]

*Third market.* According to the *A Tipping Point: The Canadian Textile Diversion Industry* report, third market includes all the textile waste that has been collected but was not sold in the thrift market.[65] The main players in this market are textile graders and rag dealers. To describe third market, Secondary Materials and Recycled Textiles (SMART) Association reports the following: "Collectors bale and sell discarded clothing products 'as is' to clothing graders or other dealers. Used clothing graders sort the items, assign a 'grade' and re-sale the graded product. The activities of collectors, graders, and used clothing brokers are instrumental in diverting solid waste from landfills and mixed-waste incinerators." Most collected textiles are exported "overseas to developing markets in Asia, Africa, Europe, or Central and South America." Alternatively, used clothing can be recycled and processed back to original fiber, or it can be used to produce wiping products, "home insulation (made from the denim of reprocessed blue jeans), stuffing for furniture, athletic equipment, pet bedding, automotive soundproofing, and carpet padding among many other new products."[66]

*Fourth market.* Fourth market is also known as the recycling market, where collected textiles are either chemically or mechanically recycled. The EPA estimates that 17 million tons of textile waste is generated annually in the United States; however, only around 15 percent of this waste is recycled.[67] There are a number of boundaries that hinder the more spread textile recycling process. Here I will mention the main ones:

- Often there is lacking information regarding the textiles content which makes it difficult to sort post-consumer textile waste.[68] According to the McCauley and Jestratijevic, "Textiles that might be ideal for particular recycling streams are more likely to be downcycled for this reason. . . . Examples of how this may impact the overall bottom line for recyclers were not found in the available literature. Two examples of enabling technologies were found in the literature: near-infrared scanning of textiles to identify material types and digital IDs that would use radio frequency identification to access embedded product information."
- The dyes and chemicals used in the fabric production, fiber blends, and materials with elastane materials create major technical challenges in recycling.
- "Harmful or banned chemicals in the feedstock may be on the resulting fiber, posing a risk that recycled fibers may not pass regulatory requirements. Additionally, the presence of chemicals on the feedstock can cause malfunctions in the solvent-recycling process; therefore, it is important that the overall system is able to remove such impurities."[69]

- "When natural fibers are recycled, their fiber length is shortened, which decreases the quality. To produce quality products, reclaimed natural fibers must be mixed with virgin fibers or must be spun as man-made fibers. For example, cotton fibers can be recycled into viscose fibers."[70]

Because of all these realistic obstacles that hinder the wider spread of recycling, innovation in this area lacks financial and strategic support from governments and fashion companies, which further prevents scaling and commercialization of recycling technologies.[71]

*Textile waste exports.* If we consider the research evidence that "70% of the global population relies on second-market clothing," the need to export secondhand clothing is understandable. However, there are great concerns that the influx of secondhand clothing, particularly in Africa, has undermined indigenous textile industry.[72] From that standpoint, it is argued that although international resale and reuse of secondhand clothing collected through charitable organizations saves natural resources needed for new production, it also creates poverty within local communities who are importing secondhand goods (instead of preserving their local textile industry and artisans).

*Keeping textile waste domestic!* "Although 98% of textiles originated abroad, outside of the US, the ideal solution is to keep the textile waste domestic"[73] and consider it as monetizable input for textile-to-textile recycling.[74] Furthermore, since there is a great demand for recycled fibers, it is important to financially support innovative recycling methods and new technologies for regeneration of both cotton and polyester fibers.[75] Also, in order to prevent increasing textile waste generation, it is necessary to require the fashion businesses to divert postconsumer textile waste from the landfill (perhaps through the extended producer responsibility policy, which will be further discussed) and to incentivize closed-loop business solutions. A **closed-loop system** indicates that recycling of a material can be done indefinitely without degradation of properties. In this case, conversion of the used product back to raw material allows the repeated making of the same product over and over again.

## Textile Waste Diversion: Best Practices

Public information on efficient textile waste diversion practice is very limited. However, here I will summarize legislative and practical examples that are promising to change the way we perceive, treat, and use textile waste in the fashion industry.

*Extended producer responsibility* (*EPR*). OECD describes EPR as an environmental policy that requires fashion brands to have full responsibility for a product after consumption stage. In practice this policy manifests in two major ways:

- The responsibility is physically or financially, fully or partially transferred upstream to producers (in our case fashion brand / retailer) and away from municipalities.
- Producer (or in our case fashion brand / retailer) is finally incentivized to account for product second life (reuse) after it has been discarded.[76]

EPR was first implemented in the European Union, but other countries around the globe accepted this legislation as well. For example, to date, "France is the only country with a national textile resource recovery program," the EPR program that "started in 2007 with aggressive targets of 50% textile waste diversion by 2013. In 2009, the textile diversion rate was 18%, and it had grown to 36% by 2017." Apart from the environmental goals of this program, the program has a social goal to "employ hard-to-employ citizens, who traditionally were employed by non-profit groups in the sector. The environmental and social impacts in France under the EPR program have proven to be of great benefit."[77]

*Textile waste collection at the city level.* At the city level, separate textile collection can be considered the entry point to clothing-related environmental policy. For example, "In Amsterdam (Netherlands), post-consumer textiles are collected in above-the-ground containers assigned by municipality. These containers are managed by charitable organizations that used to pay a fee to municipality to operate."[78] According to research published by Maldini et al., since 2009 formal regulation was established that required these organizations to collect all textiles and accessories regardless of their quality and to make collection instructions clear in their communication to citizens. Furthermore, in Germany, textile waste management strategies vary between regions. For example, "In Berlin, all waste must be handed over to the main waste collection organization in accordance with Section 7 of the Closed Substance Cycle Waste Management Act." However, this act also clarifies that "other entities can also collect waste with a notice, if they prove that the waste is disposed of properly and in a harmless manner." Next, Norway has different collection systems for wearable (reusable) and non-wearable clothing items. "In 2018, charitable organizations collected 79% of all separate textiles, while municipal waste companies and private organizations collected 13% and 8%, respectively." For example, in Oslo, "Wearable textiles for reuse are collected by charities and private organizations. . . . The municipality is involved by appointing city space for collection boxes and approximately 350 boxes administered by the charities (Fretex and UFF) are placed all over the city."[79]

In the United States, the city of Austin is committed to becoming the most circular city across the nation. In 2021 it had a waste diversion rate of 41.96 percent while having the ambitious goal to reduce the amount of trash sent to landfills by 90 percent by the year 2040. In terms of textile waste collection, the city partnered with Goodwill Central Texas to offer a free on-call curbside collection service for unwanted clothing, shoes, accessories, toys, linens and housewares for reuse or recycling.[80]

*Innovative start-up solutions.* Circular Thrift, an environmental start-up, was recently launched in Columbus, Ohio, to test, facilitate, and propose a novel, hyper-local, scalable, and replicable approach for apparel reuse. Unlike linear business models in fashion, which are guided by cradle to grave philosophy, where garments are produced and disposed, the Circular Thrift business model is based on the cradle to cradle philosophy, aiming to bring prematurely discarded apparel items back into circulation for reuse. Specifically, Circular Thrift facilitates unwanted clothing collection (pick-up services), donations (drop-off stations), swaps (thematic and seasonal swaps), resale (pop-up thrift events), and repair (upcycling projects and mending events). All of these promote thrifting and secondhand apparel consumption as a sustainable alternative to new product consumption.[81]

## Other Opportunities for Textile Waste Diversion

The EPA reports that at least 15 million tons of textile waste are generated annually in the United States, while only around 15 percent of this waste is recycled. According to the McCauley and Jestratijevic, "When considering that the average landfill tipping fee is $55 per ton, the cost associated with dumping textile materials into landfills would be approximately $700 million annually across the US,"[82] although some studies estimate much higher figures, even reaching over $3 billion.[83] When discarded to the landfill, synthetic items may take between twenty and two hundred years to decompose.[84] For example, one pair of shoes made from blended materials takes at least one hundred years to decompose if discarded in a trash bin, from which they are sent directly to landfills. Here are some other problematic facts:

- In a coauthored study titled "Measuring the 'Clothing Mountain': Action Research and Sustainability Pedagogy to Reframe (Un) Sustainable Clothing Consumption in the Classroom," we discovered that over a twelve-week period, my students (n=755) reported (cumulatively) purchasing 10,931 apparel items (for a total value of $754,239).
- From all these items, we further discovered that during this twelve-week time period, every sixth item was not worn. This means that perhaps 1,821 recently purchased items (approximately 17 percent) were added to students' collections of inactive wardrobe pieces.
- The remaining 9,110 of the recently purchased items were worn on average five times, while every fourth item was trashed and sent directly to the landfill.
- This means that within twelve weeks, the 755 students discarded 2,732 items (or approximately 25 percent of newly purchased items) into a local landfill.
- Surprisingly, most students were more likely to trash their wearable clothing items rather than to donate them. In fact, only every tenth student reported donating wearable clothes to local charities such as Goodwill and/or the Salvation Army.[85]

Although this data is not generalizable to the general population, as this research was done using student sample, the results are shocking! Yet our study validates previous studies showing that today average consumer buys more clothing items than ever before while keeping them for very short periods of time, which further leads to increased accumulation of textile waste.[86]

The challenge is obvious: How can we reduce the number of textiles ending up in landfills in a meaningful way while also making sure they can be reused in one form or another? For this to become reality will require innovation and collaboration from all parties involved in the textile creation, collection, and diversion processes. The benefits of textile waste industry growth are endless, but major ones definitely include new jobs, waste reduction, and community protection.[87] Here are three action items for the support of further textile waste industry development:

1.  *Innovation in the recycling area.* The first action item for the support of further textile waste industry development includes innovation in the recycling area. Below is table 16, showing the key impacts a single T-shirt has on our environment. As you can see from the data, if a single shirt is recycled and not wasted, the water savings are significant.

**Table 16** The key impacts a single T-shirt has on our environment

| *A T-Shirt's Impact* |
| --- |
| • Recycling a single T-shirt saves 594 gallons of water (2,700 liters). |
| • We could reduce our carbon footprint by 20–30 percent by extending the life of our garments by a mere nine months. |
| • The global warming effect of gases produced in the manufacture of T-shirts is twenty-five times higher than that of carbon dioxide because they include methane gas, creating a sizable contribution to climate change. |
| • 210 billion gallons (954.6 billion liters) of water could be saved, and 1 million pounds of CO2 could be eliminated, if every person in North America recycled a single T-shirt. |

*This table was adapted from NACTRS, *A Tipping Point: The Canadian Textile Diversion Industry: An In-Depth Look at the Current Industry and the Prospects for the Future,* April 2019, accessed June 10, 2023, https://nactr.ca/wp-content/uploads/2022/02/The-Canadian-Textile-Diversion-Industry-April-2019.pdf.

As stated throughout this book, one of the critical strategies to reduce textile waste is to recycle discarded textiles. Textiles can be recycled in two ways. The first is the mechanical method, and the second is the chemical method.

**Mechanical recycling** refers to mechanical shredding of textiles, which does not change the basic structure of the materials. For example, ideally cotton waste that consisted of one fiber (pure cotton) can be mechanically processed into recycled cotton through the process of fabric cutting, shredding, and then pulling the material apart into fibers. Once the cotton is recycled it is usually mixed "with virgin cotton or polyester to improve the quality because recycled cotton has short fiber lengths and is weaker than its virgin counterpart." It is common to see that many major brands now include a portion of the recycled cotton in their clothing (for example, all Mud Jeans consist of recycled cotton).[88]

Recycled polyester (known as RPET, with *R* standing for recycled and *PET* standing for polyethylene terephthalate) is made primarily from discarded plastic bottles which are "an excellent waste stream because there is an abundant supply, and plastic bottles are fairly clean . . . they are often clear, do not contain pigments, and have relatively few chemical additives." Interestingly for apparel and footwear products recycled polyester commonly originate from "plastic water bottles and not polyester textile waste." Recycled polyester is mostly used to produce shoes and bags (for example, the fashion brand Rothy's is known for their RPET shoes and bags).[89]

**Chemical recycling** is the process where chemicals are used to recycle and break down materials back to monomers, components which then can be used to create new fibers and materials. Chemical recycling is used to recycle clothing and apparel that contain more than one fiber since they cannot be easily separated. For example, Worn Again and Ambercycle companies launched innovative chemical recycling technologies that are used to "separate fabric blends to create textile waste streams that can be further processed into recycled products, including recycled fibers." While recycling often means converting materials into something of lesser value (shredded pieces), upcycling includes the performance of a value-added activity on the material or disassembled garment in such a way as to create a product of higher quality or value than the original. For example, Econyl is a relatively new upcycled "nylon yarn manufactured by the Aquafil Group through depolymerization which occurs through a series of chemical reactions that convert nylon pieces into nylon monomers." Raw materials for Econyl production are old fishing nets and other textile waste found in the water.[90]

2. *By-product networks for closed-loop textile waste systems.* The second action item for the support of further textile waste industry development includes creation of **by-product networks**. The by-product networks unite various companies together in order to create a closed-loop system in which one company uses waste from the other company as raw materials in their production process. Because in such a system waste is reused as input for new production cycles, by-product networks are ideal solutions to support business circularity. For example, in Columbus, Ohio, there is a by-product network called Ohio Materials Marketplace (supported by the Ohio EPA) that unites entrepreneurs to exchange waste from their streams in this meaningful way.[91] Currently, this network has around a thousand members that use each other's "wasted materials" to divert nearly 3.7 million pounds of material from Ohio landfills. Members of this network have "significant economic savings by sourcing cheaper feedstocks from both industrial by-products and post-consumer recycled materials. On the flip side, businesses using the marketplace to find outlets for their by-products and waste materials are able to avoid costly landfill tipping fees and waste hauling services. Many businesses participating in Materials Marketplace projects are able to generate a significant amount of revenue from recycling and reuse. General Motors, for example, has generated nearly $1 billion in annual revenue through the reuse and recycling of its by-products."[92] In Texas I have discovered a similar by-product network called the Austin Materials Marketplace, a city-led project that has facilitated reuse, recycling, and waste exchange since 2014.[93]

In recent times, by-product networks have also become more common forms of successful collaboration in the fashion industry. The following are some examples.

*Vegea wine leather.* The Italian company Vegea won the Global Change Award for innovative solutions in which eco-friendly vegan leather is produced from wine industry leftovers. In this case, new products are created as the outcomes of by-product collaboration between agricultural products and technology. In particular, Vegea is collaborating with Italian wineries and using innovative technological methods to process the "wine waste grape marc, which is composed of grape skins, stalks, and seeds discarded during wine production." Most importantly, there are "no heavy metals, toxic solvents, or substances dangerous for humans and the environment involved in the production process."[94] The vegan coated fabric that is produced represents a sustainable alternative to oil-based and animal-based derived materials. The vegan fabric has applications across industries, including the fashion, furniture, packaging, and automotive industries.

The official website of the Vegea company shares an interesting story about its business venture.[95] According to their findings, around 27 billion liters of wine are produced in the world each year. With it, huge quantities of wine leftovers are produced as well. Everything that does not make it into the bottle, around seven billion tons of stalks, skins, and seeds, represents the leftovers from this industry. These by-products, collectively referred to as "pomace," are a nutrient-rich organic mix often used as organic fertilizer or animal feed. Vegea represents an animal-friendly alternative with numerous environmental benefits. It feels like conventional leather although no water is needed for its production (unlike conventional leather, which has a huge water footprint). Wine leather also does not require a complex and toxic tanning process, which commonly involves heavy metals and hazardous chemicals. Lastly, but not less important, all products of the Vegea company are compliant with the most stringent European regulations (REACH); they are solvent-free, eco-friendly, and made in Italy.[96]

*Fish-skin lab.* The development of "fish leather was initiated in 2018 when Elisa Palomino researcher at UAL's Centre for Sustainable Fashion at London College of Fashion was funded by the European Commission, EASME, under COSME 2014–2020 to produce a collection of bags made of fish leather (using it as an alternative to exotic leathers from endangered species), developing new embellishments and eco-friendly digital printing." According to the researcher findings, "Fish leather has been used for centuries by the Inuit, Yup'ik, and Athabascan peoples of Alaska and Canada; Siberian peoples, such as the Nivkh and Nanai; the Ainu from the Hokkaido island in Japan and Sakhalin Island, Russia; the Hezhe from northeast China; and Icelanders." Because there is an abundance of fish skin waste, Fishskin Lab promises to put this waste into commercial production, which can potentially divert nearly thirty-two million tons of fish waste annually.[97]

*Redress and the R Collective.* Redress is a Hong Kong-based NGO established in 2007 that is committed to preventing sending unwanted clothes and textiles to landfills. The main goal of this organization is to creatively reuse discarded textile waste and help support formation of by-product networks. Redress established R Collective as a upcycled fashion brand created with a mission to design clothes using discarded textile materials.[98]

3. *Influencing municipal and federal governments to implement textile diversion programs.* The third action item for the support of further textile waste industry development includes implementation of textile diversion programs at municipal and federal levels. Influencing municipal and federal governments to implement textile diversion programs to reduce waste and contribute to environmental initiatives is an urgent need in today's society. Given this urgency and importance, all the successful initiatives mentioned above in the textile diversion industry sector should be celebrated. At the same time, there is a need to increase public awareness that this sector features a great opportunity for growth, including opportunities for job development, market development, and economic growth. It will be a quick win for any municipal and federal government if they seize this opportunity and invest in further development of the

industry. Innovation in the area of recycling and diversion programs, as has been required for some other forms of wasted materials (e.g., batteries or tires), must be carried out in the textile waste sector as well.

## Packaging Waste

Apart from the textile waste that the fashion industry generates each year, discarded packaging represents another problematic waste generation area in the local municipalities. According to the EPA 2018 report, in the United States, packaging accounted for 82.2 million tons of generated waste or 28.1 percent of total solid waste generation in the same year. In the same year, according to Eurostat's estimates, the total amount of packaging waste generated in Europe was 77.7 million tons. Of that amount, 14.8 million tons included plastic packaging.

As reported by Jestratijevic et al., "Conventional packaging materials used for apparel and footwear wrapping, protection, and shipping come largely from petrochemical-based sources, which are not eco-friendly or biodegradable. This means that when one shopping bag is discarded directly into the natural environment, the plastic materials contained may persist for hundreds of years in the natural environment while releasing greenhouse gasses and contaminating soil, air, and water." Consequently, single-use plastic packaging is one of the greatest environmental threats worldwide. On the positive side, efforts to reduce packaging waste are emerging. Australia and Canada significantly advanced sustainable packaging, while the United States and Europe have committed to ban single-use plastic bags. In the retail sector worldwide, companies are committed to reduce packaging size and weight, reduce or limit plastic content, and increase packaging recyclability and/or the decomposability of the packaging components.[99]

## Sustainable Packaging Solutions in Use among Fashion Brands

Although some innovative packaging solutions are already available consumers, admit that they lack a general understanding of technical jargon used to promote sustainable packaging solutions since various terms (such as natural, compostable, recyclable, biodegradable, green, eco, organic, etc.) are used interchangeably.[100] Consequently, even in the cases in which improved sustainable packaging solutions exist for fashion products of consumers choice, consumers opt for conventional packaging because the benefits of sustainable packaging are not clearly communicated, nor are they well understood. If the sustainable packaging solutions were adequately promoted among the leading fashion brands, sustainable packaging would be substituted for conventional packaging faster.

While researching sustainable packaging in the fashion industry extensively in the recent past, I became familiar with initiatives created by the Responsible Packaging Movement (RPM), and I will briefly describe them here. RPM represents a collaborative network among sustainability-oriented fashion brands that are committed to sharing sustainable packaging learnings. The RPM initiative was launched by the fashion brand prAna, with the following sustainable packaging goals that RPM members target:

1. *Ban and exclude plastic packaging.* RPM members argue that all plastics from the packaging must be eliminated, "including bio-based plastics, compostable plastics, and plastics with additives, as all these 'alternative' options to petroleum plastic do not solve the problems created by the plastic."[101]

2. *Source natural fibers responsibly.* Even when brands decide to go plastic-free, it is not enough unless they carefully "consider the source of their natural fiber alternatives." As stated by the RPM members, brands that do not consider the source of their natural fiber alternatives "can unintentionally create more environmental damage" than benefits. According to Canopy, an award-winning environmental not-for-profit organization, when businesses are improving their packaging, the following hierarchy of sources should be considered in order from the "most to the least preferred: post-consumer waste; post-industrial waste; agricultural residue fibers; Forest Stewardship Council (FSC) certified and free of Endangered and High Conservation Value Forest Fiber."[102]

Now, the first question is, What does RPM consider to be plastic free packaging? Just as there is much debate about the preferred definition for *sustainable*, there is no standardized definition of plastic-free. EcoEnclose, a well-established ecommerce sustainable packaging supplier, has explored the plastic-free concept deeply and developed following definition of plastic-free: "plastic-free packaging is packaging that does not contain ANY form of plastic, which means that even if the packaging itself is plastic-free but still contains synthetics and polymers in the forms of the glue that holds box together, or silicone strips that close and seal mailers," packaging cannot be considered plastic-free. For this reason, when brands promote plastic free packaging, it is also necessary to disclose if and how they are ensuring that all adhesives are plastic free.[103]

The second question is, What does RPM consider to be a responsible source of natural fiber? For example, in their guide to environmentally responsible paper, Canopy provided the following instructions for responsibly sourced paper:

**Table 17**  Instructions for responsibly sourced paper according to Canopy*

| Type of Paper | Requirements |
|---|---|
| Environmentally inferior paper | Has no environmental attributes<br>Meets no minimum criteria<br>Has no or minimal recycled content<br>Virgin tree fibers without FSC certification that may be sourced from protected and endangered forests |
| Environmentally improved paper | At least 50% of fiber has environmental attributes, meaning it meets the following minimum criteria:<br>– Minimum 30% consumer recycled content.<br>– FSC certification required on papers with virgin tree content |
| Environmentally superior paper | All fiber (100%) has environmental attributes meaning it meets the following criteria at minimum:<br>– Minimum 50% consumer recycled content.<br>– Virgin tree paper cannot contain wood from protected and endangered forests.<br>– Must be processed chlorine free or totally chlorine free |

*This table is adapted from "The Paper Steps," *Canopy*, 2021, https://canopyplanet.org/resources/the-paper-steps/.

In table 18 I will review sustainable packaging solutions used by fashion brands to showcase some efficient examples of improved packaging in the fashion industry.

**Table 18** Highlights of the innovative packaging solutions used among fashion brands

| Brand | Innovative Packaging Solution |
|---|---|
| A Woven Plane | Paper mailers made from post-consumed coffee cup waste |
| Afends | Renewable, compostable, custom cornstarch courier satchel bags |
| Corkor | Paper bags sewn to avoid using glue or plastic tapes |
| Elvis & Kreese | Packaging made from reclaimed materials, including rescued parachute nylon, rescued tea sacks, and recycled cardboard |
| Monday's Child | Recycled cardboard shoes boxes that can transform into a doll house, which gives them a fun new practical purpose |
| Nu-In | "Exact composition of the box and certification of the paper: Exterior paper FSC Kraft liner 115 g/m² + Wave B recycled strong FSC paper 115 g/m² + Interior Paper FSC Kraft liner 110 g/m²"[104] |
| Panagia | TIPA compostable packaging |
| Zara | Boxes with a Past art projects |
| Isla in Bloom | Compostable and biodegradable mailers made from corn-starch and cassava root |
| Aardes | Packaging boxes "made from recycled cardboard and printed with water-based inks. Garment wrapped in recycled tissue paper and sealed with an FSC certified paper sticker, printed with soy ink. Paper tape to seal the package biodegradable. Garment swing tags made from recycled cotton t-shirt offcuts"[105] |

Moving forward, I believe that fashion retailers will continue to innovate, providing newer packaging formats. In a recent sustainable packaging report published by McKinsey, an international pool of consumers was surveyed on their perceptions about the importance of sustainability in packaging. The results showed that a majority of international consumers said they would pay more for sustainable packaging. The highest willingness to pay more for sustainable packaging was in China (86 percent of consumers said they were willing to pay a lot or a bit more), followed by Indonesia (75 percent), the US (68 percent), and Brazil (66 percent). In Japan and France, the percentage of consumers willing to pay more for sustainable packaging was somewhat lower at 48 percent of consumers in both cases. Additionally, the survey showed that better labeling on the packaging is needed, clearly explaining all the sustainable attributes of the package and its full content (100 percent). Given the availability of such packaging, these attributes would encourage at least 23 to 61 percent of consumers surveyed to buy it as opposed to conventional packaging.[106] Taking all these findings into account, we can conclude that sustainable packaging represents a strong value proposition for packaging suppliers.

## Case study 8: Circular solutions for sustainable businesses

*Chicfashic fashion startup.* Fabiola Polli, a former postdoc researcher at the University of Groningen (the Netherlands), is an LCA trainer and course creator for Climate Impact Forecast and winner of two MIT Dutch grants that she used to pursue her research on textile fibers. She is also the founder of two start-ups: Chicfashic,[107] a sustainable fashion start-up, and BioFashionTech, a biotech startup that transforms textile waste into valuable new raw material; it also upcycles plastics fibers and dyes that are usually blended in the textile.[108] Chicfashic is a unique blend of education, shopping, and community that creates a circular economy by turning unused resources into community assets instead of designing them to become waste. "It makes use of an online platform to educate people about the significance of second-hand fashion in combating climate change and the adverse impacts of the fast fashion industry. Additionally, the platform allows people to rent, swap, or sell or buy clothes locally and directly from other individuals, making shopping cheaper than it has ever been since it avoids the many conventional layers of packaging that create masses of waste and consume many resources and removes emissions from packaging and shipping."[109] Furthermore, the Chicfashic community helps people to meet new, like-minded friends and to spread awareness of environmental justice and sustainability. For example, while traveling people can rent clothes and accessories from other individuals around the planet. This is very convenient because it minimizes people's impact when traveling as they no longer need to transport everything. Chicfashic's educational programs range from sewing workshops to coaching on how to recycle and reduce waste. Chicfashic works with more than twenty international organizations such as the University of Manchester, UNICEF, Erasmus Student Network, Sand BikeRacer Amsterdam, and the Global Slow Fashion Movement. Chicfashic's long-term goal is to change how people consume clothing by creating an educational dialogue on fast fashion issues and circular fashion benefits.[110]

*Renew by Eileen Fisher.* Eileen Fisher is a pioneer in reselling its own used designs. Their program Taking Back started in 2009, when the company "established a program to take back old clothes from customers and refurbish and resell them or to convert them into other products such as pillows."[111] With time this take-back and resale program became more popular, and the Eileen Fisher team decided to rebrand it as Renew. The concept is simple: supply relies completely on what customers send back to the company. "Customers are invited to return a pre-owned Eileen Fisher garment to any Eileen Fisher or Renew retail store, or alternatively they can send the garments via post. In return, they are awarded a $5 reward card for each item." The company stated that since the project initiation in 2009, "the company had received 1.5 million garment pieces from its customers. Garments that are brought to a physical store are bagged and shipped to the recycling center, where a team of specialists sorts them by condition. Garments ready to be resold are machine-washed or professionally dry-cleaned with environmentally responsible cleaning processes."[112] The company also used external assessment services from the NYU Stern CSB team called return of sustainability investment, known also as the ROSI methodology.[113] ROSI is used to help companies and investors bridge the gap between sustainability commitments and strategies and actual financial performance. Using the ROSI methodology, they calculated the money invested in running this program and "four benefit categories which included 1) the Renew profit that is generated for Eileen Fisher, 2) earned media generated due to increased visibility from the Renew program, 3) the incremental profit generated for the brand due to Renew customers' buying additional parent company products and 4) reductions in customer acquisition costs due to attracting new customers." Because the company

> incentivizes customers to participate in the Renew program, one $5 gift card is provided per garment. If the customer returns a garment by mail, the cost of shipping to warehouses is paid by the customer. However, shipping costs rose as sellable items were sent from the recycling locations to stores. For clothing items not in sellable condition, Eileen Fisher incurred costs to discard or to shred the fabric into fibers for recycling. For garments in sellable condition, there were costs associated with refurbishment such as overdyeing or resewing. Other costs included downstream operating costs to prepare the garment to be resold in-store.[115]

As a result of ROSI assessment, findings showed that $1.8 million was earned in 2019, which was considered as Renew profit. Additionally, another benefit was "earned media generated due to increased visibility from the renew program," which included approximately $391,406 of avoided cost of earned media. Another benefit was a new customer base, which means that the Renew program attracted new customers that were not previously shopping for Eileen Fisher products. In the conclusion, the company stated that they have tangible evidence that the Renew circular apparel program generated a total net benefit of $1.8 million in 2019; the Eileen Fisher company team attests that their circularity program provided both environmental and financial benefits.[116]

**Student Activity:** Explore circular solutions for used textiles in the fashion industry. Discuss with your peers which circular strategies (e.g., recycling, resale, reuse, repurposing) fashion brands commonly implement and why.

## Sustainability Expert Profile: Dr. Jana Hawley

*Building a career focused on the three legs of sustainability.* Dr. Jana Hawley serves as dean and professor at the University of North Texas. Previously, she was director of the Norton School of Family and Consumer Sciences at the University of Arizona, chair at the University of Missouri and Kansas State University, and faculty at Mizzou, the University of North Texas, and Indiana University. As a PhD student at the University of Missouri, she fell in love with qualitative research methods and conducted a year-long study of the business practices of the Old Order Amish. She and her two sons lived, worked, and played among the Amish of Jamesport, Missouri, while she collected data. That experience led her into a career of research that focuses on using observations to answer research questions rather than testing hypotheses. As her preferred method of research, Dr. Hawley enjoys the process of deep questions that help us understand human behavior and believes that stories give life to data, and data gives authority to stories. Dr. Hawley sees research as an endless discovery and expression of true behavior. In other words, her research allows her to understand the world from others' points of view.

As an assistant professor at the University of North Texas in the late 1990s, Dr. Hawley searched for a topic that could deliver personal meaning to her. Rather than studying why and what people buy, she started to explore how and why people discard. That led to a career of research focused on sustainability. Her most cited article is "Digging for Diamonds," published in 2006 in the *Clothing and Textiles Research Journal*.[117] She has also published numerous other articles and book chapters on the topic. She takes a holistic approach to the subject of textile and apparel recycling, with the hopes that consumers will learn more about how and why we should not put our old clothing in landfills. Instead of putting clothes in the trash, Dr. Hawley encourages everyone to take their clothes, no matter the condition, to their favorite charity. An international network of recycling partners works with each other to help move used clothing from their closets to the appropriate next stage, whether that be charity shops, exportation of used clothing, wiper rags, or insulation for houses and automobiles. When Dr. Hawley gives talks about textile and clothing recycling, she encourages consumers to recycle everything. She reports that even underwear has a place in the recycling pipeline and suggests that underwear be bagged separately from other donations. Shoes should be kept in pairs by tying laces together or putting rubber bands around them. Once shoes are separated at recycling houses, it is nearly impossible for mates to be put together again. Even clothing that is torn, missing a button, or stained has a place in the pipeline, although it will likely end up as housing insulation or as part of soil erosion materials.

Dr. Hawley's work in recycling has included serving as a consultant for many companies and on the board of directors for the Council of Recycled Textiles. As one of the first researchers in the United States to conduct research on textile recycling and apparel sustainability, she is delighted that many other scholars are now conducting research on sustainable practices, all leading to a significant body of literature on the topic.

In more recent years, Dr. Hawley has changed the focus of her research to the sustainability of communities and traditional craft through the development of a global marketplace for folk artisans. In 2021 she completed her ninth year as a volunteer for the International Folk Art Market (IFAM) in Santa Fe, New Mexico. "IFAM was launched in 2004 as a way to share and celebrate traditional crafts of the world. When the market first started, the intent was to preserve traditional crafts, have an impact, and support social change. While some of the artists are time-honored traditional masters of their craft, others are young creators reinterpreting the tradition" with fresh ideas.[118] As IFAM states, "IFAM envisions a world that values the dignity and humanity of the handmade, honors timeless cultural traditions, and supports the work of artists serving as entrepreneurs and catalysts for positive social change."[119]

Today, IFAM celebrates artisans and helps build sustainable communities that are supporting families, villages, or cultures. Even in 2021, with COVID-19 still looming, more than 115 artisans were represented and more than 9,000 people from all over the country attended the festival market. The market brought in more than $2.2M in proceeds, with most of the money returning to the artisans' communities.[120] Stories abound of artisans who have been able to establish schools for girls, clean water systems, and employment for many of the community members.

In 2021 Women Weave, a charitable trust located in the state of Maheswar, India, was juried into IFAM for the first time. This global not-for-profit group assists handloom weavers to create innovative designs on their looms. Dr. Hawley and Dr. Nancy Rutherford were artisan partners for Women Weave because the weavers themselves could not come to the United States due to the pandemic. The woven scarves and shawls were held up in customs, and after arriving a day late, they still sold out in two days, earning nearly $10,000 for the cooperative. Not only does the market provide a global marketplace for artisans, giving the cooperatives, communities, and families economic viability, but it also assures that the handloom tradition is valued and thus will be sustained into the future.

Another group that Dr. Hawley has worked closely with is Multicolores of Guatemala. This group has also gained economic viability and sustainability from the sales of their latch-hook rugs at IFAM. Multicolores was founded in 2006 by a team of four women who had a passion for textiles and supporting economic development.[121] From the onset founders hoped to offer holistic support to the artisans and their communities. The average annual salary for a Guatemalan woman is about $12,000. In 2010, when cotton prices soared, Guatemalan weavers could not afford the cotton warp yarns for their backstrap weaving. A grant was obtained so that each woman had fifty dollars to buy colorful T-shirts at the local *pacas*, or used clothing stores. *Pacas* are recipients of clothing exported from the United States. The women bought colorful used T-shirts and were taught how to make latch hook rugs with strips of the shirts. They were encouraged to continue creating traditional designs inspired by their environment. The first year that Multicolores was in the marketplace, they sold $60,000 in rugs in two and a half days of the market.[122] This substantial amount is life changing for women in rural Guatemala. Guatemala experienced a civil war between 1960 and 1996, leaving many women as sole providers for their families because they have lost their husbands and sons to the war. In addition, the success of the rug project has increased the number of women in the Multicolores cooperative exponentially, contributing to economic impact. Not only has the Multicolores project helped sustain communities and traditional crafts, it has also created a new use for old T-shirts.

Dr. Hawley's volunteer work at IFAM extends to artists from Uzbekistan, Peru, India, Mexico, Guatemala, Kyrgyzstan, Niger, and Afghanistan. Each artisan group has been able to grow the economic viability of their communities and at the same time sustain the folk-art traditions. She finds this work to be rewarding and has published several articles and chapters on immersive participant observation research. For example, see her article in the journal of *Fashion Style & Popular Culture*, coauthored with Judy Frate.[123]

Dr. Hawley believes strongly that we all gain when we look at the world through a sustainability lens and embrace citizens and cultures different from our own. She has led study groups to India, Guatemala, Mexico, Peru, Turkey, Europe, Uzbekistan, and South Korea. As she says, "When people are exposed to the world, they develop a global view that allows them to accept new things."[124] Her work sustains her, and she hopes it can sustain you, too.

## Chapter Summary

This chapter discusses the applications of the circular economy principles (such as cradle-to-cradle, recycling, reusing, upcycling, repurposing, composting, etc.) within wasteful and linear fashion industry systems (with a take-make-trash mindset). In this chapter we discussed sustainability problems related to overconsumption processes and how textile, apparel, and packaging waste generation in the fashion industry impact the environment and human well-being. Special focus was placed on textile waste by explaining why, in the context of a circular economy, it must be considered as a valuable resource for the next production cycle. This chapter overviews the issues related to packaging waste by identifying sustainable packaging solutions already in use among international fashion brands. Case studies on circular solutions for sustainable businesses reviewed how discarded textiles can be reused through innovative business examples such as the Chicfashic fashion startup, which transforms textile waste into value new raw material, and Renew by Eileen Fisher, which takes back old clothes from customers and refurbishes and resells them in their store. The sustainability expert profile in this chapter centers on Dr. Jana Hawley (dean of the College of Merchandising, Hospitality, and Tourism, University of North Texas), who pioneered research on clothing and textile recycling.

# References

1. Kate Fletcher, *Sustainable Fashion and Textiles: Design Journeys* (London: Routledge, 2013)., 76.
2. Ibid.
3. Ellen MacArthur, "Towards the Circular Economy," *Journal of Industrial Ecology* 2, no. 1 (2013): 23–44.
4. Ellen MacArthur Foundation, *Towards the Circular Economy*, accessed on June 15, 2023, https://www.werktrends.nl/app/uploads/2015/06/Rapport_McKinsey-Towards_A_Circular_Economy.pdf.
5. Ana Brismar, "What Is Circular Fashion?," 2017, accessed on May 20, 2022, https://greenstrategy.se/circular-fashion-definition/.
6. Iva Jestratijevic and Nancy A. Rudd, "Six Forms of Sustainable Fashion," *Latest Trends in Textile and Fashion Designing* 2, no. 4 (Aug. 2018): 220–22, http://dx.doi.org/10.32474/LTTFD.2018.02.000145.
7. Brismar, "What Is Circular Fashion?"
8. Jonathan Chapman, *Emotionally Durable Design: Objects, Experiences and Empathy* (London: Routledge, 2012).
9. Isobella Wolfe, "Made-By Environmental Benchmark for Fibres," *Good on You*, June 17, 2020, https://goodonyou.eco/made-by-environmental-benchmark-for-fibres/.
10. "Waterless Jeans," *Levi's*, accessed on June 29, 2022, https://www.levi.com/US/en_US/blog/article/how-we-make-jeans-with-less-water/.
11. William McDonough and Michael Braungart, "Design for the Triple Top Line: New Tools for Sustainable Commerce," *Corporate Environmental Strategy* 9, no. 3 (2002): 251–58.
12. Fletcher, *Sustainable Fashion and Textiles.*
13. McDonough and Braungart, "Design for the Triple Top Line."

14. Jana M. Hawley, "Textile Recycling: A Systems Perspective," in *Recycling in Textiles*, ed. Youjiang Wang (Manchester, UK: Woodhead, 2006).

15. Fletcher, *Sustainable Fashion and Textiles*.

16. A. Khatri and M. White, "Sustainable Dyeing Technologies," in *Sustainable Apparel: Production, Processing, and Recycling*, ed. R. S. Blackburn (Manchester, UK: Woodhead, 2015), 135–60.

17. Fletcher, *Sustainable Fashion and Textiles*.

18. "Product as a Service," M*ud Jeans*, accessed on June 13, 2022, https://mudjeans.eu/pages/lease-a-jeans.

19. Irene Maldini, Laura Duncker, Lidian Bregman, Gunilla Piltz, Lisa Duscha, Gwen Cunningham, Marc Vooges, Theresia Grevinga, Rens Tap, and Fioen van Balgooi, *Measuring the Dutch Clothing Mountain: Data for Sustainability-Oriented Studies and Actions in the Apparel Sector*, 2017, https://dataaccess.saxion.nl/resolver/getfile/EA10D5A3-B490-43EE-87E4F21472E296A9.

20. Levi's, *Life Cycle Assessment*, 2015, accessed on June 20, 2022, https://www.levistrauss.com/wp-content/uploads/2015/03/Full-LCA-Results-Deck-FINAL.pdf.

21. Iva Jestratijevic, Irina Maystorovich, and Urška Vrabič-Brodnjak, "The 7 Rs Sustainable Packaging Framework: Systematic Review of Sustainable Packaging Solutions in the Apparel and Footwear Industry," *Sustainable Production and Consumption* 30 (2022): 331

22. Ibid, 337.

23. Hawley, "Textile recycling."

24. Fletcher, *Sustainable Fashion and Textiles*.

25. T. Karthik and D. Gopalakrishnan, "Environmental Analysis of Textile Value Chain: An Overview," *Roadmap to Sustainable Textiles and Clothing: Environmental and Social Aspects of Textiles and Clothing Supply Chain* (2014): 158.

26. Ibid, 159.

27. Ibid, 161.

28. "Organic Cotton Plus," *Organic Cotton Plus*, accessed June 10, 2023, https://organiccottonplus.com/pages/learning-center.

29. Ibid.

30. Ibid.

31. Ibid.

32. Ibid.

33. "Sustainability", Tencel, accessed June 10, 2023, https://www.tencel.com/sustainability.

34. Karthik and Gopalakrishnan, "Environmental Analysis of Textile Value Chain."

35. Ibid.

36. Ibid.

37. Ibid.

38. Subramanian Muthu, *Textiles and clothing sustainability: Recycled and Upcycled Textiles and Fashion* (Singapore: Springer, 2017).

39. "Solid Waste and Hazardous Waste Exclusions," *EPA*, accessed on June 12, 2023, https://www.epa.gov/hw/criteria-definition-solid-waste-and-solid-and-hazardous-waste-exclusions#tablesw.

40. Subramanian, *Textiles and Clothing Sustainability*.

41. Evan, McCauley and Iva Jestratijevic, "Exploring the Business Case for Textile-to-Textile Recycling Using Post-Consumer Waste in the US: Challenges and Opportunities," *Sustainability* 15, no. 2 (2023): 1473.

42. Subramanian, *Textiles and Clothing Sustainability*.

43. McCauley and Jestratijevic, "Exploring the Business Case for Textile-to-Textile Recycling."

44. Subramanian, *Textiles and Clothing Sustainability*.

45. Ibid.

46. Ibid, 92.

47. Ibid.

48. "In Latin America and the Caribbean, the Closure of Aging Dumps Is Helping to Clear the Air," *UNEP*, September 7, 2020, https://www.unep.org/news-and-stories/story/latin-america-and-caribbean-closure-ageing-dumps-helping-clear-air.

49. "A New Textile Economy," *Ellen MacArthur Foundation*, accessed on June 10, 2023, https://ellenmacarthurfoundation.org/a-new-textiles-economy.

50. "Facts and Figures about Materials Waste and Recycling," *EPA*, accessed on August 1, 2023, https://www.epa.gov/facts-and-figures-about-materials-waste-and-recycling/nondurable-goods-product-specific-data#ClothingandFootwear.

51. NACTRS, *A Tipping Point: The Canadian Textile Diversion Industry: An In-Depth Look at the Current Industry and the Prospects for the Future*, 2019, accessed on June 10, 2023, https://nactr.ca/wp-content/uploads/2022/02/The-Canadian-Textile-Diversion-Industry-April-2019.pdf.

52. EPA, "Facts and Figures."

53. Ibid.

54. Ibid.

55. NACTRS, *Tipping Point*.

56. Ibid.

57. Ibid.

58. K. Vladimirova, Y. Samie, I. Maldini, S. Iran, K. Laitala, C. Henninger, S. Alosaimi, K. Drennan, A. Copeland, L. Lam, A. Teixeira, and I. Jestratijevic, "What If Export of Textile Waste Is Not an Option? Towards Sustainable Urban Textile Waste Management: Learnings from Nine Cities in OECD Countries," *Journal of Cleaner Production*, forthcoming.

59. McCauley and Jestratijevic, "Exploring the Business Case for Textile-to-Textile Recycling."

60. Ibid.

61. "Goodwill's History," *Goodwill*, accessed on June 28, 2023, https://www.goodwill.org/about-us/goodwills-history/.

62. NACTRS, *Tipping Point*.

63. "Salvation Army," *Forbes*, accessed on August 1, 2023, https://www.forbes.com/companies/salvation-army/?sh=5eb2ee4ccb57.

64. "ThredUP Resale Report," *ThredUP*, 2022, accessed on August 1, 2023, https://www.thredup.com/resale/2022/#size-and-impact.

65. NACTRS, *Tipping Point*.

66. Ibid, 16.

67. McCauley and Jestratijevic, "Exploring the Business Case for Textile-to-Textile Recycling."

68. NACTRS, *Tipping Point*.

69. McCauley and Jestratijevic, "Exploring the Business Case for Textile-to-Textile Recycling."

70. NACTRS, *Tipping Point*.

71. McCauley and Jestratijevic, "Exploring the Business Case for Textile-to-Textile Recycling."

72. NACTRS, *Tipping Point*.

73. Ibid.

74. McCauley and Jestratijevic, "Exploring the Business Case for Textile-to-Textile Recycling."

75. NACTRS, *Tipping Point*.

76. "Extended Producer Responsibility," *OECD*, accessed on June 10, 2023, https://www.oecd.org/environment/extended-producer-responsibility.htm.

77. NACTRS, *Tipping Point*.

78. Irene Maldini, Iran Samira, Kirsi Laitala, Gunnar Vittersø, Iva Jestratijevic, Amaral Mirena, and Katia Vladimirova, "Dress and the City: A Comparative Study of Clothing and Textiles Environmental Policy in Five European Cities," *Proceedings of the 20th European Roundtable in Sustainable Consumption and Production* (2021), accessed July 26, 2021, https://www.hva.nl/binaries/content/assets/subsites/kc-fdmci/fashion/measuring-the-dutch-clothing-mountain_final-report-1.pdf.

79. Ibid.

80. "Austin Resource Recovery's 2021 Annual Report," city of Austin, Texas, accessed on June 1, 2023, https://data.austintexas.gov/stories/s/sabp-xcz6.

81. "Circular Thrift," *Circular Thrift*, accessed on June 29, 2023, https://www.circularthrift.org/.

82. McCauley and Jestratijevic, "Exploring the Business Case for Textile-to-Textile Recycling."

83. Marisa Adler, *Textile Recovery in the US: A Roadmap to Circularity*, June 30, 2020, http://recycle.com/wp-content/uploads/2020/09/2020-Textile-White-Paper-sept-15-2020.pdf,

84. "Textile and Garment Recycling Facts and Figures," *Liveabout*, accessed on June 1, 2023, https://www.liveabout.com/textile-recycling-facts-and-figures-2878122.

85. Iva Jestratijevic and Julie L. Hillery, "Measuring the 'Clothing Mountain': Action, Research and Sustainability Pedagogy to Reframe (Un)sustainable Clothing Consumption in the Classroom," *Clothing and Textiles Research Journal* 41, no. 1 (2023): 10–25.

86. Liveabout, "Textile and Garment Recycling Facts and Figures."

87. NACTRS, *Tipping Point*.

88. "Fiber Recycling Uses Mechanical and Chemical Processes," *Cattermole Consulting*, accessed on May 10, 2023, https://www.cattermoleconsulting.com/fiber-recycling-using-mechanical-and-chemical-processes/.

89. Ibid.

90. Ibid.

91. "Impact," *Ohio Materials Marketplace,* accessed on May 10, 2023, https://ohio.materialsmarketplace.org/impact.

92. "Cost Savings," *Ohio Materials Marketplace,* accessed on May 10, 2023, https://ohio.materialsmarketplace.org/cost-savings.

93. "Austin Materials Marketplace," *Austin Materials Marketplace*, accessed on May 10, 2023, https://austinmaterialsmarketplace.org.

94. "Do Organic Leather Alternatives Have a Place in Fashion's Future?," *Luxiders,* accessed on August 1, 2023, https://luxiders.com/organic-leather/.

95. "Vegea," *Vegea*, accessed August 1, 2023, https://www.vegeacompany.com/.

96. Lydia Skrabania, "Vegea: Eco-Friendly Vegan Leather from Wine Industry Leftovers," Reset, May 21, 2018, https://en.reset.org/blog/vegea-eco-friendly-vegan-leather-wine-industry-leftovers-05212018.

97. Cat Cooper, "Bringing Fish Skin to Market as the Sustainable New Leather," UAL, March 30, 2020, https://www.arts.ac.uk/about-ual/press-office/stories/bringing-fish-skin-to-market-as-the-sustainable-new-leather.

98. "The R-Collective," Avery Dennison, accessed August 1, 2023, https://rbis.averydennison.com/en/home/our-solutions/apparel-and-footwear-branding/avery-dennisons-brand-partnerships-program_20/the-r-collective.html.

99. Jestratijevic, Maystorovich, and Vrabič-Brodnjak, "7 Rs Sustainable Packaging Framework."

100. Ibid.

101. "Responsible Packaging Movement," Prana, accessed August 1, 2023, https://www.prana.com/sustainability/responsible-packaging-movement.html.

102. "The Future of Sustainable Packaging and Shipping Supplies, Delivered," EcoEnclose, accessed August 1, 2023, https://www.ecoenclose.com/responsible-packaging-movement.

103. Ibid.

104. "Cardboard Boxes," *Nu-In*, accessed August 1, 2023, https://nu-in.com/pages/packaging?nopreview=.

105. "Responsibility," Aardes, accessed August 1, 2023, https://www.aardes.com/responsibility.

106. "Sustainability in Packaging: Inside the Minds of Global Consumers," McKinsey & Company, December 16, 2020 https://www.mckinsey.com/industries/paper-forest-products-and-packaging/our-insights/sustainability-in-packaging-inside-the-minds-of-global-consumers.

107. "Chicfashic: Stylish. Sustainable. Together," *Reflow*, accessed August 1, 2023, https://reflowproject.eu/best-practices/chicfashic-stylish-sustainable-together/.

108. "BioFashionTech," *BioFashionTech*, accessed August 1, 2023, https://biofashiontech.com/.

109. "About Us," *Chicfashic*, accessed August 1, 2023, https://chicfashic.com/about-us-3/.

110. Ibid.

111. Sophie Rifkin, Rithu Raman, Chana Rosenthal, and Christine Tan, *The Business Case for Sustainable Apparel at Eileen Fisher*, January 2021, https://www.stern.nyu.edu/sites/default/files/assets/documents/EILEEN%20FISHER%20Case.pdf.

112. Ibid.

113. "Return on Sustainability Investment (ROSI) Methodology," *NYU Stern*, accessed August 1, 2023, https://www.stern.nyu.edu/experience-stern/about/departments-centers-initiatives/centers-of-research/center-sustainable-business/research/return-sustainability-investment-rosi.

114. Rifkin, Raman, Rosenthal, and Tan, *Business Case for Sustainable Apparel at Eileen Fisher*.

115. Ibid.

116. Ibid.

117. Jana M. Hawley, "Digging for Diamonds: A Conceptual framework for Understanding Reclaimed Textile Products," *Clothing and Textiles Research Journal* 24, no. 3 (2006): 262–75, https://doi.org/10.1177/0887302X06294626.

118. Judy Frater and Jana M. Hawley, "A Hand-Crafted Slow Revolution: Co-Designing a New Genre in the Luxury World," *Fashion, Style & Popular Culture* 5, no. 3 (2018): 299–311.

119. "Our Mission," IFAM, accessed August 1, 2023, https://folkartmarket.org/our-mission.

120. IFAM Weekender. (July 21, 2023). An Update from IFAM.

121. "Multicolores," Multicolores, accessed August 1, 2023, http://multicolores.org

122. Dr. Jana Hawley's personal data collection from the folk market. Dr. Hawley has a long involvement with IFAM and Multicolores.

123. Frater and Hawley, "Hand-Crafted Slow Revolution."

124. Personal communication with Jana Hawley, January, 15, 2021.

# Chapter 5

# Sustainability Communication among Fashion Brands

## Chapter Introduction and Learning Objectives

In this chapter we will elaborate on how fashion businesses can manage economic and reputational risks by communicating their sustainability efforts. Although this chapter demonstrates that sustainability initiatives

179

bolster sustainability credentials, it also shows that communicating sustainability is not an easy task. There are various marketing ploys and greenwashing tactics in use, and thus when analyzing promotional tools used by fashion brands, we need to navigate through a myriad of green, natural, organic, and recycled options that all promise the same "sustainable" value. Thus, this chapter intends to equip readers with the knowledge and expertise in sustainable product and certification areas, helping readers not to fall into the fashion greenwashing trap. Contribution of the students in the Student Voices sections of this chapter is significantly important because in both the fashion transparency and Federal Trade Commission product recalls projects, students are positioned as storytellers and collaborators who advocate for sustainability-driven change in our industry.

This chapter has following learning objectives:

- Recognize the tools used by businesses to report sustainability efforts.
- Describe how sustainability credentials can help promote business sustainability.
- Explore why transparency in sustainability communication is critical to secure brand trust.
- Elaborate on the sustainable products and certifications currently offered.
- Analyze industry cases in order to learn how to recognize greenwashing tactics and traps.

**Key Terms**

| | |
|---|---|
| greenwashing | sustainability reporting |
| sustainability certificates | transparency |
| sustainable | triple bottom line |
| shareholders | stakeholders |

# Fashion Business and Sustainability Reporting

In 1994 the work of John Elkington manifested an early effort to codify the relationship of sustainability to business, meaning that businesses should make measurements, report them, and be held accountable to stakeholders for their performance in regard to their environmental and social impacts as well as their economic performance. To date, Elkington's triple bottom line has been well received as a framework that business can use in framing their sustainability agendas and in reporting results. His work has provided a significant boost to what has become an industry within an industry—the preparation of annual sustainability reports. Broadly speaking, we can say that the term "**sustainability reporting** refers to voluntary, non-financial public disclosure made by companies on the social and environmental impacts of their businesses."[1] As the content of such reports began to expand, many companies, in the full spirit of striving for sustainability, have moved them to a digital format. Investors are a prime audience for the reports of public and private investor-owned companies, as they contain information useful in gauging investment risk. Other audience groups include not only consumers and nongovernmental institutions but also early-career jobseekers interested in working for sustainably oriented businesses.

*The GRI reporting framework.* In the early years of sustainability reporting (the 1990s), every company that issued a sustainability report used its own format, and often the format changed from year to year. This made it difficult for stakeholders to track progress. The Global Reporting Initiative (GRI) was founded to bring more uniformity to sustainability reporting and today provides related services to reporting entities in over one hundred countries.

Founded by CERES (the organization we discussed in the previous chapter of this book) and the Tellus Institute in 1997, the GRI provides a framework for all organizations to report on a full range of impacts resulting from their operations.[2] Developed with the support of the UN, the GRI is closely linked to the UN Global Compact (UNGC), so users can easily use the GRI when filing their related Communication of Progress (COP) reports. With thousands of organizations reporting from more than one hundred countries, the GRI has become internationally recognized as the most widely used standard for disclosing sustainability performance. According to the GRI, 92 percent of the world's largest 250 corporations report on their sustainability performance, and 74 percent of them use the tool to do so.[3] An important aspect of the GRI system is placing sustainability performance in the context of how the organization contributes or plans to contribute in the future in each area of social, economic, and environmental sustainability. Many well-known fashion brands such as H&M and Nike use the GRI reporting framework. Such reporting is a transparent and credible way of enhancing brand trust and trustworthiness. Reporting is done using corporate websites or through integrated or independent sustainability reports, and companies are advised to report key performance indicators (or KPIs), which include, among other things, information about sourcing practice, energy and water usage, biodiversity, carbon emissions, waste and chemical management, innovation, and life cycle.[4]

> External drivers for sustainability reporting in the fashion industry come from various directions; they include new regulations, NGO pressures, and industry practices. In the United States, the California Transparency Supply Chain Act (CATSCA) requires retailers to trace their supply chain and to disclose on their website the efforts they make to eradicate human abuse in the production process. In the United Kingdom, the UK Modern Slavery Act was established for the same purpose. In the European Union, the REACH (Registration, Evaluation, Authorization and Restriction of Chemicals) Act was created to direct chemical management and information reporting and disclosure. Non-governmental associations also foster corporate disclosure. Clean Clothes, PETA (People for the Ethical Treatment of Animals), and Greenpeace are pressuring companies to improve the ethical treatment of workers, animals, and the environment and to report on the remediation processes they use to resolve these issues.[5]

*The UN Guiding Principles on Business and Human Rights Framework.* In addition to the GRI reporting framework, apparel brands frequently use the UN Guiding Principles on Business and Human Rights Framework.[6] The framework was developed in 2011 when the UN Human Rights Council introduced the Guiding Principles on Business and Human Rights to guide implementation of the UN's Protect, Respect, and Remedy Framework. The foundational principles for business enterprises include the responsibility to respect human rights as expressed in the Declaration on Fundamental Principles and Rights at Work, put forward by the ILO.

The foundational principles require companies to carry out due diligence on human rights, which includes assessing actual and potential human rights impacts, taking action upon making findings, and transparently communicating how impacts are addressed.

According to the UN Guiding Principles on Business and Human Rights Framework, apparel brands must identify "salient human rights" that are applicable to their own supply chain network, provide definitions and explain the relevance of the issues that are identified, and discuss remediation of the emerging issues.[7] Table 19 shows how some of those silent issues are defined and includes a brief recommendation for issue-reporting guidance.

**Table 19** Salient issues and reporting recommendations*

| Salient Issue | Definition | Reporting Recommendation |
|---|---|---|
| Fair Living Wage | "Everyone who works has the right to just and favorable remuneration ensuring for the self and the family an existence worthy of human dignity and supplemented, if necessary, by other means of social protection. Livable compensation is a comparison of the costs of living in a community/region with compensation levels. A typical US livable compensation measure is a wage rate per hour enough that one wage earner can afford a 2-bedroom apartment while paying no more than 30% of their gross income (before taxes) for total housing costs."[8] | "Fashion companies interested to report this issue must provide information, policies, and roadmaps to a living wage. Also, brands may want to consider joining a fair-trade initiative and commit to sustainable wage and fair labor conditions."[9] |

(*Continues*)

**Table 19** Continued

| Salient Issue | Definition | Reporting Recommendation |
|---|---|---|
| Health and Safety | "Facilities and working conditions that ensure the wellbeing and safety of workers, employees, and customers" is provided.[10] | This issue is of special concern in the fashion supply chain and its internal operations. Fashion producers should provide information on relevant policies (e.g., the Bangladesh Accord on fire safety, "the US Clean Air Act, the EU's REACH regulations, and Taiwan's Occupational Safety and Health Act all provide representative examples for the establishment and enforcement of standards related to public health."[11] |
| Forced and Child Labor | "Forced labor is any work or services which people are forced to do against their will under the threat of some form of punishment. Child labor is defined as work that deprives children of their childhood, their potential, and their dignity and that is harmful to their physical and mental development (UN CRC, CRBP, ILO Conventions). The problem occurs when children are directly or indirectly impacted by business activities throughout the production chain."[12] | A Ceres and Sustainalytics 2014 survey of 613 large US publicly traded companies found that only 31 percent have "formal policies or statements protecting the human rights of their direct employees," and only 13 percent mention both forced and child labor explicitly in their human rights policies or statements.[13] Fashion retailers must provide policies, regulations (e.g., CATSCA), and information on partnerships they have established in order to avoid having forced or child labor issues in their supply chain (e.g., joining the Better Cotton Initiative). Additionally, fashion retailers must define the minimal working age separately for each country in their supply chain (please note that the minimal age often varies among countries). |

*(Continues)*

**Table 19** Continued

| Salient Issue | Definition | Reporting Recommendation |
|---|---|---|
| Freedom of Association | A worker has the "right to join and/or form organizations of his/her own choosing and to bargain collectively (ILO Convention 87, 98, 135, 154)."[14] | Fashion retailers must report policies that support workers' rights to join or leave groups voluntarily, the right to pursue interest of association, and the right to accept or decline membership based on certain criteria. Corporate partnerships with ACT or ILO, for example, are preferable.[15] |
| Social security and well-being | Social security involves access to health care and income security, particularly in cases of old age, unemployment, sickness, invalidity, work injury, maternity, or loss of a main income earner.[16] | The issue is "the responsibility of the State as defined by the UN Guiding Principles, but it is relevant especially in supply chain countries and some retail markets where a lack of legal frameworks or institutional capacity sufficiently addressing this issue is common."[17] Fashion company outsourcing from the suppliers in the specific country should share the commitment in accordance with the regulation in the country of the producer and the specific regulations they have. Also, fashion companies must consider specific policies that apply to refugees and immigrant workers in the particular locality and in the region. |
| Working hours | "Working hours must comply with national law, ILO Conventions, or collective agreements, whichever affords the greater protection of the workers and their right to health and family life."[18] | Fashion companies must share adequate policies showing their commitment to prevent worker exploitation. Companies also need to show evidence of how regular working hours are inspected and ensured throughout the supply chain. |

*(Continues)*

**Table 19** Continued

| Salient Issue | Definition | Reporting Recommendation |
|---|---|---|
| Access to water | Access to water and a sufficient supply of water which is "accessible and affordable for personal and domestic use is needed in communities in the value chain in both production and retail markets."[19] | Fashion companies must disclose water safety policies and regulations related to water waste treatment and chemical management practices. |

*Please note that this list is not exhaustive. Each value chain has its own salient issues that deserve special attention. Most of the reporting definitions are adapted from H&M, "H&M Group Sustainability Report 2017," accessed July 29, 2023, https://about.hm.com/content/dam/hmgroup/groupsite/documents/masterlanguage/CSR/reports/HM_group_Sustainability Report_2017_FullReport.pdf.

Beside the GRI reporting framework and the UN Guiding Principles on Business and Human Rights framework, other reporting frameworks also exist. For example, "the Sustainability Accounting Standards Board (SASB), a non-profit organization founded in 2011, has developed sustainability accounting standards for 77 industries."[20] "The standards identify the subset of environmental, social, and governance (ESG) issues most relevant to financial performance in each industry."[21] Apparel, accessories, and footwear sustainability accounting standards can be downloaded from the official website of this organization.[22]

Lastly, the Sustainable Apparel Coalition has also developed "the Higg Index, a standardized value chain measurement suite of tools that help apparel, footwear, and textile industry brands measure and report their sustainability improvements across their value chain." To learn more about their standards, please visit the official website of the Sustainable Apparel Coalition.[23]

# Fashion Transparency Index and Transparency among Fashion Brands

"The journeys made by our clothes remain largely unseen. They may have started life in a field and then travelled across a vast network, in many countries, through the hands of hundreds of workers, working for dozens of different companies, before reaching our wardrobes." The fashion supply chain complexity was brought into question after the Rana Plaza factory collapse in Bangladesh (2013) when "major fashion brands could not determine whether they were sourcing from that particular factory despite their clothing labels' being found in the rubble."[24] Brands dismissed allegations of responsibility in the tragedy, transferring responsibility to their contractors. Likewise, brands claimed that they did not track their supply chains, meaning that they were not responsible for their supplier actions, or for their effects.[25] Something similar happened earlier in the fashion practice as well. For example, "In the 1990s, Nike's CEO dismissed sweatshop allegations at Nike's Indonesian factories, transferring responsibility to Nike's contractors."[26] "In 1996, Life magazine ran a report on child labor that included photos of a 12-year-old Pakistani boy sewing a Nike soccer ball. Nike has strongly denied such claims in the past, suggesting the company has little control over sub-contracted factories."[27] However, after facing a backlash, Nike has established long-term commitment to audit factories, and improve relationships with its suppliers. Also, as a result of its transparency commitments, Nike was the first apparel retailer to launch interactive supplier mapping systems on its official website, on which manufacturer information was publicly shared, "including the facility name, location, and subcontracting status for suppliers."[28]

Similarly, "In 2009, Anti-Slavery International (ASI) reported that Bangladesh Beximco Textiles, a major cotton supplier for famous fashion brands, had admitted that 45–50% of their raw cotton was imported from Uzbekistan, a country known for forced child labor. ASI urged international retailers to improve supplier tracing, preventing further human exploitation."[29] Soon after, international fashion retailers, including H&M and Adidas, among many others who sourced from Beximco Textiles, signed a global pledge to oppose child labor in Uzbekistan's cotton harvests and to commit to stopping sourcing from this country until the government of Uzbekistan ended the practice of forced child labor in its cotton sector.[30]

*Why is transparency important for sustainability and fashion leadership?* Transparency is one of the main prerequisites for ethical and sustainable business. "Increasing transparency through sustainability reporting encourages business scrutiny and also signals the readiness and openness of the business for further advancement. From that perspective, transparency in the fashion industry does not constitute the final business goal but rather represents a basic precondition for achieving systematic industry change."[31]

*The Fashion Transparency Index.* Since 2016 the Fashion Transparency Index has been launched annually to rank the global fashion brands according to the level of "information they have disclosed on their website(s), on their parent company website(s), or within annual/sustainability reports." Creation of this index helps to benchmark and track various levels of transparency across reporting areas. Reporting areas include following: "policies (referring to the social and environmental standards the business adheres to); governance (referring to the level of visibility of top management and the responsibility it holds); traceability (referring to the visibility of suppliers and production networks); audits (referring to the information on the producer's last audits, corrective plans, and remediations); and sustainability issues or negative impact reporting (covering mapping the social and environmental impacts of the business)."[32]

*Insights in the Fashion Transparency Index Rankings among mass market and luxury brands.* In 2020, I collaboratively published the study exploring Fashion Transparency Index data comparing transparency levels among 100 luxury and mass market fashion brands. We relied on raw Index data which included publicly shared information divided into the five above-mentioned areas. Our findings showed two main things. First, we discovered that there was an 80% chance that brands were scored higher in corporate policies than in any of the supply chain transparency areas (including traceability, audits, and sustainability issue reporting) which further means that fashion brands prioritized to publish corporate policies. Next, we found that the sub-sample of the mass-market brands ($n = 27$) had higher transparency scores compared to the sub-sample of luxury brands ($n = 13$), meaning that broadly speaking, transparency is higher among brands operating in the mass market sector than among the brands which constitute the luxury sector. We can assume that mass market brands are increasing transparency because mass-market brands are more often publicly scrutinized for supply chain exploration. However, we also need to acknowledge that the least transparent areas for both group of brands were traceability and sustainability issue reporting. This further raises important concerns: "Firstly, it suggests that companies have solid knowledge about their suppliers' production procedures and impacts, but due to reputation-associated risks, they intentionally avoid releasing such data. Secondly, the absence of such information might also suggest that the company does not yet have enough supply chain knowledge; thus, it is impossible for it to estimate supply chain impacts and to disclose those data" (please see the full paper if you are interested in learning more about this study's findings).[33]

## Fashion Brands' Strategies for Transparency in Sustainability Reporting

In 2021 I collaboratively published another study, titled "To Disclose or Not to Disclose? Fashion Brands' Strategies for Transparency in Sustainability Reporting" in an effort to explore possibility that fashion brands have strategic approaches to transparency. For this purpose the research team accessed Fashion Transparency Index data diachronically (using four indexes published between 2017 and 2020), analyzing scores across areas for ninety-eight fashion brands. Research findings confirmed that there are four strategic approaches to sustainability disclosure in the apparel sector, which we named measurable, ambiguous, policy only, and secretive strategy. Brands with an ambiguous strategy (n=56) created either wittingly or unwittingly distracting disclosures. This means that brands with this strategic approach (see the table 20) "often flood their sustainability reports and official websites with excessive levels of self-selected information that distract stakeholders from focusing on more questionable practices." For example, these brands do not update regularly information on their website and in their sustainability report, or they publicly share information, which is commonly outdated, incomplete, or obfuscated.[34]

**Table 20** Fashion brands with ambiguous reporting strategies*

| Ambiguous strategy (n = 56) | | |
|---|---|---|
| Victoria's Secret | George at ASDA | Gap |
| Zara | Forever 21 | Express |
| Urban Outfitters | Dior | Dillard's |
| Triumph | Columbia Sportwear | Coach |
| TJ Maxx | Claire's Accessories | Calzedonia |
| Saks Fifth Avenue | Burlington | Burberry |
| S. Oliver | Bershka | Banana Republic |
| Russel Athletic | Asos | Anthropologie |
| Puma | American Eagle | Chanel |
| Pull & Bear | Calvin Klein | Gildan |
| Primark | Lacoste | Levi's |
| Prada | Ralph Lauren | Target |
| Old Navy | Tesco | Tommy Hilfiger |
| Next | Uniqlo | Mango |
| Miu Miu | Giorgio Armani | Guess |
| Michael Kors | Hudson Bay | J. Crew |
| Massimo Dutti | JCPenney | Louis Vuitton |
| Macy's | Loft | L. L. Bean |
| Lands' End | Kohl's | |

* This table is adapted from I. Jestratijevic, J. O. Uanhoro, and R. Creighton, "To Disclose or Not to Disclose? Fashion Brands' Strategies for Transparency in Sustainability Reporting," *Journal of Fashion Marketing and Management: An International Journal* 26, no. 1 (2022): 36–50. Brands reported here had ambiguous strategy during investigated time period (2017–2020).

On the positive side, of ninety-eight explored brands, twenty-nine had a consistent progress toward greater transparency and improvement was "measurable" over the years (see table 21). "For example, after their inclusion in the Index (and concluding with 2020 when this research was executed), H&M, Adidas, C&A, and Esprit were among the highest-scoring brands across sustainability reporting areas. Information disclosure for these four brands increased by approximately 10% points annually, reflecting their continual dedication to improving transparency in the sustainability reporting areas."[35]

**Table 21**  Fashion brands with measurable reporting strategies*

| *Measurable strategy (n = 29)* | | |
|---|---|---|
| YSL | Zalando | Wrangler |
| Walmart | Under Armour | Timberland |
| The North Face | Reebok | New Look |
| New Balance | Monsoon | Matalan |
| Lululemon | Hanes | Hermes |
| Jack & Jones | Gucci | Champion |
| Esprit | C&A | Bottega Veneta |
| Adidas | Benetton | Asics |
| Amazon | Abercrombie and Fitch | Nordstrom |
| H&M | Marks & Spencer | |

* This table is adapted from Jestratijevic, Uanhoro, and Creighton, "To Disclose or Not to Disclose?" Brands reported here had ambiguous strategy during investigated time period (2017–2020).

Next, "of the 98 explored brands, 9 (see table 22) had focused almost exclusively on greater transparency of business-related policies, while supply chain reporting areas were largely ignored." For instance, these brands commonly publish corporate policies for worker safety but supply chain policies for worker safety are not published. "Because information in the cases of these brands is released in preferential order, it is impossible to know whether and how business policies are implemented in day-to-day supply chain operations."[36]

**Table 22**  Fashion brands with policy-only reporting strategies*

| *Policy-only Strategy (n = 9)* |
|---|
| Top Shop |
| Ross Stores |
| Hugo Boss |
| Jordan |
| Nike |
| Ermenegildo Zegna |
| Costco |
| Converse |
| Chico's |

* This table is adapted from Jestratijevic, Uanhoro, and Creighton, "To Disclose or Not to Disclose?" Brands reported here had ambiguous strategy during investigated time period (2017–2020).

Of the ninety-eight brands explored, four brands (Neiman Marcus, Mexx, Heilan Home, and Aeropostale) "had no commitment to transparency as their approach was secretive and they chose not to release sustainability information publicly." Because these brands do not disclose any business information it is not certain whether these brands have made any sustainability improvements.[37]

## Case study 9: Fashion Transparency Index

The Fashion Transparency Index, published by the nonprofit organization Fashion Revolution, annually ranks global fashion brands according to the level of transparency in the business information they publicly share within five sustainability reporting areas. The sustainability reporting areas, as reported in the index,[38] include the following:

- *Policy and commitment:* Information in this area covers corporate, social, and environmental policies, as well as supply chain polices. In addition, this area should contain information on how the retailer puts those policies into practice at both the corporate and the supply chain level.
- *Governance:* Information in this area should showcase who in the company is responsible for the sustainability management and policies implementation. Also, this area should contain information, names, and contact details for all senior executives at the company.
- *Traceability:* Information in this area should showcase if and in what detail the brand publishes a list of its suppliers, from final manufacturing and processing to the suppliers at the raw material level. Also, this area reveals how many details companies share about each supplier.
- *Know, show, fix (audits and remediation):* Information in this area should showcase whether supply chain policies are implemented in daily supply chain operations. This area should reveal how the brand fixes problems found in its supplier facilities. Also, it should showcase who is in charge of audits and how audits are conducted. If it does so, it should also reveal whether the brand reports assessment findings and the process of problem remediation.

- *Spotlight issues (negative impact reporting):* Information in this area should showcase what the brand is doing to identify, report, and improve salient social and environmental issues identified at the supply chain level. For example, it should showcase whether the garment workers are being paid a living wage and whether the company supports workers' freedom of association. Other examples may include information on how the company manages its production waste or what the brand is doing to reduce consumption of natural resources.

Students are required to download the FTI index for the desired year (preferably more recent editions) from the Fashion Revolution website. Then the student, individually or working in groups, should select one brand and extract transparency scores across all areas for the selected brand. For easier analysis, the scores extracted for the selected brand should be organized in a separate table (see the example in table 23).

**Table 23** Examples of fashion transparency index (FTI) scores for Chanel (2017)*

| *Brand Listed in FTI 2017* | *FTI Scores* |
| --- | --- |
| Chanel | Final Score: 1% |
| | Policies and Commitments: 3% |
| | Governance: 17% |
| | Traceability: 0% |
| | Know, Show, Fix or Audits: 0% |
| | Spotlight Issues: 0% |

*Scores displayed in the table are extracted from different score sections of the 2017 FTI: "Fashion Transparency Index 2017," *Fashion Revolution*, accessed June 20, 2022, https://issuu.com/fashionrevolution/docs/fr_fashiontransparencyindex2017.

Next, using ratings and FTI raw data provided by the INDEX for the selected brand and selected year, students should provide responses in the following three ways:

1. Students should compare the scores in the table and identify the strongest and the weakest areas for the selected brand.
2. Student should address area(s) that the selected brand needs to improve in order to become more transparent.

> 3. Students should describe why transparency is a precondition for responsible business communication.

## Student Voices: Fashion Transparency Index

In table 24 below, I provide some interesting insights in the representative parts of this case study that my students completed during a previous semester. I hope that their work will inspire others to investigate transparency issues in the fashion industry and to collectively support greater accountability among fashion brands.

**Table 24** Students' evaluations of fashion transparency index scores for selected brands*

| Adidas (FTI 2020) | Question 1) Results: (Student 1) Strongest area for Adidas: Policies (99%) |
|---|---|
| Within the Fashion Transparency agency under the policy and commitment results, Adidas scored in the top percentile with a score of 99%. The FTI measures policy and commitment scores by scoring over 20 areas of sustainability both socially and environmentally. I am going to list each area with its respective score. Each area is either scored half a point (0.5) or given a score of 0. The commitments and policies are scored on both the corporate and the supply chain level. I am starting with the analysis of policies at the corporate level. Adidas scored 0.5 in Animal welfare, 0.5 in annual-leave and public holidays, 0.5 in anti-bribery, corruption, and false information, 0.5 in biodiversity and conservation, 0.5 in community engagement, 0.5 in contracts and terms of employment, 0.5 in anti-discrimination, 0.5 in diversity and inclusion, 0.5 in energy and carbon emissions, 0.5 in equal pay, 0.5 in freedom of association, right to organize, and collective bargaining, 0.5 in harassment and violence, 0.5 in health and safety, 0.5 in maternity rights and parental leave, notice period, dismissal, and disciplinary action, 0.5 in the restricted substances list, 0.5 in wages and financial benefits, 0.5 in recycling and waste of packaging, 0.5 in recycling and waste of textile materials, 0.5 in water usage and footprint, and 0.5 in working hours and rest breaks. The company itself ended up with a perfect score of 10.5. The FTI also evaluates the vendors and suppliers with a few different requirements having to do with labor rights. Adidas suppliers and vendors received a score of 15, only losing half a point on community engagement. With all tiers being measured in a similar way, Adidas received an overall score 46.5 for policy and commitment (Fashion transparency index 2020). The scores really do align with Adidas' commitments on their website. ||

*(Continues)*

**Table 24**  Continued

| Brand **United Colors of Benetton** (FTI 2020) | Question 2) Results: (Student 2) Weakest area for United Colors of Benetton: Policies (20%) |
|---|---|

United Colors of Benetton had the lowest score of 20% in the spotlight issues category. This score weighed heavily on their overall score of a 55% and was 17% lower than their second lowest score of 37% in know, show, fix. While United Colors of Benetton scored higher than the industry average in this category, they did not outscore it by much (only by 5%). This category is the first and most pressing that United Colors of Benetton needs to improve in order to become more transparent and socially responsible. In reporting, the company breaks this category down into the four Cs of conditions, consumption, composition, and climate. These four Cs align with the United Nations Sustainable Development Goals. According to the Fashion Transparency Index, this category tasks companies to proactively tackle spot areas in their entire supply chain as they pertain to the aforementioned four Cs. The key word in the previous sentence is proactive. It is not enough to assume or hope that partners or third-party vendors are doing their part to develop and implement sustainable practices. United Colors of Benetton needs to proactively ensure all people and entities they do business with promote and adhere to transparent and sustainable practices. An area where they could improve in order to raise this score is ensuring that modern slavery is not being used by any entity in their supply chain. This pertains to the conditions portion of the four Cs. Another area in which they need to improve is the consumption portion of the four Cs. They can monitor how much waste is created and how much is recycled as opposed to simply reporting what has been discarded or destroyed. Furthermore, they need to increase the usage of sustainable materials in their production (pertaining to the Composition portion of the four Cs). Finally, they can improve in the climate portion of the four Cs. For example, they should disclose the carbon footprint created in their supply chain. Lastly, let me note that a researcher need only review the sustainability page on the United Colors of Benetton website. They state that they "ask our suppliers in Europe and around the world to agree to a Code of Conduct" (United Colors of Benetton Sustainability). This sounds as if it is a very good stance to take, and in a vacuum, it is; however, simply *asking* their suppliers in Europe to adhere to a Code of Conduct is not only extremely vague; simply *asking* does not press the issue enough with regard to the category of spotlighting issues when it comes to the four Cs and their alignment with the United Nations Sustainable Development Goals. This category needs much improvement by United Colors of Benetton if the company is to become more transparent and socially responsible.

*(Continues)*

**Table 24** Continued

| **Fashion Transparency Index, 2020** | Question 3). Student 3. Why is transparency a precondition for responsible business communication? |
|---|---|

Transparency should be at the forefront of retailers' business models as it helps them protect their workers as well as create trust with consumers. Since the disastrous Rana Plaza incident in 2013, there has been a call to retailers to expose more of what goes on behind the scenes of their brands' production and sourcing. Consumers should know where their products come from, how the workers are treated, and if the products are sustainably made. The Fashion Transparency Index shows that more often than not, most brands have a long way to go to become transparent. The disclosure of information to the public allows consumers to make educated purchase decisions. Unfortunately, even when brands do disclose information, it is typically hard to find or not detailed enough. In addition to helping consumers make informed purchase decisions, transparency also holds the brand accountable. There is no room to hide when everything is disclosed to the public. This keeps facilities' workers safe and well paid and in general puts human rights first. Brands like Patagonia and Warby Parker disclose detailed information on human rights and environmental risks. Patagonia discloses every aspect of the supply chain and has a section of their website dedicated to sharing such information. Warby Parker consistently posts updates on how they are improving supplier standards. When consumers learn from transparent brands, their eyes are opened to how other brands might not be as transparent. Part of transparency is answering consumer questions. In order to be transparent, brands must be prepared to answer the difficult questions from consumers on the behind-the-scenes of production. It is important that consumers know not only brand policies and standards but also how the brand is actually enforcing them in their facilities. Transparency has become a hot topic lately. Consumers have more desire than ever to support brands that produce ethical and sustainable products. Making information readily available and easy to locate on the website encourages more consumers to make better choices. Through the publication of real information and actual data, consumers are also able to understand whether the brand is greenwashing or is truly sustainable.

*Table quotes students' answers on the topics we have discussed in the following course: UNT 4560 Sustainable Strategies.

# Stand Earth: Fossil-Free Fashion Scorecards and Fashion Brand Rankings

Stand Earth (formerly ForestEthics) was founded in 2000 as an environmental organization whose goal was to transform corporate policy and governmental laws in order to protect endangered forests.[39] As a part of their activism, in 2020 Stand Earth published a report emphasizing the steps that the fashion industry must take to reduce their carbon footprint.[40] The report, titled *Fashion Forward: A Roadmap to Fossil-Free Fashion*, identifies five critical focus areas companies should tackle in their efforts to reduce carbon emissions:

1. "*Ambitious Commitments + Accountability Through Meaningful Transparency.*" In the report it is stated that fashion brands only in the recent past began reporting their climate pollution targets. "Starting with Levi's commitment in 2018, the move by global fashion brands to set supply chain climate pollution targets has represented a critical step forward. However, commitments must go hand-in-hand with regular and detailed reporting on the energy performance of suppliers and material inputs throughout the supply chain to drive a race to the top in decarbonizing the fashion sector and to prevent the greenwashing that has been far too commonplace in corporate sustainability reporting efforts."[41]

2. "*Renewable Energy at the Center of Supply Chain Decisions.*" The report also states that "companies that set a 100% renewable energy goal for their supply chains send a powerful signal to the market that preference will be given to suppliers and locations that can rely more heavily on renewable sources of electricity. However, unless brands are willing to retake ownership of key segments of production to regain greater control over energy inputs and performance, a new partnership between brands and suppliers is most urgently needed to drive the renewable energy transition."[42]

3. "*Renewable Energy Advocacy.*" The report further argues that "companies with strong climate and renewable energy commitments must also use their standing to put pressure on governments to help their suppliers build back green with policies that incentivize suppliers and their

customers to make the technology investments needed to decarbonize and compete in the global market. Corporate demand for renewable energy, when combined with government policy advocacy, has been shown to be a powerful driver not only for investing in renewable energy but increasingly also for requiring utilities to divest from fossil fuel based energy generation."[43]

4. *"Low Carbon and Long Lasting Materials."* "Polyester and other fossil fuel-based plastic materials have also become a key driver in the growth of the cheaper, shorter-lived clothing associated with the fast fashion business model that has emerged over the past decade, fueling higher rates of consumption and higher emissions. By moving to lower-carbon materials and by steadily phasing out the use of virgin fossil fuel based plastic fabrics and shifting instead to a circular production model that involves long-lasting fabrics made from recyclable materials, the fashion sector can dramatically reduce emissions and its reliance on fossil fuels."[44]

5. *"Greener Shipping."* "As one of the largest customers of both ocean and air freight, fashion and apparel brands have an opportunity to serve as critical catalysts in reducing emissions from air freight and to drive the investment needed in both ships and port infrastructure to decarbonize cargo vessels by the end of the decade. Several global brands have begun to take pilot approaches to reducing their shipping footprint, but much stronger demand for decarbonization, along with near-term demands requiring the elimination of the use of toxic heavy fuel oil by cargo ship fleet operators serving major fashion brands, could help trigger much-needed investment in zero-emission ocean freight."[45]

In conclusion, as suggested in *Fashion Forward: A Roadmap to Fossil-Free Fashion Report*, fashion brands committed to reducing and eliminating fossil fuels from their supply chain are required to transition to renewables; source lower-carbon materials; eliminate plastics, which originate from fossil fuels (such as polyester); and invest in green shipping. The report also advises fashion brands to avoid "greenwashing initiatives like renewable energy credits and carbon offsets; but also supporting false 'clean' energy transitions from coal to fracked gas or from coal to biomass; and they should avoid increasing the amount of materials sourced from fossil fuels like fracked gas and coal."[46]

In the summer of 2021, during the pandemic, Stand Earth released another Fossil-Free Fashion report, titled the "Fossil-Free Fashion Score-card Report," which assessed forty-seven fashion brands that are committed to eliminating fossil fuels from their operations. Those brands are "Adidas, ALDO, Allbirds, American Eagle Outfitters, Arc'teryx, Armani, Asics, Boohoo, Burberry, C&A, Capri Holdings, Chanel, Columbia, Eileen Fisher, Esprit, Everlane, Gant, Gap, Guess, H&M, Hugo Boss, Inditex, Kering, Levi's, Lululemon, LVMH, M&S, Mammut, MEC, New Balance, Nike, On Running, Patagonia, Pentland, Prada, Primark, PUMA, PVH, Ralph Lauren, REI, Salomon, Salvatore Ferragamo, SKFK, Under Armour, UNIQLO, VAUDE Sports, and VF Corp."[47]

The scorecard report assessed the performance of global fashion brands across the five areas elaborated in Stand Earth's 2020 Roadmap. Here I will briefly review the results:

1. "*Climate commitments*: Companies are failing to set strong enough climate targets, putting the industry on a trajectory far surpassing the 1.5C pathway recommended by the U.N. Paris Agreement. Only three of the companies assessed—Asics, Mammut, and REI—have committed to slashing absolute emissions across the supply chain by 55% or greater by 2030 (the goal recommended by the U.N.)."[48]

2. "*Renewables in manufacturing*: The industry continues to rely heavily on coal to power its manufacturing processes, contributing to rising climate emissions and air pollution in countries like Vietnam and Bangladesh. Few companies reported taking meaningful steps toward financial incentives or direct investments encouraging suppliers to purchase renewable energy, but seven of the companies assessed—Mammut, Nike, Asics, Levi's, Adidas, Esprit, and PUMA—ranked highly in this area for setting renewable energy targets in their supply chains or working with manufacturing partners to phase out coal-fired boilers. A broad range of companies loudly tout efforts to deploy renewable energy in their head-quarters and stores, but these decarbonization efforts would cancel only a small percentage of their climate pollution."[49]

3. "*Renewables advocacy*: Companies are not doing enough to seek better access to renewables from governments in the countries where their

factories are located. Despite this lack of progress, advocacy opposing new investment in coal-fired electricity is an important bright spot, with several companies signing on to a letter to Cambodia cautioning against plans to increase coal-fired power and a letter to Vietnam seeking a pilot program for purchasing renewables. Notably, H&M, Levi's, and VF Corp signed both letters, contributing to their high ranking in this area."[50]

4. "*Low-carbon materials*: Many companies have recently announced 'sustainable material' commitments to phase out virgin polyester or other fossil fuel fabrics such as nylon but are doubling down on the use of fibers recycled from plastic waste, which prevents them from fulfilling any promises of circularity as these fibers are ultimately destined for the landfill. Several of the sportswear and fast fashion companies assessed—including Lululemon, Under Armour, Zara, and Uniqlo—will face major challenges in transitioning to the use of low-carbon materials since fossil fuel-derived fabrics like polyester make up a large proportion of their materials mix."[51]

5. "*Greener shipping*: The fashion industry is one of the largest customers of ocean and air shipping, which contributes to significant air pollution worldwide. With the industry's shipping needs expected to increase dramatically in the coming decades, it is imperative for companies to advocate for zero-emissions vessels and infrastructure. Fewer than half, only 20 companies assessed—including Adidas, Mammut, Nike, and PUMA—included shipping in their supply chain emissions reduction targets. Swiss outdoor gear brand Mammut set a new precedent in the sector by being the only company to commit to switching to the use of zero-emission shipping vessels by 2030."[52]

The results showed that following fashion brands are best performing across evaluated metrics: Mammut, Asics, Nike, PUMA, VF Corp, Adidas, Arc'teryx, Patagonia, Levi's and H&M. However, it is critical to mention that none of these companies scored higher than a B-.[53]

In conclusion, the report states that brands' commitments to reducing their carbon footprints are inconsistent with their practices. "Of the 47 companies evaluated in the Scorecard, only Asics, Mammut, and REI Co-op have made commitments to slash their GHG emissions across the value chain by at least half by 2030—by 63%, 55% and 55%, respectively. With the exception of Burberry (46%), Allbirds (42%), American Eagle Outfitters (40%), H&M (41%), and Levi's (40%), all other companies have either set supply chain emission reduction targets or 30% or lower or have committed to intensity-based targets that fall short of achieving the necessary 2030 reductions." In reality, we can see that fashion brands still rely on nonrenewable energy in their supply chain, despite their supply chains being responsible for 90 percent of GHG emissions. Moreover, fashion brands falsely promote becoming "carbon neutral" or "climate positive," as such marketing statements are often not backed up by strong emissions reduction or renewables targets. As a matter of fact, according to the report findings, in many cases, "these increasingly popular buzzwords provide a false impression about companies' decarbonization efforts." For example, "Gap has set a target to become 'carbon neutral' by 2050; however, the company's absolute emissions reduction target of 30% by 2030 for its supply chain remains far below the trajectory it needs to set. Gap has also not set a renewable energy target for its manufacturing, which suggests that the company will likely rely on carbon offsets and unbundled renewable energy credits to claim credit toward achieving its climate goals." Similarly, "Ralph Lauren has committed to a 'net zero' target by 2040 by relying largely on 'carbon credits' and 'nature-based carbon removal' but has not set a renewable energy target for its manufacturing."[54] Likewise, H&M fashion brands heavily promoted their "climate positive" supply chain, but after facing public criticism the company announced that they are moving away from climate positive strategy "as it is vague and lacks scientific support." However, H&M stated that they are now committed to reach "net-zero" standard, which "focuses on reducing GHG emissions as much as possible before balancing out any emissions that cannot be avoided using permanent carbon dioxide removals."[55]

## Sustainable Products and Certifications

What makes a sustainable product? This is a question that many companies, consumers, and governments are asking. First, it must be admitted that creating a truly sustainable product with no impact is hardly possible, although some companies are seriously committed to improving the quality, durability, safety, and circularity of goods they are creating. Let me first clarify the main challenges in creating sustainable products. In our society, "The life cycle for most products is still linear, beginning with the design process and including the stages of raw material extraction, manufacturing, packaging/distribution, and consumption/use, and ending with disposal in a landfill or incinerator. At each stage there are material, energy, and labor inputs, waste outputs," but also other negative social, economic, and environmental impacts which are sometimes very difficult to capture. For example, "extracting and processing raw materials is often hazardous to workers, but these processes might also degrade the environment and harm local communities. The manufacturing process poses additional occupational hazards, creates hazardous and solid waste, and causes air, water, and soil pollution." The impact of packaging is also hard to capture, but packaging, transport, and distribution stages often require the use of significant amounts of energy. These and similar examples are suggesting that most of the products (if not all of them) we see in today's market still have such wide-ranging impacts throughout their life cycle. Sometimes, even if toxins are eliminated from a final product, supply-chain workers are exposed to toxins through various sections of the production cycle. For this reason we cannot consider a product as being sustainable if it harms the local community during the production process. Because the demand for safe and healthy products is growing, it is very important that circularity of the product be considered at the design stage of the process. "It has been estimated that 70% of the life cycle cost of products can be determined at the design stage." Therefore, legislation in many countries has targeted a policy known as extended producer responsibility (EPR), which states that not only producers but also importers and sellers (retailers) of products should bear a significant degree of responsibility for the negative impacts of the product, through its entire life cycle.[56]

In the wake of demands for healthy products, faced with safety concerns and product recalls, consumers must "learn how to ask questions through which they can determine whether a product is safe for them and their family." *The Lowell Center Framework for Sustainable Products* recommends that consumers ask questions such as the following: "What are the conditions under which this product was made? Is the production process safe for workers? What resources were used in making the product, and what is the environmental impact of this product in its production, use, and disposal? Do workers receive a living wage? Do profits support local community development?" To clarify which characteristics a sustainable product must certainly possess, *The Lowell Center Framework for Sustainable Products* provides an unambiguous definition to ensure that the "sustainable product" is meaningful as a concept. Here I will refer to their proposed definition, which states that "sustainable products minimize environmental and social costs throughout the product life cycle and aim to maximize environmental and social benefits to communities, while remaining economically viable."[57] For clarity, table 25 lists the recommendations for a sustainable product checklist proposed by *The Lowell Center Framework for Sustainable Products*.

**Table 25**  The Lowell Center Framework for Sustainable Products*

| |
|---|
| *A sustainable product is healthy for consumers.* This means that it avoids chemicals that cause cancer or mutations; damage the reproductive, nervous, endocrine, or immune systems; are acutely toxic; or accumulate or persist in the environment . . . it is safe for use, meaning it is not flammable, explosive or corrosive; does not cause lacerations, choking or strangling, or burns/shocks; and does not damage hearing or injure eyes. |
| *A sustainable product is safe for workers.* This means that the workplace in which the product is made "is safe, clean, well lit, ventilated, with good air quality, well designed ergonomically, free of exposure to toxins, and equipped for fire safety and other emergencies. Further, it means that workers receive adequate health and safety training, working hours and pace are not excessive, and workers have some job control and input into the production process. If workers are housed in dormitories, the living quarters are clean, and workers have sufficient food, access to potable water, and sanitation. Workers also need to be treated fairly and with respect and dignity; there is no corporal punishment, verbal abuse, coercion, discrimination, or harassment. Child or forced labor is not permitted. Workers have freedom of association and the right to collective bargaining. |

*(Continues)*

**Table 25** Continued

*A sustainable product is environmentally sound.* This means that chemical and material inputs/outputs are not hazardous. Water, energy, and materials are used efficiently in the production cycle, and renewable resources and energy are utilized in production and use. Further, waste is prevented and/or minimized throughout the product life cycle. Next, the product and its packaging are durable and can be reused, repaired, recycled, or composted. The product itself is designed for disassembly—it can be taken apart and remanufactured. Scarce resources are conserved, and ecosystems are not damaged in extracting resources for production. Critical habitats are preserved during extraction, production, and use.

*A sustainable product benefits the communities in which it is made.* This means that workers receive a living wage and can support their families without additional government assistance. This further means that the work design is supportive of family life—e.g., families are not separated, and good-quality childcare is available for workers' children. The work design promotes equity and fairness in the community—e.g., there is no age or gender discrimination. It is also expected that some of the corporate profits accrue to the local community to be used for public improvements (such as in education and health care).

A sustainable product is economically viable for the company or organization. This means that innovation is encouraged to anticipate market needs. The company is stable in terms of ownership and philosophy. The company reinvests in its facilities to improve its capacity for further production. The product is priced for economic viability and the company also aims to internalize costs so that production can be environmentally sound and socially just. The company is recognized for its corporate social responsibility: this includes programs that support and value employees as well as programs that benefit the community and the environment.

*Table text is quoted from Sustainable Production, *The Lowell Center Framework for Sustainable Products*, accessed July 24, 2023, http://www.sustainableproduction.org/downloads/LowellCenter-FrameworkforSustainableProducts11-09.09.pdf.

Although there is "increased pressure on manufacturers to increase transparency about what products are made of and how they are made so that consumers can better understand the products' health, environmental, and social impacts consumers are not routinely provided with detailed information about products such as their chemical and material ingredients, energy use, the conditions under which they are made, or hazards during use or disposal." Although companies are increasingly using various self-declared "eco-labels" to support their sustainability claims, it is important to understand that only third-party certificates truly secure credibility for a sustainability claim because the product is tested by the third party; thus, the product value and the validity of the sustainability claim is objectively verified by experts. Therefore, we can conclude that third-party certified labeling programs "help consumers make informed decisions about the products they buy. These programs focus on specific attributes such as energy efficiency, carbon footprints, and forest management. However, most labeling programs address only one aspect of sustainability and are not comprehensive. Therefore, consumers must still make decisions with incomplete information."[58]

In table 26, I provide examples, descriptions, and the meanings of the verified third-party **sustainability certificates** that are most commonly used among fashion brands to support sustainability claims for their products and their business and supply chain practices.

**Table 26** Verified third-party sustainability certificates most commonly used among fashion brands*

| Certification | Type (Environmental/Social/ Economic); Commodity Category | Overview | Certification Credibility |
|---|---|---|---|
| Cradle to Cradle Certified (CM) Products Program | Environmental, social, economic; all commodities | "The Cradle to Cradle Certified™ Product Standard guides designers and manufacturers through a continual improvement process that looks at a product through five quality categories—material health, material reutilization, renewable | "Product assessments are performed by a qualified independent organization trained by the Institute. Assessment Summary Reports are reviewed by the Institute, which certifie |

*(Continues)*

**Table 26** Continued

| Certification | Type (Environmental/Social/ Economic); Commodity Category | Overview | Certification Credibility |
|---|---|---|---|
| | | energy and carbon management, water stewardship, and social fairness. A product receives an achievement level in each category—Basic, Bronze, Silver, Gold, or Platinum—with the lowest achievement level representing the product's overall mark."[59] | products meeting the Standard requirements and licenses the use of the Cradle to Cradle Certified™ word and design marks to the product manufacturer. Every two years, manufacturers must demonstrate good faith efforts to improve their products in order to have their products recertified."[60] |
| Fair Trade Certified | Social; all commodities | Classification as a Fair Trade Certified™ good indicates that the product has met certain social, environmental, and economic criteria that support the sustainable development of small-scale producers and agricultural workers.[61] | Fair Trade USA ensures it has information sufficient to determine the extent to which outputs and short and medium-term results are being achieved. Fair Trade USA ensures that data is collected on an ongoing basis to track and report progress on current performance monitoring indicators. |

(Continues)

**Table 26** Continued

| Certification | Type (Environ-mental/Social/ Economic); Commodity Category | Overview | Certification Credibility |
|---|---|---|---|
| | | | Fair Trade USA compiles, analyzes, and produces reports on the results observed through performance moni-toring at least once per year.[62] |
| bluesign standard | Environ-mental and economic; clothing | "The bluesign® system is the solu-tion for sustainable textile production. It eliminates harm-ful substances right from the beginning of the manufacturing process and sets and controls standards for environmentally friendly and safe production. This not only ensures that the final textile product meets very stringent consumer safety requirements worldwide but also provides confidence to the consumers that they are acquir-ing a sustainable products."[63] | "The bluesign® system helps opti-mize the process' efficiency by minimizing both energy and material input. . . . Water emission control includes the return of purified water into the water cycle and reducing of the aquatic envi-ronment impact to a minimum. . . . During the entire production process chain, only compo-nents and tech-nologies that have the lowest possible impact on human health and environ-ment are applied."[64] |

(*Continues*)

**Table 26** Continued

| Certification | Type (Environmental/Social/ Economic); Commodity Category | Overview | Certification Credibility |
|---|---|---|---|
| Fair Labor Association | Social; all commodities | The FLA accredits businesses for their social compliance programs to indicate the presence of systems and procedures required for successfully upholding fair labor standards throughout their supply chains. The FLA was created as a collaborative effort of universities, civil society organizations, and socially responsible companies dedicated to protecting workers' rights around the world.[65] | The Fair Labor Association's (FLA's) Sustainable Compliance Initiative (SCI) advances workers' rights by encouraging progressive and sustained improvements in employment practices and working conditions. "SCI represents a new approach to social compliance, where the paradigm is shifted away from snapshot auditing and quick fixes at the factory level and towards collaboration between multiple stakeholders to bring sustained improvements. By focusing on the workers' employment cycle, starting from when workers are hired to when they leave the company, SCI assessment tools are created at each stage to identify labor violations and evaluate management systems."[66] |

(Continues)

**Table 26** Continued

| Certification | Type (Environmental/Social/Economic); Commodity Category | Overview | Certification Credibility |
|---|---|---|---|
| B Corporation | Environmental, social, economic; all commodities | B Corporation is a certification for an entire business, not a specific product. "A B Corporation is a new type of corporation which uses the power of business to solve social and environmental problems. B Corporations are unlike traditional responsible businesses because they meet comprehensive and transparent social and environmental performance standards, institutionalize stakeholder interests, and build a collective voice through the power of a unifying brand. Individually, B Corporations are businesses that meet the highest standards of verified social and environmental performance, public transparency, and legal accountability and aspire to use the power of markets to solve social and environmental problems."[67] Examples of certified B-Corp businesses in the fashion industry include Patagonia, Toms, Eileen Fisher, and Athleta. | "The B Impact Assessment is a digital tool that can help measure, manage, and improve positive impact performance for environment, communities, customers, suppliers, employees, and shareholders; receiving a minimum verified score of 80 points on the assessment is also the first step towards B Corp Certification."[68] |

(Continues)

**Table 26** Continued

| Certification | Type (Environmental/Social/Economic); Commodity Category | Overview | Certification Credibility |
|---|---|---|---|
| Better Cotton Initiative | Environmental, social, economic; clothing | "The Better Cotton Initiative (BCI) exists to make global cotton production better for the people who produce cotton, better for the environment it grows in, and better for the sector's future by developing Better Cotton as a sustainable mainstream commodity."[69] | "A critical component of the Better Cotton Standard System is the Better Cotton Principles and Criteria, which lay out the global definition of Better Cotton through seven guiding principles. Principle 1: BCI Farmers minimize the harmful impact of crop protection practices; Principle 2: BCI Farmers promote water stewardship; Principle 3: BCI Farmers care for soil health; Principle 4: BCI Farmers enhance biodiversity and use land responsibly; Principle 5: BCI Farmers care for and preserve fiber quality; Principle 6: BCI Farmers promote decent work; Principle 7: BCI Farmers operate an effective management system.[70] |

(Continues)

**Table 26** Continued

| Certification | Type (Environmental/Social/Economic); Commodity Category | Overview | Certification Credibility |
|---|---|---|---|
| Carbon*free* Certified | Environmental and economic; clothing | "The Carbon*free* Product Certification is a meaningful, transparent way for [businesses] to provide environmentally-friendly, carbon-neutral products to [their] customers. By determining a product's carbon footprint, reducing it where possible and offsetting remaining emissions through our third-party validated carbon reduction projects, [companies] can differentiate [their] brand and product, increase sales [and market share], improve customer loyalty, [and] strengthen corporate social responsibility & environmental goals."[71] | "The quantified greenhouse gas or carbon reductions must represent actual emission reductions. These reductions are based on approved methodologies or protocols which require rigorous monitoring, reporting, and verification (MRV) of the project's activities. The greenhouse gas or carbon reductions must result from projects whose performance can be readily and accurately quantified, monitored, and verified by independent third-party auditors."[72] |
| ECOLOGO | Environmental; plastic drinkware, plastic collectables, etc. | "ECOLOGO Certified products, services, and packaging are certified for reduced environmental impact. ECOLOGO Certifications are voluntary, multi-attribute, life cycle based environmental certifications | "All products certified to an ECOLOGO standard must meet or exceed specific criteria before receiving the mark. ECOLOGO Certification is |

(*Continues*)

**Table 26** Continued

| Certification | Type (Environ-mental/Social/ Economic); Commodity Category | Overview | Certification Credibility |
|---|---|---|---|
|  |  | that indicate a product has undergone rigorous scientific testing, exhaustive auditing, or both to prove its compliance with stringent, third-party, environmental performance standards."[73] | classified as an ISO (International Organization for Standardization) Type 1 ecolabel and has been successfully assessed by the Global Ecolabeling Network, further demonstrating its credibility."[74] |
| Fair for Life | Environmental and social; all commodities | "Fair for Life is a certification program for fair trade in agriculture, manufacturing, and trade. It was created in 2006 by the Swiss Bio-Foundation in cooperation with the IMO Group. In 2014 it was taken over by the Ecocert Group to meet a specific demand from organic farming stakeholders. Beyond the inherent concept of fair pricing, and from the very beginning of its creation, Fair for Life has been aware of the notion of responsible supply chains having a long-term vision, making a sincere commitment and acting responsibly throughout the supply chain."[75] | "After the initial evaluation and certification decision, the annual evaluations will be organized based on a 3-year cycle through surveillance and renewal evaluations."[76] |

(Continues)

**Table 26** Continued

| Certification | Type (Environmental/Social/Economic); Commodity Category | Overview | Certification Credibility |
|---|---|---|---|
| Forest Stewardship Council (FSC) Certified | Environmental; wood-derived products | "The Forest Stewardship Council's mission is to promote environmentally sound, socially beneficial, and economically prosperous management of the world's forests. Forest management shall respect all applicable laws of the country in which it occurs, along with international treaties and agreements to which the country is a signatory, and comply with all FSC Principles and Criteria."[77] | "Monitoring shall be conducted — appropriate to the scale and intensity of forest management — to assess the condition of the forest, yields of forest products, chain of custody, management activities, and their social and environmental impacts."[78] |
| MADE SAFE | Environmental and social; all commodities | MADE SAFE means that a product has passed MADE SAFE certification and gone on to be lab-tested to ensure that it—in its totality—is not toxic.[79] | "Products seeking the MADE SAFE (*Made With Safe Ingredients*™) seal are screened to ensure that over 6,500 Banned / Restricted List substances have been avoided or constrained, thereby eliminating the worst hazards commonly found in products used in our homes and daily routines."[80] |

*(Continues)*

**Table 26** Continued

| Certification | Type (Environmental/Social/ Economic); Commodity Category | Overview | Certification Credibility |
|---|---|---|---|
| SCS Global Services Recycled Content Certification For Products and Recycling Programs | Environmental; all commodities | "Recycled content certification demonstrates a company's commitment to conserving natural resources, helps it meet customer specifications, can qualify its products for LEED and environmentally preferable purchasing (EPP) programs, and supports its sustainability goals. Manufacturers of carpet, textiles, building products, wood and paper products, insulation, clothing, jewelry, and more seek this trusted certification label."[81] | "The manufacturer shall provide a diagram and/or a description of the manufacturing process showing how recycled materials are tracked and how a chain of custody is maintained. It shall also describe all inputs of materials, all internal material flows (e.g., reuse or recycling of scrap), and all material outputs (including, but not limited to, finished products, intermediary products, and waste)."[82] |
| Global Organic Textile Standards (GOTS) | Environmental, social, economic; textiles | "The aim of the Global Organic Textile Standard (GOTS) is to define requirements to ensure organic status of textiles, from harvesting of the raw materials, through environmentally and socially responsible manufacturing up to labeling in order to provide a credible assurance to the end consumer."[83] | "The GOTS logo can be applied to the final product only if all stages comply with the GOTS criteria. Therefore, all processors, manufacturers, and traders of textiles must be certified."[84] |

(*Continues*)

**Table 26** Continued

| Certification | Type (Environmental/Social/Economic); Commodity Category | Overview | Certification Credibility |
|---|---|---|---|
| Global Recycled Standard (GRS) | Environmental; textiles | "The Global Recycled Standard is intended for use with any product that contains at least 20% Recycled Material. Each stage of production is required to be certified, beginning at the recycling stage and ending at the last seller in the final business-to-business transaction."[85] | "Under the Textile Exchange accreditation system, each certification body is independently accredited by an authorized accreditation body."[86] |

* This table reflects student gathered data. Research was concluded in January 2022. If there are any later changes in the approved certificate would not be captured here.

# Greenwashing and Deceptive Product Labeling

**Greenwashing** is an act of "insincere engagement in sustainable business" practices. The term "was first used in 1986 by New York environmentalist Jay Westerveld, who criticized the hotel practice of placing green 'save the environment' cards in each room asking guests to help them 'save the environment' by reusing their towels." This "example is noteworthy given that most hotels at that point had poorly-implemented sustainability programs, with few or no environmentally friendly aspects." Similar to this case, today greenwashing refers to deceptive business practices where the advertising and promotion misleadingly indicates that the product or service is more sustainable than it really is.[87] There are numerous examples that showcase the fact that, unfortunately, greenwashing is widespread in our industry. For example, a fast fashion brand, H&M, which predominantly produces cheap, low-quality garments, describes its collections as "conscious." On the official website, H&M disclosed the following statement:

"Shop our selection of sustainable fashion pieces that make you both look and feel good. Our range of organic and sustainable clothing offers you a variety of new wardrobe favorites—everything from soft knits and stylish t-shirts to the latest denim looks and comfortable underwear."[88] However, H&M company was accused of greenwashing for not providing sufficient "information about the sustainable nature of its 'sustainable style' collection. . . . The Norwegian Consumer Authority (CA) has said that they had found that the information given regarding sustainability was not sufficient, especially given that the Conscious Collection was advertised as a collection with environmental benefits. The information on the collection was general and did not specify the actual environmental benefit of each garment sufficiently; for example, the amount of recycled material used in each garment" was not specified.[89]

To investigate whether the practice of greenwashing is prevalent among fashion retailers, in 2021 the Changing Markets Foundation published the *Synthetics Anonymous* report,[90] assessing the validity of sustainability claims among twelve fast fashion, luxury fashion, and online brands: "Asos, Boohoo, Forever 21, George at Asda, Gucci, H&M, Louis Vuitton, Marks & Spencer (M&S), Uniqlo, Walmart, Zalando, and Zara." They found that for the twelve brands, "60% of the sustainability claims involved greenwashing." For the purpose of the product and label analysis, researchers collected and examined 4,028 products. They found that "39% of the products assessed came with sustainability-related claims such as recycled, eco, low-impact, or simply sustainable. The Foundation assessed whether these claims stood up against the Competition and Markets Authority's (CMA's) new guidelines on avoiding greenwashing, which cover accuracy, the avoidance of ambiguity, not hiding or omitting important information, enabling comparison between products, covering impacts across the product life-cycle, and ensuring claims can be substantiated." In conclusion, none of the explored products had a legitimate third-party verified sustainability label. Similarly, 59 percent of the brands did not adhere to the CMA guidelines described above. H&M, ASOS, and M&S fared worse on greenwashing with 88% and more false sustainability claims. For example "H&M was highlighted as a particular concern in the report; its Conscious Collection was found to contain more synthetic materials than its main collection, with labels on many items failing to reveal the percentage of these materials that were recycled."[91]

As a part of the solution, fashion brands are advised to use verified third-party certificates to support their sustainability claims. Also, the European Commission said that they will end greenwashing and require companies to publish "reliable, comparable, and verifiable information for consumers."[92] As a result of these efforts, "The European Commission is working on two new legislative initiatives that should include measures to avoid greenwashing and make sustainability claims more reliable—frameworks titled *Empowering Consumers for the Green Transition* and *Substantiating Green Claims*."[93]

## Case study 10: Federal Trade Commission product recalls

Sustainability certifications for products were developed to support product quality and safety, promote improved product features, and facilitate consumers' purchasing decisions. However, only a small number of products are sustainable or of improved quality. Many of the products still offered for sale do not undergo valid testing, and chemical ingredients or manufacturing defects in these products may cause harm to consumers. Mandatory and voluntary clothing and footwear product recalls are happening more frequently because of the tremendous speed of fashion trends and the larger quantity of products entering the global market. For example, the International Organization for Economic Co-operation and Development (OECD) has registered 162 apparel product recalls that were issued between January and July of 2019.[94] In the United States, the Consumer Products Safety Commission (CPSC) publishes and maintains a list of recalls of toys, clothing, and apparel gear in an effort to protect consumers.[95]

**Student Activity**: To investigate product safety issues and product recalls in the fashion industry, students are invited to participate in the Federal Trade Commission Product Recalls case study. Students are asked to visit a publicly searchable database of reports of harm on the Consumer Protection and Safety Commission website.[96] Then students are instructed to identify one recall for the branded product of their interest and to investigate and describe the reasons behind that particular product recall.

# Student Voices: Federal Trade Commission Product Recalls

To investigate product safety issues and product recalls in the fashion industry, students were invited to participate in the Federal Trade Commission Product Recalls case study. Students were asked to visit a publicly searchable database of reports of harm on the Consumer Protection and Safety Commission website. Then students were instructed to identify one recall for the branded product of their interest and to investigate and describe the reasons behind that particular product recall. Table 27 below presents a brief summary of the insights in the students' findings on Federal Trade commission product recalls.

**Table 27** The insights in the students' findings on Federal Trade Commission product recalls*

| Brand | Product | Problem/Recall |
| --- | --- | --- |
| Levi's | Jeans | In 2013, a 54-year-old man noticed that his legs had begun to itch and break out after he had worn a pair of Levi's for a short period of time. He then discovered that sulfur dyes had been used to set dye in the jeans. He had an allergy to sulfur dyes. The customer reported that Levi's never answered him regarding how to neutralize the negative impact of sulfur dyes so he would not have a reaction. |
| Haute-look (Nord-strom) | Acrylic Sweater | In 2012, a 40-year-old woman noticed a strong chemical smell on the sweater she had recently purchased at Hautelook.com. After wearing the sweater for only 3 hours, the woman began to develop a very bad headache; she soon became dizzy, and her vision became blurry as well. Hautelook, a subsidiary of Nordstrom, is a discount member-only apparel shopping platform. The brand of the sweater was Hazel Clothes by Hazel & Jaloux. The sweater itself was manufactured in China and was made of 100% acrylic. |

*(Continues)*

**Table 27** Continued

| Brand | Product | Problem/Recall |
|---|---|---|
| Cat & Jack (Target) | Infant/ Toddler Girls' One-Piece Rashguard Swimsuits | Target recalled over 400,000 kids' clothing items from their private label brand called Cat & Jack due to a choking hazard associated with the material used. In terms of one particular style, the Infant-Toddler Girls' One-Piece Rashguard Swimsuits were recalled because the snaps could break or detach, posing choking and laceration hazards to children. There have been 27 reports of snaps breaking or detaching, including one report of laceration. According to the report, there was an incident in which the child suffered cuts from wearing the swimsuit. |
| Nike | Air Face Up Basketball Shoe | Nike recalled 350,000 pairs of Air Face Up shoes. The shoe was a men's basketball shoe that came in multiple colors, and they were sold in major athletic stores and department stores nationwide for about four months before they had to be recalled. The issue with the sneakers was that they had a small metal rivet on the outside of the shoe that could, over time, bend and form a sharp edge. Nike received approximately 35 reports of high school and college basketball players receiving cuts on their lower legs from the metal rivets, and two players required stitches. Customers who had bought the shoes were asked to immediately return them to the stores to exchange for a different product or to receive store credit. This took place in 1998. |
| Victoria's Secret | Silk Kimono Top | In 2002, silk tops were voluntarily recalled by Victoria's Secret because they were made of material that did not meet the fabric flammability standards (federal Flammable Fabrics Act). Information on the website said the outer shell of the fabric could readily ignite, which could cause burns and injuries. Around 500 pieces of this clothing were manufactured, and 57 were sold. |

* Table quotes work created by students enrolled in following course: UNT MDSE 4560 Sustainable Strategies (100 percent online).

After students individually researched the product recalls, we gathered as a group and discussed their findings. Students were asked to provide answers to the following prompt: Based on your understanding of sustainability issues and information in selected product recalls, please address what area(s) the selected brand needs to improve in order to prevent product failure and to ensure product safety in the future.

This activity can be replicated in original or modified form as appropriate to engage students in similar types of investigations. In addition to the proposed question, students can be asked to propose adequate third-party certificates that would manifest optimal product improvement in a category in which the product had previously failed.

## Chapter Summary

In this chapter we examined several methods used by companies to report their sustainability efforts and to track their improvements over a specific time period. Among these methods is the GRI Reporting Framework, currently the most widely used reporting tool. Reporting frameworks such as this are becoming increasingly important as consumers demand company transparency where social, economic, and environmental issues are concerned. In one of the case studies in this chapter, we examine the Fashion Transparency Index, a report that was established in 2016 to help benchmark and track the annual transparency status of sustainability disclosures among fashion retailers. This chapter also discusses Stand Earth's 2020 Roadmap for reducing fossil fuel usage within the fashion supply chain and the importance of doing so. Lastly, while discussing problems of greenwashing, this chapter attempts to clarify what constitutes a "sustainable" product and reports the certificates available within the industry for company recognition concerning their sustainable efforts. In that regard, the second case study and student voices sections of the chapter explore the implications of FTC product recalls in the fashion sector.

# References

1. Iva Jestratijevic, Nancy A. Rudd, and James Uanhoro, "Transparency of Sustainability Disclosures among Luxury and Mass-Market Fashion Brands," *Journal of Global Fashion Marketing* 11, no. 2 (2020): 99–116.

2. "Global Reporting," *Global Reporting*, accessed July 24, 2023, https://www.globalreporting.org/.

3. Ibid.

4. Jestratijevic, Rudd, and Uanhoro, "Transparency of Sustainability Disclosures."

5. Ibid.

6. "Guiding Principles on Business and Human Rights Framework," *OHCHR*, accessed June 19, 2023, https://www.ohchr.org/sites/default/files/Documents/Issues/Business/Intro_Guiding_PrinciplesBusinessHR.pdf.

7. Ibid.

8. "H&M Group Sustainability Report 2017," H&M, accessed July 29, 2023, https://about.hm.com/content/dam/hmgroup/groupsite/documents/masterlanguage/CSR/reports/HM_group_SustainabilityReport_2017_FullReport.pdf.

9. "ISSP-SPA Study Guide," *Scribd*, accessed August 1, 2023, https://www.scribd.com/document/633819872/ISSP-SA-Study-Guide-2020-pdf.

10. H&M, "H&M Group Sustainability Report 2017."

11. Scribd, "ISSP-SPA Study Guide."

12. Ceres and Sustainalytics, *Gaining Ground: Corporate Progress on the Ceres Roadmap for Sustainability*, 2014, https://www.ceres.org/sites/default/files/reports/2017-03/Ceres_GainingGround_FullReport_112316.pdf.

13. H&M, "H&M group Sustainability Report 2017."

14. "ILO Convention," *ILO*, accessed June 16, 2023, https://www.ilo.org/dyn/normlex/en/f?p=NORMLEXPUB:12100:0::NO::P12100_ILO_CODE:C087.

15. H&M, "H&M Group Sustainability Report 2017."

16. Ibid.

17. Ibid.

18. Ibid.

19. Ibid.

20. "Sustainability Accounting Standards Board," *WikiMili*, accessed June 30, 2023,https://wikimili.com/en/Sustainability_Accounting_Standards_Board.

21. "About Sabs," *SABS*, accessed June 30, 2023, https://www.sasb.org/about/.

22. "Apparel, Accessories, and Footwear Sustainability Accounting Standards," *SABS*, accessed June 30, 2023, https://www.sasb.org/wp-content/uploads/2015/09/CN0501_Apparel-Accessories-Footwear_Standard.pdf.

23. "About Sustainable Apparel Coalition," *Sustainable Apparel Coalition*, accessed June 30, 2023, https://apparelcoalition.org/about/.

24. Jestratijevic, Rudd, and Uanhoro, "Transparency of Sustainability Disclosures."
25. Ibid.
26. "Nike Sweatshops," *Wikipedia*, accessed July 24, 2023, https://en.wikipedia.org/wiki?curid=25173995.
27. Jestratijevic, Rudd, and Uanhoro, "Transparency of Sustainability Disclosures."
28. Ibid.
29. Ibid.
30. "Unprecedented US and European Apparel Companies Sign Pledge Elimination Child Labor Uzbekistan," Sourcing Network, accessed August 1, 2023, https://www.sourcingnetwork.org/press-release-unprecedented-us-european-apparel-companies-sign-pledge-elimination-child-labor-uzbekistan.
31. Jestratijevic, Rudd, and Uanhoro, "Transparency of Sustainability Disclosures."
32. Ibid.
33. Ibid.
34. Iva Jestratijevic, James Ohisei Uanhoro, and Rachel Creighton, "To Disclose or Not to Disclose? Fashion Brands' Strategies for Transparency in Sustainability Reporting," *Journal of Fashion Marketing and Management: An International Journal* 26, no. 1 (2022): 36–50.
35. Ibid.
36. Ibid.
37. Ibid.
38. "Fashion Transparency Index 2017," *Fashion Revolution*, accessed June 20, 2022, https://issuu.com/fashionrevolution/docs/fr_fashiontransparencyindex2017.
39. "Our Story," *Stand Earth*, accessed July 4, 2023, https://stand.earth/about/our-story/.
40. Stand Earth, *Fashion Forward: A Roadmap to Fossil Free Fashion*, accessed July 29, 2023, https://old.stand.earth/sites/stand/files/standearth-fashionforward-roadmaptofossilfreefashion.pdf.
41. Ibid.
42. Ibid.
43. Ibid.
44. Ibid.
45. Ibid.
46. "New Report Gives Fashion Brands a Roadmap to Ditching Fossil Fuels in the Supply Chain," *Stand Earth*, last modified August, 20, 2020, https://stand.earth/press-releases/new-report-gives-fashion-brands-a-roadmap-to-ditching-fossil-fuels-in-the-supply-chain/.
47. "Stand Earth Scorecard Fails Fashion Industry on Efforts to Tackle Climate Change," *Stand Earth*, last modified August 24, 2021, https://stand.earth/press-releases/stand-earth-scorecard-fails-fashion-industry-on-efforts-to-tackle-climate-change/.
48. Ibid.

49. Ibid.
50. Ibid.
51. Ibid.
52. "Stand Fossil Free Fashion Scorecards," *Stand Earth*, accessed August 5, 2023, https://old.stand.earth/sites/stand/files/stand-fossil-free-fashion-scorecard.pdf.
53. Ibid.
54. Ibid.
55. "Circularity and Climate Change," H&M group, accessed August 2, 2023, https://hmgroup.com/sustainability/circularity-and-climate/climate/.
56. Sustainable Production, *The Lowell Center Framework for Sustainable Products*, accessed July 24, 2023, http://www.sustainableproduction.org/downloads/ LowellCenterFrameworkforSustainableProducts11-09.09.pdf.
57. Ibid.
58. Ibid.
59. "Cradle to Cradle Certificate," *Impakter*, accessed July 1, 2023, https://impakter. com/index/cradle-to-cradle-certificate/.
60. "C2C Certified," *Healthy Printing*, accessed July 2, 2023, https://www.healthyprinting.eu/c2c-certifiedtm/.
61. "Why Fair Trade," *Fairtrade Certified*, accessed August 1, 2023, https://www. fairtradecertified.org/why-fair-trade/.
62. "How Do We Measure Impact," *Fairtrade Certified*, accessed July 25, 2023, https://www.fairtradecertified.org/what-we-do/impact-management-system/.
63. "bluesign to develop the first comprehensive sustainable chemistry index for the Textile Industry in Partnership with SCTI," *Texintel*, accessed June 25, 2023, https://www.texintel.com/eco-news/bluesign-to-develop-the-first-comprehensive-sustainable-chemistry-index-for-the-textile-industry-in-partnership-with-scti.
64. Bluesign, *Bluesign System*, accessed June 15, 2023, https://www.bluesign.com/ downloads/criteria-2020/bluesign_system_v3.0_2020-03.pdf.
65. "FLA Popsockets Accreditation Report," *Fair Labor*, accessed June 27, 2023, https://www.fairlabor.org/wp-content/uploads/2022/10/FLA-PopSockets-Accreditation-Report.pdf.
66. "Fact sheets," *Standardsmap*, accessed June 23, 2023, https://standardsmap.org/ en/factsheet/18/resources.
67. "B Corporation," *Eco Label Index*, accessed Jul 18, 2023, https://www.ecolabelindex.com/ecolabel/b-corporation.
68. "B Impact Assessment," *B Corporation*, accessed July 30, 2023, https://www. bcorporation.net/en-us/programs-and-tools/b-impact-assessment/.
69. "Better Cotton Principles and Criteria," *Better Cotton*, last modified March, 2018, https://bettercotton.org/wp-content/uploads/2019/06/Better-Cotton-Principles-Criteria-V2.1.pdf.
70. "Defining Better: Our Principles and Criteria," *Better Cotton*, accessed July 23, 2023, https://bettercotton.org/what-we-do/defining-better-our-standard/.

71. "CF products FQA," *Carbon Fund*, accessed July 1, 2023, https://carbonfund. org/wp-content/uploads/2020/10/CF-Products-FAQs-2020.pdf.

72. "Quality Assurance Protocol," *Carbon Fund*, accessed July 28, 2023, https:// carbonfund.org/quality-assurance-protocol/.

73. "Ecologo Certification Program," *UL*, accessed Jun 25, 2023, https://www. ul.com/resources/ecologo-certification-program.

74. "Ecologo," *Ecolabel Index*, accessed June 3, 2023, https://www.ecolabelindex. com/ecolabel/ecologo.

75. "Fair for Life," *Better World Products*, accessed June 3, 2023, https://www. betterworldproducts.org/fair-for-life-standard/#:~:text=Fair%20for%20 Life%20is%20a,cooperation%20with%20the%20IMO%20Group.

76. "Fair for Life," *Fair for Life*, accessed July 31, 2023, https://www.fairforlife. org/pmws/indexDOM.php?client_id=fairforlife&page_id=become_7&lang_ iso639=en.

77. "Forests for All Forever," *FSC*, accessed July 3, 2023, https://us.fsc.org/en-us/ what-we-do/mission-and-vision.

78. Ibid.

79. "Certification Process," *Madesafe*, accessed June 3, 2023, https://madesafe.org/ pages/certification-process.

80. Ibid.

81. "Recycled Content Certification," *Envirolink*, accessed July 28, 2023, https:// www.envirolink.me/recycled-content-certification/.

82. "Recycled Content Standard," *SC Global Services*, accessed July 30, 2023, https://cdn.scsglobalservices.com/files/standards/scs_stn_recycledcontent_ v7-0_070814.pdf.

83. "Global Organic Textile Standard," *OTA*, accessed July 24, 2023, https://ota.com/ advocacy/organic-standards/fiber-and-textiles/global-organic-textile-standard- gots.

84. "Global Organic Textile Standard Ecology and Social Responsibility," *Global Standard*, accessed August 1, 2023, https://global-standard.org/certification-and- labelling/who-needs-to-be-certified.

85. "Global Recycled Standard," *Textile Exchange*, accessed June 5, 2022, https:// textileexchange.org/app/uploads/2021/02/Global-Recycled-Standard-v4.0.pdf.

86. "Accreditation," *Textile Exchange*, accessed July 31, 2023, https://textileex- change.org/accreditation/.

87. The Sustainable Business Case Book," *Archive*, accessed June 1, 2023, https:// archive.org/stream/TheSustainableBusinessCaseBook/The+Sustainable+Busi- ness+Case+Book_djvu.txt.

88. Lyric Chassin, "How Companies and Consumers Are Making the Switch to Sustainable Fashion," *Mycenaean*, October 14, 2019, https://www.themyce- naean.org/2019/10/how-companies-and-consumers-are-making-the-switch-to- sustainable-fashion/.

89. "H&M Called Out for 'Greenwashing' in Its Conscious Fashion Collection," *3novices,* accessed June 14, 2023, http://3novices-india.blogspot.com/2019/08/3novicesh-called-out-for-greenwashing.html.

90. "Synthetic Anonymous," *Changing Markets,* accessed June 1, 2023, http://changingmarkets.org/wp-content/uploads/2021/07/SyntheticsAnonymous_FinalWeb.pdf.

91. "60% of Sustainability Claims by Fashion Giants Are Greenwashing," *Edie,* accessed August 1, 2023, https://www.edie.net/report-60-of-sustainability-claims-by-fashion-giants-are-greenwashing/.

92. "European Commission. Consumer Protection: Enabling Sustainable Choices and Ending Greenwashing," *EC Europa,* accessed June 12, 2023, https://ec.europa.eu/commission/presscorner/detail/en/ip_23_1692.

93. Edie, "60% of Sustainability Claims."

94. "Consumer Product Recalls," *International Organization for Economic Co-operation and Development (OECD),* accessed May 12, 2023, https://www.oecd.org/sti/consumer/product-recalls/.

95. "Safe Products*," Consumer Protection and Safety Commission,* accessed June 20, 2023, https://www.cpsc.gov/safety-education/safety-guides/general-information/log-saferproductsgov.

96. Ibid.

# Chapter 6

# Sustainability and Engagement

# Chapter Introduction and Learning Objectives

In this chapter we will explore why purposeful engagement of various stakeholder groups in sustainability activities is needed to support sustainable transformation in the fashion industry. The idea is quite simple. The SDGs in the fashion industry can be achieved only if all the parties involved in the fashion production and consumption process work together. This means that all actors—including businesses, governments, NGOs and consumers—have a role to play in sustainable development, and as discussed in this chapter, this need for stronger partnerships to reach goals is becoming particularly evident now, after the global COVID crisis. The sustainability expert whose work is presented in this chapter is Dr. Elena Karpova because she is researching sustainable apparel consumption, and she has created a list of simple practices that readers of this book can implement in their daily lives in order to consume fashion more sustainably.

This chapter has following learning objectives:

- Understand the importance of stakeholder's engagement for sustainable development.
- Discuss implications of the COVID-19 pandemic on business and sustainability.
- Overview sustainable career opportunities students should consider.
- Acquire the vocabulary of the sustainability discipline by using the glossary of key terms.

### Key Terms

---

| | |
|---|---|
| Living wage | multistakeholder engagement |
| Registration, Evaluation, Authorization and Restriction of Chemicals (REACH) | sharing economy |
| | shared value |
| sustainable | |

# Multistakeholder Engagement

What does **multistakeholder engagement** mean? Multistakeholder engagement is a strategic and structured process that a company may use to ensure that a range of perspectives is included in decision-making.[1] In a practical sense, it means that before making any business plan, the company need to consider how this new plan will (positively or negatively) affect various groups of stakeholders. Thus, in today's business world, representatives have had to rethink what it means to be a responsible company. It is not just about doing the right thing or "doing well by doing good." It is about creating value for not only shareholders but also employees, suppliers, customers, and local and global communities. Organizations seeking to address social sustainability issues need to understand the social issues we discussed at the beginning of this book. They also need to understand and engage the myriad stakeholders that are impacted by the organization's activities.

The idea that businesses have a responsibility beyond earning a profit is nothing new. "Business giving and business involvement in community issues was familiar turf to many leading companies in the first half of the 20th century. Its roots reach back at least into the 19th century, and far earlier if one recognizes that the earliest 'corporations' were chartered with public interest objectives as well as private economic objectives in mind."[2]

This issue is beginning to be addressed by companies in the mining industry. For example, the Australian Commonwealth Scientific and Industrial Research Organization (CSIRO) works with mining companies to benchmark social performance and facilitate stakeholder engagement.[3] The companies' social license to operate is considered as essential as the fulfillment of formal regulatory conditions. Today, various forms of corporate social responsibility (CSR) typically encompass environmental performance as well as a range of employees, supply chain, product safety, and community concerns. Surveys have shown the increasing importance of such activities among consumers. "The 2015 Cone Communications Global CSR Study (conducted in nine countries) found that Global consumers view CSR as a personal responsibility to be integrated and championed across the things they buy and the companies they work at and invite into their neighborhoods—and are willing to make sacrifices to address social and environmental issues. Ninety percent of the over 10,000 consumers surveyed said they would switch to brands that supported responsible causes."[4]

Despite such popular desire for CSR initiatives, efforts to adopt them can face resistance. More than 40 percent of executives and investors in a 2004 survey by the *Economist* cited "cost implications and unproven benefits" as the biggest obstacles to implementation.[5] Measuring the specific business value of such initiatives can be difficult, as noted by McKinsey and Co.: "The perceived importance of corporate environmental, social, and governance systems has soared in recent years as executives, investors, and regulators have grown increasingly aware that such programs can mitigate corporate crises and build reputations. But no consensus has emerged to define whether and how such programs create shareholder value, how to measure that value, or how to benchmark financial performance from company to company."[6] The HBS Social Enterprise Institute's research made similar conclusions: "There is increasing pressure to dress up CSR as a business discipline and demand that every initiative deliver business results. That is asking too much of CSR and distracts from what must be its main goal: to align a company's social and environmental activities with its business purpose and value."[7]

A further challenge is that some companies, especially those primarily concerned with reputational benefits, may view corporate responsibility as an easier-to-achieve substitute for the rigors of implementing truly sustainable practices. This is because there is no specific definition for when an enterprise has attained "responsibility" to its stakeholders. In addition, the enterprise may not include future generations in its definition of stakeholders. In this case, the organization may be guilty of greenwashing.

Organizations have a responsibility to keep their stakeholders informed about the issues that negatively impact them and the efforts to mitigate their causes. Providing a mechanism for these individuals and groups to offer feedback on the policies and practices that most affect them is central to successful stakeholder engagement.

## Engaging Employees

Each stakeholder group has unique needs, and the impacts they experience do not occur in isolation. In the following sections, I will highlight some specific stakeholder issues that sustainability professionals should understand and take into account when planning how to engage employees in the sustainability agenda of their company.

*Engaging employees through workplace health and safety programs.* Public safety and health have been a foundation of environmental and occupational health protection regulations and enterprise sustainability management systems. For example, the US Clean Air Act, the EU's REACH (Registration, Evaluation, Authorization, and Restriction of Chemicals) regulations, and Taiwan's Occupational Safety and Health Act all provide for the establishment and enforcement of standards related to public health. Many enterprises combine human health and safety goals with environmental sustainability efforts using environmental management systems (EMSs). In the Plan-Do-Check-Act process that is part of such a system, organizations set important health and safety goals.[8] For example, goals to reach zero workplace injuries, limit overtime, and increase employee fitness program participation all improve the work environment.

*Engaging employees through paying livable compensation.* A living wage, or a just wage, is a human right defined in the UDHR: "Article 23: Everyone who works has the right to just and favorable remuneration ensuring for himself and his family an existence worthy of human dignity and supplemented, if necessary, by other means of social protection."[9]

As described in chapter 2, a **living wage** is defined as the theoretical income level that an individual must earn to pay for basic essentials such as shelter, food, and water in the country where the individual resides. Hence, in the United States for example, a living wage is the wage rate per hour sufficient that one wage earner can afford a two-bedroom apartment while paying no more than 30 percent of their gross income (before taxes) for total housing costs. However, the unfortunate reality in the fashion industry is that workers often live in poverty, even when they are compensated at the minimum levels required by law. The Organization for Economic Cooperation and Development (OECD) Guidelines for Multinational Enterprises, adopted by forty-six countries, calls for the best possible wages that can satisfy the basic needs of the workers and their families.[10]

*Engaging employees through employee ownership programs.* Employer ownership commonly means that employees own shares in the company where they are employed. According to the employee ownership attorney Deborah Groban Olson, employer ownership helps enhance productivity, which further promotes corporate sustainability in two ways:

1. *Economic*: Local people are employed, typically at higher wages, which means that profit-retention benefits the local economy.
2. *Environmental*: Local owners are more likely to protect the local environment.[11]

*Engaging employees through engagement programs and work-life balance programs.* To engage their employees in sustainability programs, business owners may use various incentive programs in which employees are incentivized to reach certain business sustainability goals. For example, one common way is to reward employees when they achieve a certain goal, which might include reduction in paper use in the workplace, water and energy savings, recycling initiatives, or bicycling or walking instead of driving to work. Additionally, to support a healthy work-life balance, many employers have considered including or have already initiated programs such as remote work, flexible schedules, family leave, optional training, well-being programs, and career development opportunities. For example, Patagonia is known for their childcare programs, which became a hallmark of the company culture. As stated by the company, "since starting this program thirty-plus years ago, Patagonia's team has an incredible 95 percent retention of the moms at the company."[12]

*Engaging employees through education and training.* Sustainability science is a complex and relatively new academic discipline. It involves many different areas, including systems thinking, life-cycle analysis, and social justice, to name just a few. While only a handful of people who work in a company might have deep interests in matters of sustainability, implementing sustainability in everyday business practice require everyone's participation. For this reason, it is important to deepen employees' awareness and understanding of sustainability issues. Recycling at the corporate level represents a simple example of the sustainability-related topics that can be addressed through education and training. The importance of employee education can also be seen within Global Reporting Initiative (GRI) guidelines, which require companies to report initiatives they have in place in this category. For example, per GRI guidelines, businesses must report the "average hours of training per year per employee by gender and by employee category" and "programs for skills management and lifelong learning that support the continued employability of employees and assist them in managing career endings."[13] Similarly, commitment to worker training is assessed for B-Corp certification. In fact B Corp website reports that B-Corps companies take care of their employees beyond their "on-the-clock" contributions, as this is a way to build caring environment and increase employees retention.[14]

## Engaging Suppliers

In the fashion industry, we have already seen many successful examples of how a supplier can be engaged in an optimal way and how the company can create positive local value for the community where the sourcing occurs. For instance, Akola is a globally inspired jewelry brand, sourced and created by women in Uganda, Africa. The name Akola means "she works" in a local Ugandan dialect. Akola's mission is "to empower women to transform their lives and communities."[15] Akola currently employs nearly two hundred women. This is what the founder of Akola brand, Brittany Merrill Underwood, says about her initiative: "In Uganda, the average person earns less than a $1.90 per day. As part of her employment, an Akola woman receives living wages that enable her and her family to live above the poverty line. But job creation isn't enough. Akola also provides a holistic curriculum of programs: training employees in leadership and financial literacy and giving them the skills that will graduate their entire family out of poverty and into long-term self-reliance."[16]

Perhaps the most inspiring ideas for supplier engagement can be borrowed from innovative social enterprises that are taking on various social challenges throughout the world. The following are two representative examples: Batik Boutique is a social enterprise located in Malaysia.[17] Batik Boutique creates fair-trade handmade batik textiles made with natural fibers. They work with artisans across rural parts of Malaysia. Women from low-income backgrounds are trained in basic sewing techniques so that they can have employment opportunities, allowing them to achieve and sustain economic freedom. The company also provides childcare and education for the artisans' children.

A similar concept is shared by Kandahar Treasure, "a social enterprise dedicated to providing employment opportunities for women in Kandahar, Afghanistan." Kandahar Treasure provides female workers with the training and support to traditional Khamak embroidered pieces.

> Khamak is a centuries-old embroidery tradition in which geometric designs are embroidered onto a base fabric counting the weave of the fabric without using a trace. Women create their own patterns inspired by Islamic Art, and this talent is embroidered onto fabrics using their inherent artistry. Women in southern Afghanistan have embellished their homes and the clothes of their loved ones with this technique for centuries, and Kandahar Treasure has brought this art form for the first time to the world market. The vision of Kandahar Treasure is to give value and importance to the fine authentic work of the women of southern Afghanistan as this work is the main form of expression of the women of this region.[18]

## Engaging Future Generations

According to the United Nations World Youth Report, "The active engagement of youth in sustainable development efforts is central to achieving sustainable societies in the near future."[19] However, in a survey conducted by the UN in August 2012, a majority of 13,000 young respondents in 186 countries expressed they feel excluded and marginalized in their societies and communities, where they have limited opportunities to participate in decision-making processes. Thus, in order to move forward with sustainable development, there is a greater need for participatory structures between the youth and companies. To support youth engagement in sustainability actions, the UNDP published the following statement: "Young people can engage in peacebuilding, leading non-violent revolutions, using new technologies to mobilize societies to bring about change. Young people have demonstrated the potential to build bridges across communities, working together—[they] are vital stakeholders in conflict and in peace-building."[20]

As local communities across the world embrace sustainability goals, young people can be engaged in various activities to support sustainable consumption. For example, young people must be educated to increase their understanding of how clothing consumption impacts our environment. It is critical, therefore, to incorporate elements of sustainability in school curricula from an early stage. A good example of this is the project The Story of Stuff by Annie Leonard, which highlighted some of the challenges that society faces resulting from excess waste generation.[21] The International Labour Organization (ILO) published guide booklets in 1996 concerning education and training to promote sustainable development.[22] It noted that sustainability education must be required at all stages of education.

An excellent example of educational programs for primary and secondary schools in Hong Kong can be seen in the case of the environmental charity Redress. Among the many impressive things they do, they are committed to teaching students in partner schools about the environmental impacts of their clothing choices. During their visits and lectures in schools, they encourage students to change unsustainable habits and make them feel excited to make a lifelong commitment to sustainability. Redress also publishes "School activity packs," which can be downloaded on their webpage.[23]

## Engaging Fashion Consumers

Drawn from the recent research findings of the Global Web Index international market research agency, here are some of the latest insights about young fashion consumers of which fashion brands should be aware:[24]

- Gen Z consumers are commonly supporting sustainability but also they are more likely to buy shoes and clothes even if they don't need them.[25]
- "Etsy's acquisition of the second-hand online shopping platform Depop reflects the fact that consumers are interested in buying secondhand and, importantly, that engagement in the circular economy is gathering momentum, especially among members of Gen Z."[26]
- Gen Z fashion consumers believe that brands need to guide them on how to mend and store their clothes. Gen Z consumers believe that these initiatives are important for sustainable development.

- "53% of Gen Z shoppers who buy sustainable products think it is important to use recycled materials."[27]
- Gen Z agrees that recommerce is important for sustainable development.
- "To gain Gen Z consumer trust, brands must be transparent and accountable for their actions."[28]

Nongovernmental entities are perhaps most proactive in the ways they stimulate consumer engagement. For example, Fashion Revolution, an NGO that publishes annual transparency rankings of companies in the fashion industry, is encouraging consumers to be more engaged in transforming the industry through activism. On their website and social media channels, they call for consumers to raise their voice and become involved.[29] The campaign is called "Who made my clothes?" and they suggest that consumers ask brands to disclose more information about workers in the supply chain networks that stand behind the clothes they sell. This is how Fashion Revolution promotes consumer-engagement initiatives:

> Your voice can change everything. Since Fashion Revolution started, people from all over the world have used their voice and their power to tell brands that things must change. And it's working. The industry is starting to change. More brands are being open about where their clothes are made. More manufacturers are making their factories safer. More producers are being seen and heard. But the story is far from over. We are only just getting started. We cannot stop until every garment worker who makes the clothes we love is seen, heard, paid properly, and working in safe conditions. Your voice does make a difference. We need to make this Fashion Revolution Week bigger and bolder than ever before. Ask brands #whomademyclothes?[30]

Fashion Revolution lists some tangible actions consumers can take to support the #whomademyclothes campaign, including sending email to a brand and sharing their voice on Twitter and Instagram posts.[31] Their annual publication *Fashion Revolution Impact Report* reported the following consumers engagement statistics for 2021: 569 million consumers total were reached on social media, 4.2 million posts with "Fashion Revolution" hashtag were made, 284,000 consumers were engaged on social media, and the organization gained 177,000 new followers on social media. Fashion Revolution is a truly people-driven movement; the organization is registered in the UK, with another 14 registered offices and voluntary teams in 78 countries around the world.[32]

## Six Forms of Sustainable Fashion: What Sustainable Fashion Should Consumers Buy?

Much of the existing knowledge on sustainable business practices comes from the fashion industry. Topics including innovation in fiber and material design, optimization of the production processes to reduce the environmental impacts of fashion, and waste management strategies are frequently discussed among fashion brands, but they are also discussed among other important industry players, including market research agencies, NGOs, fashion media, and various activist groups. However, the question of how fashion consumers can improve their own clothing consumption practices has received much less industry attention. In order to explore opportunities in that important but often neglected area, in Fall of 2020 I joined the Sustainable Fashion Consumption Network, which helped me to make contact with a group of academic researchers and practitioners interested in topics related to fashion consumption.[33] To date, our international community has published extensive research in the area of sustainable fashion consumption, and many of the topic areas are related to consumer engagement in sustainability. For instance, some of the collaborative research papers published by group members cover the following areas: sustainable alternatives to fast fashion, secondhand shopping, clothing swaps, clothing rental, the sharing economy, collaborative consumption, trends of fashion minimalism, downsizing, wardrobe decluttering, and mindful consumption. Based on my recent research findings in the sustainable consumption area, I will here elaborate on two points. First, I will discuss how we as consumers can influence fashion brands to further advance sustainability, because both consumers and producers/brands must act together in order to support industry transformation. Second, I will define what sustainable fashion truly means and will propose six paths for sustainable fashion consumption that any sustainability-oriented consumer can easily adopt in everyday life. Let's get started.

First, it is clear that we as consumers have a right to know by whom, where, and under what working conditions the branded apparel we consider purchasing was produced.[34] For that reason, transparency in the fashion industry is critically important. Because many brands still rely heavily on promoting falsely claimed sustainable practices, in a practice known as greenwashing, we must demand more information from brands we like in order to support them financially through our purchases. Similarly, it is urgent to replace fancy sustainability commitments with tangible and verifiable evidence of sustainability. For example, manufacturing maps and supplier lists with factory names and addresses should be accessible online. Videos showing real-time conditions in factories can be streamed in the store and online. Likewise, material traceability should be easier, as to date we as consumers still do not know the full lists of apparel components, nor do we know the origin of all (100 percent) of the material sources.

Second, we as consumers have a right to be given an option to select among a greater variety of sustainable products. If we exclude all brands that self-proclaim the sustainability of their products, our choice of truly sustainable products remains very limited. In practice, this means that brands should offer only garments, accessories, and shoes that are officially certified with legitimate third-party certificates in order not to deceive consumers by promising sustainable attributes they cannot deliver. Third-party certificates are important to showcase production ethics and guarantee consumption safety. All other value-free and illegitimate "sustainability" certificates should be banned as deceptive. This would help prevent many brands from monetarizing on self-proclaimed green, natural, organic, eco-friendly, and sustainable qualities their products do not have.

Third, we as consumers must have greater accessibility to sustainable services. For example, fashion retailers should provide in-store circular opportunities for consumers to repair, redesign, and customize their items. The option to buy fashion on-demand is still limited, but it might become one of the mainstream paths for sustainable fashion businesses in the future. Similarly, fashion brands need to consider selling their unsold (discounted) merchandise from previous seasons, as well as their secondhand items. Those practices would substantially encourage consumers to buy products that have already been produced and sold once, and it would help to prevent overproduction of new and unneeded items.

With this information in mind, as consumers we already have various options available to improve our consumption practices and influence brands to advance fashion in a more sustainable and circular direction. However, we also must be aware that sustainable fashion has become a topic of a keen debate, with the result that thousands of brands and fashion media outlets have dedicated themselves to answering the question of what sustainable fashion is and what consumers should buy. "Particularly within the fashion media, sustainability has often been promoted misleadingly. For example, in the 1990s fashion magazines, environmentally friendly fashion or the so-called green chic was described as 'natural,' 'pure,' 'green,' and 'recycled,' regardless of the ethics of its production and the material provenance." Similar misconceptions are part of the context today. For example, "Fashion brands commonly compartmentalize sustainability as an environmental issue. Even through natural resource scarcity and ongoing climate change severely affect the lives of individuals, regions, and communities, sustainability is often not seen as an equally important social problem." Moreover, "Brands tend to promote sustainability commitments primarily through pro-environmental improvements such as resource circularity, recycling, and repair, while their pro-social business activities such as workers' rights, anti-discrimination, living wage, child labor, etc., especially in their supply chain, remain essentially unknown and certainly less advertised." Similarly, some apparel products are "mislabeled as eco, conscious, or sustainable even when they clearly lack official certification or have ambiguous material lists and unclear information about the product's country of origin." This practice creates "great uncertainties on the part of consumers, who report that they are not sure what sustainability truly means and what social and/or environmental consequences fashion production and consumption entails."[35] To make it easier to avoid possible misconceptions that that may be systematically produced by various industry players, I will first summarize what we have learned so far about the true meanings of sustainable fashion. Next, I will elaborate on how we as fashion consumers can consume fashion in six sustainable ways to support progress toward sustainability in the fashion industry.

As argued throughout this book, the most common understanding of sustainability advancements is related to the business itself. For this reason, it seems clear that "sustainable fashion is embedded in the entire business model and that it determines how, where, and under what conditions products are made. It also determines how the products are packaged, labeled, and promoted while ensuring that product declarations clearly instruct consumers how to maintain, repair, and/or dispose of goods they have bought."[36]

To summarize, the fashion that sustainability-conscious consumers should buy have the following forms and characteristics.

1. *Sustainable fashion is circular.* Rationale: In order to "shift from the linearity reflected in take-make-dispose logic, sustainable fashion is grounded in a circular mentality in which things are used and re-used. Aligned with that philosophy, sustainable fashion aims to reduce waste, preserve already-created products, and save natural resources. Therefore, all newly created products must fit into one of two categories and be ether a) biodegradable, i.e., naturally decomposable, or b) recyclable in either a mechanical or a chemical way."[37] Practically, this means that consumers should seek repairable, high-quality products preferably made from 100 percent pure materials which can have a long life-cycle, as well as another life after being used, reused, and recycled.

2. *Sustainable fashion is considered sustainable luxury.* Rationale: "Sustainable fashion is well grounded in a conscientious aesthetics in which products are designed to last." Sustainable luxury is well-crafted and produced in a small quantity. In practice, this means that sustainable luxury products are "valuable, high-quality goods that can be passed on to others to use for the same purpose."[38]

3. *Sustainable fashion includes second-hand, vintage, and swapped items.* Rationale: "Sustainable fashion is grounded in the principle of connectivity and shared values. Aiming to extend the life cycle of already-existing whole products, sustainable fashion supports product re-use that may involve redistribution and resale. In addition to its social significance, sharing pre-owned clothes with others in need brings important environmental savings as reselling clothes preserves resources otherwise needed for new production."[39]

4. *Sustainable fashion can be repaired, upcycled, and repurposed.* Rationale: Sustainable fashion is waste-free fashion. For this reason, instead of new production, it always prioritizes the usage of "repaired, upcycled, and upgraded products that were previously discarded but can be repurposed to gain new life."[40]

5. *Sustainable fashion is ethically produced.* Rationale: "Sustainable fashion is intended to generate wellbeing for all the various stakeholders and individuals involved in or affected by the sourcing, production, use, reuse, and disposal of textiles. Opposed to fast, and disposable fashion, sustainable fashion truly aims to reattach people to the clothing they wear. It reconnects consumers with various producers, starting from the person who stitched, dyed, or labeled the product and continuing to the person who put it on the retail shelves."[41]

6. *Sustainable fashion is officially certified.* Rationale: Sustainable fashion is never deceptive. It stands for what it stays. Sustainable fashion is "officially certified, and it includes products labeled with an approved trademark that guarantees product safety, quality, and production ethics."[42]

**Table 28**  Forms of sustainable fashion*

| *Sustainable Fashion Form* | *Qualities* | *Examples* |
|---|---|---|
| Circular | 100% "Biodegradable or Recyclable" | The plant shoe by Native, Rothy's |
| Sustainable luxury | "Produced in small scales Based on unique designer/ artisan expertise Custom-made Durable/Repairable High quality" | Patagonia (B Corp), Eileen Fisher (B Corp) Prota Fiori (B Corp), Another Tomorrow (B Corp) |
| Secondhand | "Pre-loved Compassionately shared Affordable | Vestiaire Collective, Renew by Eileen Fisher |
| Vintage | | |
| Swapped | Unique finds" | |

(*Continues*)

**Table 28** Continued

| Sustainable Fashion Form | Qualities | Examples |
|---|---|---|
| Repaired | Upgraded quality and/or functionality | The Zero Waste Collection by Alabama Chanin |
| Upcycled | New purpose | |
| Repurposed | Prolonged life cycle | |
| Ethically made | "Free from human exploitation Ethically sourced and produced" Authentic, traditional art forms Local expertise | B-Corp certified fashion businesses Artisan brands (e.g., Lemlem, The Peruvian connection) |
| Officially certified | "Approved and verified quality Legally compliant" | *GOTS, GRS, Fairtrade NoNasties—100% certified organic, vegan clothing |

*Table is reproduced and quotes from Iva Jestratijevic and Nancy A. Rudd, "Six Forms of Sustainable Fashion," *Latest Trends in Textile and Fashion Designing* 2, no. 4 (Aug. 2018): 220–22, http://dx.doi.org/10.32474/LTTFD.2018.02.000145.

Since the sustainability in our industry continuously evolves, this table of sustainable consumption will certainly grow in the future. For this reason, I recommend that readers follow updates on other current and inspiring sustainable consumption practices. For example, Redress, an environmental charity, frequently shares updates on these and similar topics on their consumer campaign page.[43] Likewise, Redress organizes various campaigns, workshops, and seminars discussing how to buy, wear, take care of, and dispose of clothing, so if you have interest in these topics, be sure to follow their online activities.

## Sustainability Expert Profile: Dr. Elena Karpova

Dr. Elena Karpova was born and grew up in Igarka, a town of twenty-five thousand people located in Northern Siberia, just above the Arctic Circle (for comparison, think *very* northern Canada). It was a close-knit, very safe community that can be reached only by plane; there are no highways, roads, or railroads. When she was twelve, Elena began making her own clothes on a treadle sewing machine. She made several skirts, upcycled a couple of her dad's shirts into cute tops, and created her own prom dress. A major barrier was that she did not know how to make patterns, so after graduating high school, she chose a major that would teach her that. Her five-year training as an apparel engineer was very rigorous. She spent months in sewing labs and studios developing patterns and then making the garments. She started to make all her clothes herself, from tops, bottoms, and dresses to outerwear made of leather and fur. She loved the process of coming up with original designs, developing patterns, working on an impeccable fit, and producing garments of high craftsmanship. For several years Elena had her own tailoring business where she designed and custom made garments to make sure they fit the customers' personalities and flattered their body shapes and skin and hair color tones.

Elena continued her education in the United States, where she received a PhD in textile products marketing from the University of North Carolina at Greensboro and went on to be a professor at Iowa State University. Fifteen years later, she returned to her alma mater as a Putman & Hayes Distinguished Professor, where she now teaches undergraduate and graduate courses in sourcing, consumer behavior, and product development and marketing.

Elena loves clothes. She loves getting dressed—choosing colors, textures, and shapes, and especially when all these magically come together to create a unique outfit. For her clothing is a form of art—you can create it every day and then wear it. Clothing can be used to express who you are and why you are. Elena also loves shopping for clothes. She does not buy much, which makes the process even more special. Instead of following trends, she follows her own style, which has been continuously evolving. When shopping, she carefully picks and chooses items that she loves and that fit her style. Most garments in her wardrobe are between seven and fifteen years old, with some twenty-plus years old that she made herself, such as a pair of leather pants or an Italian boiled-wool cropped top.

At the same time, Elena is keenly aware that the fashion industry is one of the most polluting of the manufacturing sectors. Her research focuses on apparel consumption—why and how people buy, use, care for, and dispose of clothes—to reduce their environmental footprint. She is also interested in how and why people consume apparel unsustainably; for instance, what drives people to adopt fast fashion—buying and disposing of clothes frequently to keep up with the latest fashion trends or to succumb to peer pressure in order to fit in? In a recent research project, Elena developed a typology of sustainable apparel consumers after carefully studying a thousand *New York Times* readers' comments posted to an article that discussed the negative environmental impact of the fashion industry. She determined that people who want to reduce the footprint of their apparel purchases can be divided into four distinct groups based on two factors: 1) how much individuals are willing and/or able to spend on clothing, and 2) how important clothing and appearance are for them.

In another research project, Elena examined swapping—an emerging type of collaborative consumption that involves exchanging garments with other people. Collaborative consumption (swapping, renting, borrowing items from clothing libraries, etc.) is good for people, because it allows them to acquire garments at a fraction of the cost of buying new clothes, and is good for the environment, because it facilitates the redistribution of unused and underutilized garments, thus reducing the need to produce new products at the cost of tons of water and other renewable resources (i.e., wood to make viscose and other cellulosic fibers) and nonrenewable resources (i.e., oil to produce polyester and other synthetic fibers). To help educate the public and especially future industry professionals, Elena devoted an entire chapter to sustainability in the book *Going Global: The Textile and Apparel Industry*[44] and coauthored another book, *The Dangers of Fashion: Towards Ethical and Sustainable Solutions*.[45]

To walk the talk, Elena has gradually altered her own clothing consumption. Here are some of her practices that she hopes might work for other individuals who want to consume sustainably:

- Stick to buying clothing you need and/or love. Ask yourself the following questions: Do I need it? Do I love it (how it looks, fits, feels)? If yes, then buy it. Don't buy it if you only like a garment or want it.

- Another question to ask yourself: Am I going to wear the garment at least thirty times? If not, pass.
- Think of fashion as an investment. Buy more expensive pieces whenever you can; high quality garments last longer, and you will take better care of them because (a) you love them, and (b) you paid more for them.
- When you need something, check out consignment or other resale stores in the neighborhood or online. You may be surprised by what you find.
- When you really need something new to wear, check the back of your closet for items you have forgotten about. Alternatively, consider swapping five to seven of your garments with a close friend who wears the same size. Sharing photos of your outfits with the friend will make it a fun, bonding experience, not to mention a significant addition to your wardrobe. The swapping can be temporary or permanent.
- Avoid using a dryer, and instead air-dry your clothes. The United States is the only country where most people use dryers, which are the energy gobblers. Besides, your clothes will last much longer when they are not damaged in a dryer. Maybe you can sacrifice the softness of your towels to save the planet.

## Case study 11: Capsule wardrobe

Clothing consumption on a mass scale is a major producer of greenhouse gas emissions. More precisely, McKinsey's research shows that in 2018, the fashion industry sector alone was responsible for about 4 percent of the global greenhouse gas emissions that originated primarily from garment manufacturing and clothes washing.[46] Moreover, statistics shows that "the number of garments produced annually has doubled since 2000 and exceeded 100 billion for the first time in 2014: nearly 14 items of clothing for every person on earth. The average consumer now buys 60% more clothing items a year and keeps them for about half as long as they did about 15 years ago." To reduce negative environmental impacts, there is an urgent need for consumers to react, and downsize their consumption.

Research shows that "extending the life of clothing by an extra nine months of active use would reduce carbon, waste and water footprints by around 20-30% each and cut resource costs by 20%."[47]

*What is a capsule wardrobe all about*? "Capsule Wardrobe projects aim to promote the idea that the most sustainable clothing is the one we already own. Thus, one of the simplest ways to reduce the negative environmental impact of our unsustainable shopping habits (e.g., impulsive buying, clothes hoarding, trend hunting and quick disposal) is to keep our clothes in use for longer and make use of what we already have."[48]

**Student Activity**: In this activity, at the beginning of the semester students create a capsule wardrobe that contains all of their clothes deemed necessary for the course of a semester in order to reflect on their consumption needs and the forces that influence them. The number of items should be minimal. Commonly students manage to wear around twenty to thirty items during fifteen weeks. Sometimes, students challenge themselves and choose only eleven to fifteen items to wear. Alternatively, students sometimes opt for a higher number of items (up to forty). At the end of the semester, students submit a final project report and photos of their capsule wardrobe. In the report they are expected to summarize the experience of wearing the capsule wardrobe.

# The Intersections of COVID-19 with Business and Sustainability

The fashion industry was turned upside-down when government-ordered lockdowns were instituted for many countries around the world due to the COVID-19 pandemic. Many small and medium-size companies have had to adapt and evolve though increased strategic dexterity, which means that they have had to entirely reconsider their business structures and attempt to learn from the success and failures of others as well as focusing on the social, environmental, technological, and economic aspects directly resulting from the pandemic.[49] The pandemic has directly influenced businesses to adopt sustainable practices at an accelerated pace. According to McKinsey and

Company's *State of Fashion 2022* report "60% of fashion executives have already invested or plan to invest in closed-loop recycling next year."[50] Executives also rank sustainability as their second most prominent challenge after supply chain disruptions.[51] *Green Biz* reported the following major trends captured in the business environment during pandemic:

1. *A sustainable recovery is needed after the crisis.* "The COVID-19 pandemic has brought many weaknesses to the surface, in particular highlighting the destructive impacts of many business models on humans and the environment. According to the OECD, for the economic recovery from the crisis to be durable and resilient, a return to business as usual with its environmentally destructive patterns and activities must be avoided. Unchecked, global environmental emergencies, such as climate change and biodiversity loss, could cause social and economic damages far greater than those caused by the virus."[52]

2. *Increased disclosure and reporting requirements.* *Green Biz* report also predicts that in the future governments are going to make sustainability reporting mandatory. New Zealand's government and the UK government announced that they will implement mandatory climate risk reporting for large companies. Although prior to the pandemic it was obvious that businesses "were making progress in disclosing their environmental impacts and governance standards, social factors had not been given the same attention."[53] There have been numerous debates on how to capture and assess data on social issues, and perhaps reporting social improvements remains one of the biggest business challenges in the future.

# The Impact of COVID-19 on Garment Workers

At the beginning of March 2020, many businesses were forced to close their brick-and-mortar locations to protect public health. However, probably the worst forms of "the hardships of the pandemic have fallen on the most vulnerable members of the supply chain: the garment workers." The Fashion Revolution NGO reports that fashion brands have "cancelled more than US $40 billion finished and in-production orders of goods from factories and suppliers." The Worker Rights Consortium (WRC) reported that during the first two months of the pandemic in 2020, "Across just 31 facilities investigated, 37,367 workers were denied US $39.8 million in wages to which they were entitled—meaning that each garment worker lost approximately five months' worth of wages. By continuing their research, WRC has identified an additional 210 garment factories and production facilities across 18 countries in the same year in which 160,000 workers were owed an estimated US $171.5 million after the outbreak of COVID-19."[54]

The Workers' Rights Consortium (WRC), in association with the Center for Global Worker's Rights (CGWR) at Pennsylvania State University published a COVID-19 Tracker naming the brands that acted responsibly (or not) towards their supply chain workers during the COVID-19 crisis. To create the report, they studied "the following sources: public statements by the corporation (including statements reported by credible news sources), direct correspondence with the WRC and/or CGWR, information provided by country-level associations of suppliers, and information provided by individual suppliers."[55] The tracker is updated regularly, but for the purpose of this book section. I will list only data from the current state of affairs for brands assessed at the time of the writing of this book section (in January 2022).

The Workers' Rights Consortium (WRC) and the Center for Global Workers' Rights (CGWR) at Pennsylvania State University disclosed the following justification of the methods they used to determine companies' commitments:

> Brands listed as having made a commitment to pay in full met the following criteria with respect to all orders placed (and on which fabric was cut) prior to the inception of the crisis:
>
> - The brand is paying the originally agreed prices for all in-production, finished, and shipped orders, with no requests for discounts or rebates;
> - The brand is not canceling orders, except with full compensation to suppliers.
> - The brand is not delaying shipping dates, or, if any delays have been imposed, they are small in scale and length and the brand is providing reasonable accommodation to affected suppliers; and
> - If the brand is delaying any payments relative to agreed terms, the brand is providing affected suppliers with access to low-cost financing so that suppliers' cash flow is unaffected.[56]

**Table 29** COVID-19 Tracker naming the brands that acted responsibly (or not) toward their supply chain workers during the COVID-19 crisis (as of January 2022)*

| *Brands Committed to Paying in Full for Orders Completed and in Production* | *Brands That Have Made No Commitment to Pay in Full for Orders Completed and in Production* |
|---|---|
| Adidas | Arcadia (TopShop) |
| Amazon | American Eagle Outfitters |
| ASOS | Balmain |
| H&M | Esprit |
| Inditex (Zara) | JCPenney |
| Lululemon | Kohl's |
| Marks & Spenser | Ross Stores |
| Moschino | Sears |
| Nike | The Children's Place |
| PVH (Calvin Klein, Tommy Hilfiger) | TJX (T.J. Maxx, Marshalls) |
| Ralph Lauren Corporation (Polo) | Urban Outfitters (Anthropologie) |
| Target | Walmart |
| Tesco | Oscar De La Renta |
| UNIQLO | Mothercare |
| Under Armour | Edinburgh Woolen Mill (Bonmarché, Peacocks) |
| VF Corp. (JanSport, The North Face, Vans, Timberland) | Li & Fung/Global Brands Group |

*This table is adapted from "COVID 19-Tracker," *Workers Rights*, accessed August 1, 2023: https://www.workersrights.org/issues/covid-19/tracker/. Please check the original source of these data to see how the status of their commitments may have changed for some brands.

## The COVID-19 Pandemic's Push Toward Sustainable Consumption

Due to the COVID-19 pandemic at the beginning of March 2020, many fashion businesses were forced to close their retail stores. With a large portion of their revenue stream cut off, numerous retailers were forced to innovate their business models to reach customers at their homes. With more time at home, many consumers were able to take the time to evaluate their consumption behaviors, leading them to place more value on sustainable businesses. This inevitably led consumers to prefer sustainable clothing retailers in line with their newfound values. Each consumer has a different set of values that led them to sustainable consumption, whether functional, social, emotional, or conditional values that consumers find within their purchasing behavior.[57] McKinsey and Company's *State of Fashion 2020* report found that many consumers were able to increase their knowledge of sustainability, bringing a new wave of consumers concerned about how their consumption affected the natural environment around them.[58] Consumers who regularly shopped with retailers like Rent the Runway or Nuuly no longer wanted clothing from those companies due to the lockdown and instead made orders from home, which led to the drying up of many companies' revenue streams. In a recent scientific study on rental platforms in fashion, it was determined that due to the increase in consumers who value the sustainable model that clothing rental retailers provide, retailers who were able to make it through the worst parts of the pandemic should see heightened financial gains when the economy starts to rebound.[59] This information is backed up by ThredUp research, which found that consumers had favorable attitudes toward clothing rental services during the pandemic, indicating that the potential of clothing contamination did not seem to be a large deterrent for the consumers.[60] The companies can capitalize on the increased awareness of sustainability efforts that many companies are making to ensure decreased waste and carbon emissions during the clothing manufacturing process.

Next, research also shows that during the lockdown, many consumers were able to reflect more on how their consumption affects not only themselves but also the environment around them. For example, in a study conducted in Israel, consumers were surveyed to examine how their recy-cling habits differed between the prepandemic period and the current moment when they must stay at home. Results showed that 40 percent of low-intensity recyclers and 20 percent of moderate/high-intensity recyclers intended to increase their recycling behavior going forward.[61] There has also been an increase in the upcycling of materials to appeal to consumers' sustainable values. This activity can be found in all areas of fashion due to the millennial and generation-Z cohorts having more time to express their creativity and sustainable values.

Also, with stay-at-home orders in place, many consumers altered their clothing consumption to reflect the "new normal," which consisted of comfortable clothing rather than their regular business attire.[62]

A study conducted during the lockdown that mined Tweets from the social media platform Twitter (now X) found that there were many shifts in consumer sentiment when it came to the consumption of clothing. Consumers were looking for more simplistic clothing that appealed to life at home since there was not a need for items driven by trends. This study also found that consumers were affected by disruption in their consumption practices, either forcing them to shop online more or increasing the amount of pent-up demand for shopping goods.[63] Also, consumers were more likely to purchase essential goods rather than nonessential items such as entertain-ment or services. To help alleviate the stress of not being able to go to stores, many consumers resorted to shopping online.[64]

## Meet the Post–COVID-19 Fashion Consumers

In the 2021 fashion resale market and trend report, ThredUp published a data-driven report about postpandemic fashion consumer behavior, providing important insights about changes in fashion consumers' shopping motivations due to the pandemic. Let's examine the most significant changes revealed in this report.

- Consumers increasingly care about sustainability. "One in three consumers state that they care more about wearing sustainable apparel now than before the pandemic."

- Consumers reduce the amount of money they want to invest into low quality fashion purchase. Every second consumer who participated in the survey said that seeking value in the products they consume is becoming more important now after the pandemic. Also, 43 percent of surveyed consumers said they prefer to buy garments they can easily resell. "Moms especially are willing to spend more on secondhand purchases in the coming years" to reduce the burden of increasing clothing costs.
- Consumers care about reducing amounts of textile waste. Fifty-one percent of consumers expressed concerns as the creation of unnecessary environmental waste is increasing due to unsustainable clothing consumption.[65]

The McKinsey 2020 report on *Consumers' Sentiments on Sustainability in Fashion* complements the above-mentioned findings by providing additional insights about relevant fashion consumer behavior:

- "While the fashion industry is reorganizing for the new normal, it should consider that fashion consumers want brands to uphold their social and environmental responsibilities amid the crisis. Of surveyed European consumers, 67 percent consider the use of sustainable materials to be an important factor in determining their purchasing choices, and 63 percent consider a brand's promotion of sustainability the same way."
- Fashion consumers said despite the pandemic they "expect brands to take care of their employees and workers" as brands need to maintain consistency in their sustainability commitments during the crisis.
- Pandemic showed that fashion brands need to "build trust and transparency with consumers, as 70 percent of consumers are sticking with brands they know and trust during the crisis."
- "88 percent of consumers are experiencing a slow recovery or a recession. As a result, consumer spending on fashion is also changing. More than 60 percent of consumers report spending less on fashion during the crisis, and approximately half expect that trend to continue after the crisis passes. As a solution, consumers are likely to cut back on

accessories, jewelry, and other discretionary categories before reducing their spending on apparel and footwear."

- Also the report showed that "the pandemic crisis has recruited new consumers to online shopping platforms. 43 percent of surveyed consumers who did not purchase fashion online before the crisis have started using online channels. That shift is unlikely to reverse, at least not among the Generation Z and millennial cohorts as nearly 28 percent of consumers in those age groups expect to buy less at physical stores."
- There is greater interest in purchasing secondhand fashion following the pandemic crisis.[66]

As there is a great consistency in the findings of these two recent reports, we can conclude that "the COVID-19 crisis should be considered as an important reset opportunity for fashion brands across a variety of sectors." I hope that fashion brands will reflect on findings from these significant reports and use them to potentially reduce emphasis on fashion seasonality and emphasize the importance of circularity in the future.[67]

## Moving Forward in Your Sustainability Career

Sustainability is a highly diverse career field that offers opportunities across many different industries, including the textile and fashion industry, the home-décor industry, the packaging industry, beauty and cosmetics, and more! So what types of positions can be considered as a part of sustainability career?

As has been suggested throughout this book, sustainability can help companies across various industry sectors to conduct business better. Therefore, I always say to my students that sustainability challenges encourage managers to "analyze complex problems, explore innovative solutions, and make informed decisions."[68] Broadly speaking, we can say that individuals with sustainability roles in any company focus on the following tasks:

- Ethical sourcing
- Circular product development and innovation

- Supply chain management
- Waste reduction
- Responsible Branding
- Sustainability reporting and management
- Ethics and governance
- Consumer engagement

In a recent years, we have witnessed a diverse range of employers advertise sustainability jobs. However, when fashion, retail, and merchandising students are searching for a job in this arena, the common problems are ambiguous and unstandardized job titles (e.g., sustainability coordinator, sustainability analysist, sustainability fellow, sustainability associate, and so forth) and the often confusing use of jargon (e.g., climate-positive consulting, net-zero consulting, green finance). Most often students in their senior years, when preparing for entry into the job market, cannot help but be confused about where to look for sustainability-oriented jobs. Then, once they find something that potentially resembles their interest, they are not quite sure what the terms in the job description truly mean. Here, I must clarify that this confusion is not because students are not familiar with sustainability terminology but because the terminology is often misused. Additional confusion arises when some companies advertise an "associate" role that requires a bachelor's degree while a master's degree is the only one considered at other firms for the very same position.

Students' frustrations are real. They often apply for forty-plus positions only to be told in an interview that the only thing they need is working experience. For greater clarity in the job market situation, I will here showcase two job postings that have crossed my desk in the past couple of years.

## H&M Regional Sustainability Manager*

Are you looking for an exciting opportunity to work in H&M, an organization that wants to change how fast fashion approaches sustainability? This might be it then! Apply today to be the Regional Sustainability manager and help us do what is right! What is Production? It's the place where design ideas are transformed into actual products. We are in over 20 sourcing markets and are the direct point of contact for local suppliers. We work to ensure our products are of good quality and produced at the best price and in a sustainable way. As the Regional Sustainability Manager, you are accountable for ensuring that sustainability goals are met for your region, guaranteeing both social and environmental standards. You are responsible for setting a vison for your region that is aligned with the global sustainability and business visions. You are responsible for setting goals and activities that will fulfill our overall business goals through collaboration with other functions in the company. You are also responsible for ensuring that the company works with only sustainable and approved vendors and suppliers in your region. You own sustainability initiatives, projects, and programs across your region and ensure that efforts are aligned with global and business goals. You regularly connect with NGOs, certification bodies, government organizations, and other companies in our industry to keep up to date with developments that impact routines and policies we already have in place. You identify upcoming challenges based on market trends and initiate projects/programs for future strategic plans. You manage a budget to drive meaningful investments which drive innovation, change, and improvements in your function's capabilities, processes, tools, and systems. Who are you? You deliver on the areas you have ownership for by living our values every day and primarily through collaboration and teamwork. You partner closely with the global sustainability team for Production to understand the global direction for the function and how to implement developments in your region. You also work closely with the supply chains to ensure they take into account sustainability topics in setting business strategies. You are solutions-oriented, constantly looking for ways for our suppliers and our internal teams to innovate and improve in the ways that we work. As the function head for Sustainability in your region, you act as a true H&M leader by being a role model of H&M's leadership expectations and by focusing on developing your people. Can you join the H&M Family? Of course, yes but only if you're comfortable in an environment with high levels of ambiguity and constant change. A place where your opinions matter right from day one, so you better have them and not be afraid to speak up. A place where 'doing what you're told' is more often 'questioning what you're told.' A place where you can make mistakes, learning from those mistakes to set an example by bringing changes for your own development. A place where you can't just work on auto-pilot completing your tasks but where you're pushed to think out-of-the-box. The good thing about it is that at H&M, we truly work together and help each other as a team, we don't just write slogans about it. This role can also be the start of a career in H&M, if earned through great results, engagement, and enthusiasm upon joining! So switch roles. Learn new skills. Take on new responsibilities. Dive off the deep end at H&M.

\* H&M job post published online in 2021 when job search was active.

When we discussed this job posting in the classroom, students found the job description to be somewhat ambiguous because the list of responsibilities was broadly described in the form of a narrative rather than in the form of the typical listing, but at least it was clear that this job targeted a sustainability professional who is probably, at minimum, in the middle of a sustainability career.

Let's consider another job ad that targeted a senior-level executive role.

## Levi's Senior Manager, Sustainability\*

Job Description: We believe that clothes—and how you make them—can make a difference. Since 1853, we've been obsessed with innovation to meet people's needs. We invented the first blue jeans. And we reinvented khaki pants. We pioneered labor and environmental guidelines for our manufacturing partners. And we work to build sustainability into everything we do. A company doesn't last 160 years by standing still. It endures by reinventing itself, striving to delight its consumers, winning in the marketplace, and remaining true to its values.

You will influence, activate, and manage the successful incorporation of LS&CO.'s sustainability initiatives into the marketplace by working with senior business leaders across Marketing, DTC (retail, ecommerce), and Commercial Operations. You will support the activation of marketing programs, sustainable product launches, and customer sustainability initiatives to drive commercial value and ensure LS&CO.'s sustainability leadership in the marketplace. You will also activate the full value of LS&CO.'s sustainability assets by influencing and catalyzing programs with enabling functions to reach key stakeholders including Finance (investors), HR (employees and potential talent), Marketing (consumers), ComOps (customers), Corporate Affairs (civil society, media), and Legal (board and shareholders). You will manage the Net Positive Board of senior leaders advising the company on sustainability, manage the company's licensees on sustainability, and develop and lead the company's strategy on the circular economy.

*Responsibilities*

- Drive consumer and customer engagement with LS&CO.'s sustainable products and sustainability programs, building brand and commercial value by influencing and catalyzing marketing and sales initiatives with commercial functions (DTC, Commercial Operations).
- Build corporate reputation and commercial value by working with enabling functions to inform key stakeholders of LS&CO.'s sustainability programs and leadership. This includes marketing and communications (employees, civil society); HR (employees and prospective talent); Finance (investors); Legal (board and shareholders); and ComOps (customers).
- Drive brand value by managing integration of sustainability programs with global licensee operations
- Support strategic development of sustainability at LS&CO. by managing the Net Positive Board of senior leaders advising LS&CO. on sustainability.

*Activate Sustainability with Consumers and Customers (50%)*

- Engage consumers by developing and managing sustainability programs in the global DTC portfolio, including clothing collection/ recycling.

- Engage DTC teams to incorporate sustainability into omni-channel sales and operations strategies, ultimately building sales of sustainability enhanced products.
- Identify and drive environmental/social impact reduction opportunities with DTC teams (e.g., packaging reduction, NexGen store initiatives) and support DTC teams in communicating sustainability to consumers.
- Support ComOps teams by providing sustainability-related communications and marketing information to sales teams and engaging wholesale customers, e.g., ASOS, Target, etc., on their sustainability initiatives
- Identify and drive environmental/social impact opportunities with ComOps teams (e.g., packaging reductions, clothing collection).
- Engage sales teams to incorporate sustainability into sales launches and operational strategies, ultimately building capabilities of the sales team to drive sustainability with customers.
- Partner with brand marketing teams to develop global omni-channel sustainability marketing programs that drive consumer awareness and engagement on company sustainability initiatives.
- Partner with Corporate Communications and Finance to drive media, stakeholder, investor, and employee awareness of company sustainability initiatives.

*Levi's job post published online in 2021 when job search was active.

When we discussed these two job posts in the classroom, master students expressed frustration with the sustainability job market. They argued that fashion brands should "stop asking for many years of experience in the sustainability field" since this is relatively new career path. Also, students argued that "these positions need the fresh perspectives of a younger generation whose members have been learning about sustainability since elementary school." So the first question here is whether "the entry-level sustainability opportunities exist, or they are just hard to find?"[69]

As stated in one *Green Biz* article, "The war for sustainability talent is real. The job market is hot right now, but it can seem that every company that has woken up to sustainability and ESG issues in the past year has suddenly started posting jobs looking for candidates with 10-15 years of ESG or sustainability experience." However, according to the author of the same article not many sustainability professionals have ten to fifteen years of sustainability experience. This statement actually indicates that more young professionals in this area are urgently needed meaning that "the sustainability job market is hot for entry-level, early career, and mid-career professionals, too." From that perspective, companies searching for sustainability candidates should let young job applicants in so that they can gain experience and become sustainability experts![70]

The second question is what kind of advice to give to young sustainability job seekers?

One commonly suggested strategy for entry-level professionals is that the "sustainability career path is NOT linear. Most sustainability practitioners have built their expertise by working across industries and sectors which help them cultivate a diverse set of skills." For example, "Liza Schillo, senior manager of global sustainability integration at Levi Strauss, started her career as an intern with the Southern Alliance for Clean Energy. She developed her environmental expertise and program management skills in early roles with World Wildlife Fund (WWF), the Southern Environmental Law Center, a U.S. Congressional office and the consulting firm Natural Capital Solutions before ultimately moving into business." When asked to describe her career path this is what she stated: "The work I did before moving into the private sector equipped me with a bigger picture perspective that serves me every day . . . I learned about stakeholder engagement, as well as diplomacy. Underlying both of these skills is the ability to empathize with the other voices in the room; this has been a huge asset for me, and was honed during my time in the nonprofit sector." From this and many similar examples, we can conclude that although the sustainability job market is tough, "The world needs more bright young professionals entering sustainability careers,"[71] hence it is a responsibility of all of us educators to guide our students to get started.

# Chapter Summary

In this chapter we explored a rising need for stronger and more strategic partnerships among various market groups, including businesses, governments, NGOs, and consumers, which all have important roles to play in the sustainable development of our societies. The need for partnerships to achieve sustainable development goals was particularly evident during the global COVID crisis when many companies had to entirely reconsider their business structures and attempt to learn from the success and failures of others. For that reason, this chapter investigates some of the more recent phenomena, including the importance of the COVID-19 pandemic in the context of sustainable development, but also the impacts that the pandemic has imposed on garment manufacturers, fashion brands, fashion supply chain workers, and fashion consumers. The sustainability expert whose work is presented in this chapter is Dr. Elena Karpova (Putman & Hayes Distinguished Professor in the department of consumer, apparel, and retail studies at the University of North Carolina, Greensboro) who is known for her research in the sustainable apparel consumption domain. Perhaps the most important section in this chapter for students is the section discussing how to move forward in your sustainability careers. In this section we review two recent sustainability-related job postings in the fashion industry sector (H&M Regional Sustainability Manager and Levi's Senior Manager, Sustainability), suggesting strategies for students to secure entry-level professional positions in this field.

# References

1. "Stakeholder engagement," BSR, accessed July 10, 2023, https://www.bsr.org/en/prs/stakeholder-engagement.
2. Kenneth Goodpaster, David Rodbourne, Barbra Hernke, and Linnea Betzler, *Corporate Social Responsibility: The Shape of a History, 1945–2004* (Minneapolis: Center for Ethical Business Cultures, 2010).
3. "The Challenge: Building Mutual Trust between Community and Industry," Australian Commonwealth Scientific and Industrial Research Organization (CSIRO), accessed July 10, 2023, https://www.csiro.au/en/work-with-us/industries/mining-resources/social-and-enviromental-performance/social-licence-to-operate.

4. "6 Key Findings on the Rising Role of Corporate Social Responsibility," Cybergrants (blog), August 3, 2023, https://blog.cybergrants.com/corporate-social-responsibility-csr-201506.html.

5. "The Good Company," *Economist*, 2005, accessed July 10, https://www.economist.com/special-report/2005/01/22/the-good-company.

6. "Valuing Corporate Social Responsibility," McKinsey, 2009, accessed July 10, Mckinsey.com/business-functions/strategy-and-corporate-finance/our-insights/valuing-corporate-social-responsibility-mckinsey-global-survey-results.

7. Rangan Kasturi, Lisa Chase, and Sohel Karim, "The Truth about CSR," *Harvard Business Review*, January–February 2015, https://hbr.org/2015/01/the-truth-about-csr#:~:text=But%20there%20is%20increasing%20pressure,its%20business%20purpose%20and%20values.

8. "Plan-Do-Check-Act Process," ASQ, accessed July 10, https://asq.org/quality-resources/pdca-cycle.

9. "Article 23," *Human Rights*, accessed July 10, https://www.humanrights.com/course/lesson/articles-19-25/read-article-23.html.

10. "OECD Guidelines for Multinational Enterprises 2011 Edition," *OECD*, accessed August 1, 2023, https://www.oecd.org/daf/inv/mne/48004323.pdf.

11. "Sustainable Business Employee Ownership Cooperatives," *Esoplaw*, accessed August 1, 2023, https://www.esoplaw.com/sustainable-businesses-employee-ownership-cooperatives.

12. Jillian Richardson, "How Patagonia Created One of the Most Generous Family Policies in the World," *Convene*, November 15, 2018, https://convene.com/catalyst/office/patagonia-family-policy-childcare/.

13. "Item 03: Employee-Worker Terminology Revisions (Part 2)," Global Reporting, accessed July 10, https://www.globalreporting.org/standards/media/2295/item-03-employee-worker-terminology-revisions-part2.pdf.

14. "Behind the B: Reasons Why Employees Appreciate Working at a B Corp," *USCA BCorporation*, March 10, 2022, https://usca.bcorporation.net/zbtcz03z22/bcm-behind-the-b-reasons-why-employees-appreciate-about-working-at-a-b-corp/.

15. "Impact Model," *Akola*, accessed July 10, 2023, https://akola.co/pages/impact-model.

16. "Founders Page," *Akola*, accessed July 16, 2023, https://akola.co/pages/founders-page.

17. "The Batik Boutique," *Batik Boutique*, accessed July 16, 2023, https://global.thebatikboutique.com/.

18. "About," *Kandahar Treasure*, accessed July 21, 2023, https://kandahartreasure.com/about/.

19. "World Youth Report 2030 Agenda," *United Nations*, 2018, accessed July 21, 2023, https://www.un.org/development/desa/youth/wp-content/uploads/sites/21/2018/12/WorldYouthReport-2030Agenda.pdf.

20. "Youth, Political Participation and Decision Making," *UN*, accessed July 21, 2023, https://www.un.org/esa/socdev/documents/youth/fact-sheets/youth-political-participation.pdf.
21. "Story of Stuff," *Story of Stuff*, accessed August 1, 2023, https://www.storyofstuff.org/movies/story-of-stuff/.
22. "International Development: Trade Unions and Environmentally Sustainable Development," *ILO*, accessed August 1, 2023, https://www.ilo.org/wcmsp5/groups/public/---ed_dialogue/---actrav/documents/publication/wcms_122104.pdf.
23. "Redress for Schools," *Redress*, accessed August 1, 2023, https://www.redress.com.hk/getredressed/schools.
24. "The Fashion Consumer," *Global Web Index*, accessed August 1, 2023, https://www.gwi.com/reports/fashionistas.
25. Tom Hedges, "Fashion for Good: Why Sustainability Is on Trend," December 7, 2021, https://blog.gwi.com/CHART-OF-THE-WEEK/SUSTAINABLE-FASHION/.
26. Ibid.
27. Ibid.
28. Ibid.
29. "Get Involved," *Fashion Revolution*, accessed July 1, 2023, https://www.fashionrevolution.org/about/get-involved/.
30. "Fashion Revolution: Do Something," *Fashion Revolution*, accessed July 1, 2023, https://www.fashionrevolution.org/wp-content/uploads/2018/03/190918_FashionRevolution_DoSomething_2018.pdf.
31. Ibid.
32. Fashion Revolution, *Fashion Revolution Impact Report*, accessed July 1, 2023, https://issuu.com/fashionrevolution/docs/fr_impactreport_2021.
33. "Sustainable Fashion Consumption Network," Sustainable Fashion Consumption, accessed May 1, 2023, https://sustainablefashionconsumption.org/.
34. Iva Jestratijevic, James Ohisei Uanhoro, and Rachel Creighton, "To Disclose or Not to Disclose? Fashion Brands' Strategies for Transparency in Sustainability Reporting," *Journal of Fashion Marketing and Management: An International Journal* 26, no. 1 (2022): 36–50.
35. Iva Jestratijevic and Nancy A. Rudd, "Six Forms of Sustainable Fashion," *Latest Trends in Textile and Fashion Designing* 2, no. 4 (Aug. 2018): 220–22, http://dx.doi.org/10.32474/LTTFD.2018.02.000145.
36. Ibid.
37. Ibid.
38. Ibid.
39. Ibid.
40. Ibid.
41. Ibid.
42. Ibid.

43. "Get Redressed Individuals," *Redress*, accessed May 1, 2023, https://www. redress.com.hk/getredressed/individuals.

44. Elena Karpova, Grace I. Kunz, and Myrna B. Garner, *Going Global: The Textile and Apparel Industry* (New York: Bloomsbury Publishing, 2021).

45. Sara B. Marcketti and Elena E. Karpova, eds., *The Dangers of Fashion: Towards Ethical and Sustainable Solutions* (New York: Bloomsbury Publishing, 2020).

46. "Fashion on Climate: How Fashion Can Urgently Act to Reduce Its Greenhouse Gas Emissions," McKinsey and Global Fashion Agenda, 2020, https://www. mckinsey.com/~/media/mckinsey/industries/retail/our%20insights/fashion%20 on%20climate/fashion-on-climate-full-report.pdf.

47. "Get Redressed Lesson Plan," *Squarespace*, accessed July 29, 2023, https:// static1.squarespace.com/static/579095c1b8a79bc4629250d1/t/5d8f23d095f-70c20d4e45eed/1569661922239/Get+Redressed+Lesson+Plan.pdf.

48. Iva Jestratijevic, "Dressed for Sustainability Success: A Capsule Wardrobe Project," chapter 34 in *Teaching and Learning Sustainable Consumption: A Guidebook*, ed. Jen Dyer (London: Routledge, Taylor & Francis Group, 2023): 29.

49. Iva Gregurec, Martina Tomičić Furjan, and Katarina Tomičić-Pupek, "The Impact of COVID-19 on Sustainable Business Models in SMEs," *Sustainability* 13, no. 3 (2021): 1098.

50. McKinsey, *The State of Fashion* 2022, accessed July 29, 2023, https://www. mckinsey.com/~/media/mckinsey/industries/retail/our%20insights/state%20 of%20fashion/2022/the-state-of-fashion-2022.pdf.

51. McKinsey, The State of Fashion 2021: In Search of Promise in Perilous Times, accessed July 29, 2023, https://www.mckinsey.com/~/media/mckinsey/industries/retail/our%20insights/state%20of%20fashion/2021/the-state-of-fashion-2021-vf.pdf.

52. Joel Makower and the editors of *GreenBiz*, *State of Green Business 2021*, accessed July 29, 2023, https://info.greenbiz.com/rs/211-NJY-165/images/state_of_green_business_2021.pdf?mkt_tok=eyJpIjoiT0RRMk5XSmlZV0ZsWWPpCaiIsIn-QiOiJ6eVpqa3J3bW1xNktLUzNvVHRkQTZnank3QkRScThieDhWOHR-WRGlNYStXZE5JUldmdzhGMWVQanp5Z2FTRUgrWUJcL3g1VWJ4V-2lWUmN6UGtqeU1mQmtxcFVTVm1Nek0xUG1lTVFhTWtcL05sR1RNOX-BQUU9YV1p4bjlrZUtcL0Z1QiJ9.

53. Ibid.

54. "COVID 19," *Fashion Revolution*, accessed August 1, 2023, https://www.fashionrevolution.org/covid19/.

55. "COVID 19-Tracker," *Workers Rights*, accessed August 1, 2023, https://www. workersrights.org/issues/covid-19/tracker/.

56. Ibid.

57. Nornajihah Nadia Hasbullah, Zuraidah Sulaiman, and Adaviah Mas'od, "The Effect of Perceived Value on Sustainable Fashion Consumption in the Era of COVID-19: A Proposed Conceptual Framework," *Int. J. Acad. Res. Bus. Soc. Sci* 1 (2020): 895–906

58. McKinsey, *The State of Fashion 2020*, accessed August 1, 2023, https://www.mckinsey.com/~/media/mckinsey/industries/retail/our%20insights/the%20state%20of%20fashion%202020%20navigating%20uncertainty/the-state-of-fashion-2020-final.pdf.

59. Taylor Brydges, Lisa Heinze, Monique Retamal, and Claudia E. Henninger, "Platforms and the Pandemic: A Case Study of Fashion Rental Platforms during COVID-19," *Geographical Journal* 187, no. 1 (2021): 57–63.

60. "2012 Resale report: Size and Impact," ThredUp, accessed July 28, 2023, https://www.thredup.com/resale/2021/#size-and-impact.

61. Anat Tchetchik, Sigal Kaplan, and Vered Blass, "Recycling and Consumption Reduction Following the COVID-19 Lockdown: The Effect of Threat and Coping Appraisal, Past Behavior and Information," *Resources, Conservation and Recycling* 167 (2021): 105370.

62. Katia Vladimirova, Claudia E. Henninger, Cosette Joyner-Martinez, Samira Iran, Sonali Diddi, Marium Durrani, Kavitha Iyer, et al., "Fashion Consumption during COVID-19: Comparative Analysis of Changing Acquisition Practices across Nine Countries and Implications for Sustainability," *Cleaner and Responsible Consumption* 5 (2022): 100056.

63. Chuanlan Liu, Sibei Xia, and Chunmin Lang, "Clothing Consumption during the COVID-19 Pandemic: Evidence from Mining Tweets," *Clothing and Textiles Research Journal* 39, no. 4 (2021): 314–30.

64. Song-yi Youn, Jung Eun Lee, and Jung Ha-Brookshire, "Fashion Consumers' Channel Switching Behavior during the COVID-19: Protection Motivation Theory in the Extended Planned Behavior Framework," *Clothing and Textiles Research Journal* 39, no. 2 (2021): 139–56

65. ThredUp, *2021 Resale Report*, accessed July 28, 2023, https://www.thredup.com/resale/2021/#resale-industry.

66. "Consumers' Sentiments on Sustainability in Fashion," *McKinsey*, July 17, 2020, https://www.mckinsey.com/industries/retail/our-insights/survey-consumer-sentiment-on-sustainability-in-fashion.

67. Ibid.

68. "Why Is Sustainability Education Important?," *Greener Ideal*, accessed July 29, 2023, https://greenerideal.com/news/0513-why-is-sustainability-education-important/#:~:text=Sustainability%20education%20goes%20beyond%20imparting,solutions%2C%20and%20make%20informed%20decisions.

69. Katie Kross, "Are Entry Level Sustainability Jobs a Needle in a Haystack?," *GreenBiz*, December 13, 2021, https://www.greenbiz.com/article/are-entry-level-sustainability-jobs-needle-haystack.

70. Ibid.

71. Ibid.

# Glossary of Terms

| | |
|---|---|
| **B Corporation** | B-Corp certification is a designation that a business is meeting high standards of verified performance, accountability, and transparency on factors ranging from employee benefits and charitable giving to supply chain practices and input materials. The *B* stands for *benefit*, and to achieve B-Corp certification, a company must undergo an assessment that attests that their business decisions routinely consider the impact of their decisions on their workers, customers, suppliers, community, and the environment. |
| **biomimicry** | Biomimicry is a design approach that guides product designers through the myriad of complex considerations while relying on processes and principles employed by nature. One example is a paint called Lotusan that leaves a coating that mimics the self-cleaning characteristics of the lotus leaf. |
| **blockchain** | Blockchain is an embryonic set of emerging digital technologies for protecting the privacy and security of transactions. A primary value of blockchain technology is that it increases the integrity of transactions among and between the parties to a business transaction, called the network, by making the records of a transaction (i.e., the ledger) available in real time across the network. With regard to sustainability, blockchain has found application to improve the integrity of supply chain transactions. |
| **by-product synergy (BPS)** | By-product synergy (BPS) brings clusters of companies together to create closed-loop systems in which one business's wastes become raw materials for another. |
| **chemical recycling** | Chemical recycling uses a series of chemical processes to recycle the waste stream back into building block chemicals called monomers. |

| | |
|---|---|
| **circular economy** | The classical, linear, take-make-waste economy is giving way to the circular economy, in which products are designed to be disassembled, remanufactured, and recycled or upcycled back into economic use. Circular economy ideas have gained traction due to the work of the Macarthur Foundation. |
| **closed-loop system** | The closed-loop system indicates that recycling of a material can be done indefinitely without degradation of properties. In this case, conversion of the used product back to raw material allows the repeated making of the same product over and over again. |
| **Cradle to Cradle (C2C)** | Cradle-to-Cradle design and manufacturing aims to reuse valuable fibers via closed-loop manufacturing methods. As mentioned by its founders, William McDonough and Michael Braungart, waste should be eliminated as a concept. The name clearly signals the shift from the traditional cradle-to-grave approach to product end-of-life approaches. |
| **economic sustainability pillar** | The economic sustainability pillar requires businesses to align with shareholders' interests but also with stakeholders' values and expectations. |
| **ecosystem services** | Ecosystem services are the functions performed and benefits provided that make human life possible. |
| **embedded vs. bolted-on sustainability** | Embedded sustainability describes an organizational approach in which sustainability principles are part of the culture. Sustainability policy and goals are transparent to all stakeholders. All employees know how their duties contribute to sustainability goals and are encouraged to make suggestions. Executives, managers, and supervisors talk frequently about progress on sustainability goals and new goals as they are established. Bolted-on sustainability occurs when selected products or services are given features that contribute a sense of being sustainable. However, overall enterprise culture and operations do not contain a conscious commitment to sustainability. |
| **environmental sustainability pillar** | The environmental sustainability pillar refers to the effective management of physical and finite resources so that they can be conserved for the future. |

| | |
|---|---|
| **environmental, social and governance (ESG) reporting** | ESG reporting refers to reporting of environmental, social, and governance issues. The performance analysis of ESG factors might be in the form of quantitative and qualitative disclosures and helps investors avoid companies that might pose a greater financial risk due to their environmental, social, or governmental practices. The criteria for ESG reporting vary slightly from one industry sector to another, as do the weights given to criteria, and they may be adjusted slightly from one year to another. This makes sense because it brings into play board-level decisions that relate closely to the strategic dimensions of a robust sustainability agenda. |
| **extended producer responsibility (EPR)** | Extended producer responsibility (EPR), also known as product stewardship, is a strategy to place a shared responsibility for end-of-life product management on producers and other entities involved in the product chain, instead of on the general public, while also encouraging product design changes that minimize negative impacts on human health and the environment at every stage of the product's life cycle. |
| **greenhouse gas (GHG) emissions** | Gases that trap heat in the atmosphere are called greenhouse gases. Greenhouse gases refer to the sum of gases that have direct negative effects on climate change. |
| **green vs. sustainable** | Green and sustainable are often incorrectly interchanged. This is understandable because in the early days of sustainability discussions, after the release of *The Brundtland Report* in 1987, the focus was on the environmental aspect of sustainability. Inclusion of social issues in the definition of sustainability brings into play factors that are often included in the domain of corporate social responsibility. Such factors include, for example, supply chain practices that might tap into exploitative labor practices, community impacts that might result from 24/7 manufacturing operations, or heavy freight traffic through neighborhoods, and cover up of product safety issues that can be traced to toxic raw materials. |
| **greenwashing** | Greenwashing is the dissemination of incorrect or incomplete information to convey an impression that the party providing the information is sustainable or environmentally responsible. Seven forms of greenwashing have been identified: hidden trade-off, no proof, vagueness, irrelevance, lesser of two evils, fibbing, and worshipping false labels. |

| | |
|---|---|
| **handprints vs. footprints** | We are all familiar with footprints as a metaphor for the damage we do to the environment as we go about our business. Handprints is a new metaphor for the good we can do. There is a significant difference. The best we can do is to reduce our footprints to zero, which none of us will probably ever achieve. But there is no limit to our handprints, the good we can do. To imbed this into corporate goals, many corporations are now talking about being net positive, the net impact of footprints and handprints, a laudable aspirational goal. Examples ae that reducing emission to zero would maximize possible footprint reduction, whereas increasing the efficiency of energy use would be a handprint improvement. |
| **Higg Index** | The Sustainable Apparel Coalition has developed the Higg Index, a standardized value chain measurement suite of tools that help apparel, footwear, and textile industry brands measure and report their sustainability improvements across their value chain. |
| **impact investing** | Impact investing refers to investments made into companies, organizations, and funds with the intention to generate a measurable, beneficial social or environmental impact alongside a financial return. Impact investments provide capital to address social and/or environmental issues. Impact investing is in contrast to socially responsible investing, which screens out investments in companies judged by the investor to have negative social or environmental impact. |
| **key performance indicators** | KPI stands for key performance indicator, a quantifiable measure of performance over time for a specific objective. KPIs are the critical (key) indicators of progress toward an intended result. |
| **leadership in energy and environmental design (LEED)** | One of the first sustainability credentials for buildings was conceived by the US Green Building Council with its program Leadership in Energy and Environmental Design (LEED). Using a point system, buildings can apply to be designated at one of four levels of LEED: certified, silver, gold, or platinum. Buildings are scored on six groups of factors relating to location and transportation, materials and resources, water efficiency, energy and atmosphere, site sustainability, and indoor air quality. |

| | |
|---|---|
| **life-cycle assessments (LCA)** | Life-cycle assessments (LCAs) are an assessment technique that aims at addressing the environmental aspects and the potential environmental impacts throughout a product's life cycle. |
| **lifestyles of health and sustainability (LOHAS)** | Lifestyles of health and sustainability (LOHAS) is a large and growing market segment of consumers interested in knowing about the sustainability credentials of products. |
| **linear economy** | A linear economy is based on the take-make-waste philosophy, where raw materials are sourced and transformed into products (consumer goods) that are then briefly used and quickly thrown away so that new products can replace them. A model of linear economy has prevailed since the second half of the twentieth century. |
| **living wage** | A living wage is sufficient to meet the basic needs of a worker and the worker's family and to provide some discretionary income. Specifically, this wage must<br>• Apply to all workers, which would mean that there would be no salary below the living-wage level<br>• Be earned in a standard work week of no more than forty-eight hours to prevent overtime work and exploitation<br>• Represent the basic net salary, after taxes and (where applicable) before bonuses, allowances, or overtime<br>• Cover the basic needs of a worker and their dependents (for Asia this can be defined as 3 consumption units, where an adult = 1 and a child = 0.5. For other regions, a calculation to define a family is needed to reflect differing family sizes and expenditure patterns.)<br>• Include an additional 10 percent of the costs for basic needs as discretionary income. |
| **manufacturing restricted substance list (MRSL)** | Manufacturing restricted substance list (or MRSL) testing analyzes the chemical formulations that are used to manufacture raw materials that go into the production of consumer goods. |

| | |
|---|---|
| **materiality** | In the context of sustainability, materiality is used to determine what aspects of sustainability, across the full spectrum of environmental, social, and economic issues, really matter to an organization and its stakeholders. For example, for a company that manufactures paper, water conservation would be material from an environmental point of view, whereas for a company with a large network of retail stores that sell products made in Asia, child labor would be a material issue from a social point of view. |
| **materiality assessment** | Materiality assessment is the process of mapping the list of material issues selected by an organization onto a 2 x 2 grid. This shows how well each issue is aligned with stakeholder priorities for that issue with the organization's priorities. Both the core and comprehensive GRI reporting formats require inclusion of a materiality assessment in a sustainability report. |
| **mechanical recycling** | Mechanical recycling takes waste and recycles it into a second material without changing its basic structure. Some common mechanical techniques for textile recycling include shredding fabrics and melting and extruding plastic fibers such as polyester. |
| **minimum wage** | According to the International Labor Organization (ILO), a United Nations agency whose mandate is to advance social and economic justice through setting international labor standards, a minimum wage is the minimum amount of remuneration that an employer is required to pay wage earners for the work performed during a given period of time. |
| **multistakeholder engagement** | Multistakeholder engagement is a strategic and structured process that a company may use to ensure that a range of perspectives is included in decision-making. In a practical sense, it means that before making any business plan, they need to consider how this new plan will (positively or negatively) affect various groups of stakeholders. |

| | |
|---|---|
| **people, planet, and profit (3 Ps)** | The social, environmental, and economic bottom line are also referred to as people, planet, and profit—components commonly recognized as the 3 Ps. |
| **product as a service** | Product as a service builds on the realization that we acquire many of the products we buy not because we want to own the product but because we want access to the service the product provides. |
| **quadruple vs. triple bottom line** | The term *triple bottom line* (TBL) refers to the social, environmental, and economic bottom line of a business. This is the notion that enterprises are accountable for performance in three accounts. In addition to the traditional economic measures are added environmental performance and social responsibility.<br>Researchers in Australia and New Zealand have suggested a fourth *P*, *purpose* (to create the quadruple bottom line), suggesting that a sustainable organization should have an aspirational purpose (beyond its mission) that speaks to why the organization exists and why anyone would want to work there. |
| **Registration, Evaluation, Authorization and Restriction of Chemicals (REACH)** | REACH represents one of the most comprehensive chemical management regulatory laws in European Union dating from 2006. REACH aims to improve the protection of human health and the environment through the better and earlier identification of the intrinsic properties of chemical substances. |
| **renewable vs. nonrenewable resources** | Renewable resources (e.g., wind, solar, plants, trees) will naturally replenish themselves over time. Nonrenewable resources will be gone forever once used (like coal, fuel, etc.). Understanding the difference between renewables and nonrenewables is key to managing natural resources for the future. |
| **resilience** | Resilience is the capacity for systems to survive, adapt, and grow in the face of turbulent change. When applied to a business or any other type of enterprise, resilience speaks to the ability of the enterprise to recover its ability to perform after some shock—a fire, a market downturn, an extended strike, a weather disaster, etc. Clearly, in order to be sustainable, a business must be resilient, and vice versa. |

| | |
|---|---|
| **shared value** | Shared value is the practice of creating economic value in a way that also creates value for society by addressing its needs and challenges. In the context of sustainable business practices, shared value results from policies and practices that contribute to competitive advantage while strengthening the communities in which a company operates. |
| **shareholders vs. stakeholders** | As commonly understood, shareholders are people (or entities) that own part of a company. Their interest in how a company performs is essentially purely financial. In contrast, a stakeholder is any person, organization or community that incurs environmental, social, or economic impacts caused by the operations of another party such as a business. Stakeholders include, for example, neighbors, employees, investors, regulators, suppliers, and customers. Stakeholder may be not only local but regional or global. For example, regional stakeholders would be a community that gets its water supply from a watercourse to which a company discharges wastewater. |
| **sharing economy** | The sharing economy, also called collaborative consumption, epitomized by public libraries, has been with us for centuries and is an example of the conserver economy. Driven in the case of libraries by scarcity and affordability of books, present day interest in sharing some assets is driven by conservation interests. For example, equipment and tools for home maintenance, which can be expensive and/ or inconvenient to store and maintain, are desired not for ownership per se but for the service they provide. Many people view automobiles and bicycles in the same manner. Accordingly, rental and leasing options for various assets have become very popular in many communities, particularly among millennials, and Gen-Z consumers. |
| **social life-cycle assessment (S-LCA)** | A social life-cycle assessment (S-LCA) is a social impact and potential impact assessment technique which assesses the social aspects of products and their potential positive and negative impacts along their life cycle, encompassing the extraction and processing of raw materials, manufacturing, distribution, use, reuse, maintenance, recycling, and final disposal. |

| | |
|---|---|
| **social sustainability pillar** | The social sustainability pillar refers to social standards to which businesses are expected to conform. |
| **social license to operate (SLO) a business** | The social license to operate or the social license to run a business is a corporate right which can be built and earned throughout the time a company proves to take good care of its employees, stakeholders, and the community where company operates directly (e.g., in the case of the location of retail stores and business headquarters) or indirectly (e.g., in the case of the location of factories, sourcing, processing, and production facilities). If a company is recognized as a responsible corporate citizen, we can conclude that it holds a social license to operate. |
| **supplier scorecard assessments** | Traditional supplier scorecard assessments are used to enable retail businesses to track, quantify, and rank supplier performance. |
| **sustainable** | The word *sustainable* is defined by Webster as "capable of being maintained at length without interruption, weakening, or losing in power or quality." |
| **sustainable development** | Sustainable development is a development that meets the needs of the present without compromising the ability of future generations to meet their own needs. This statement contains within it two key concepts: <br>1. the concept of the *essential needs*, and<br>2. the idea of *limitations* imposed by the state of the environment, as well as limits to economic welfare and social limits to economic progress. |
| **Sustainable Development Goals (SDGs)** | The Sustainable Development Goals (SDGs) were released by the UN in 2015 as a universal call to action to end poverty, protect the planet, and ensure that by 2030 all people enjoy peace and prosperity. There are seventeen SDGs, and the underlying detailed road map for action is integrated in the sense that they recognize that action in one area will affect outcomes in others, and that development must balance social, economic, and environmental sustainability. |
| **sustainability credentials** | Sustainability credentials are a means to communicate commitment to sustainability and are available for buildings, people, companies, and products. |

| | |
|---|---|
| **sustainability certificates** | Third-party sustainability certificates are commonly used among fashion brands to support sustainability claims for their products and their business and supply chain practices. |
| **sustainability reporting** | Sustainability reporting refers to voluntary, nonfinancial public disclosure made by companies on the social and environmental impacts of their businesses. |
| **sustainability vs. compliance** | Compliance is typically rooted in following the letter of the law and rarely going beyond established legal limits. Sustainability, on the other hand, guides companies to be more responsible with regard to their environmental and social impact. Additionally, compliance is typically focused on the present or reactive to current events, whereas sustainability is focused on being proactive for the future. |
| **systems thinking** | Systems thinking is a mindset that promotes thinking holistically about all the components of a problem or issue versus dealing with the components piecemeal. This is essential when working in sustainability because all the components of sustainability problems and solutions are typically interrelated in complex ways. |
| **textile waste management** | Textile waste management explores and explains the latest technologies and best practices for an integrated approach to the management and treatment of wastes generated in this industry. |
| **transparency** | Transparency is a practice of open, accessible, reliable, and relevant business communication. |
| **triple bottom line (TBL)** | Triple bottom line (TBL) is a phrase coined in 1994 by John Elkington, a British scholar and entrepreneur. The concept is that businesses should measure, report, and be held accountable to stakeholders for their performance in regard to their environmental and social impacts as well as their economic performance. |

# Index

3 Ps. *See* people, planet, and profit